# CONTE1

# LIST OF ILLUSTRATIONS

# FOREWORD: PHOONSUK ON
# *PRIDI BY PRIDI*

There have been many books on Pridi Banomyong's life and times, as well as his quest for social justice, peace, humanity, and the betterment of the lives of his beloved countrymen. Yet only a handful are in English. Therefore I would like to express my deep gratitude to Dr Chris Baker and Professor Pasuk Phongpaichit for their monumental efforts in selecting and painstakingly translating these excerpts and putting them together in a coherent manner for readers to learn from and enjoy.

*Pridi by Pridi* is composed of selected excerpts from Pridi's own works. It takes the readers through Pridi's life and times, his thoughts and deeds. It does not at all try to reach any conclusion. I am sure Nai Pridi would have approved of this. When expounding his ideas, Nai Pridi always asked his audience to digest them and decide for themselves whether to believe or disregard them. He would also ask his audience to think logically and with scientific spirit, and never accept "hearsay" easily.

This edition of *Pridi by Pridi* is timely indeed, as Nai Pridi would have been one hundred years old on 11 May 2000. This book will provide a good record of Nai Pridi's legacy for us and the younger generation to absorb and learn how meaningful a life has been, or could have been.

Phoonsuk Banomyong
February 2000

# ACKNOWLEDGEMENTS

We would like to express our great thanks to Thanphuying Phoonsuk Banomyong and the Pridi Banomyong Foundation for their permission and their help on this project. We would also like to thank Dr Chokchai Suttawet, Dr Chatthip Nartsupha, Dr Charnvit Kasetsiri, Dr Phanom Aiumprayoon, Dr Charivat Santaputra, and Dr Nakharin Mektrairat for advice, assistance, and encouragement; the Thammasat archive for providing photographs; Julian Gearing, Chaiyos Jirapreukpinyo, and Paul Handley for locating sources; Domnern Garden for help in translating some legal terms; and Trasvin Jittidecharak and Susan Offner of Silkworm Books for their helpful attitude and professionalism.

# INTRODUCTION

Pridi Banomyong (1900–83) is one of the great figures in the modern history of Thailand. In his mid-twenties, he took the leading part in founding a movement to overthrow Siam's absolute monarchy and bring in the first constitution. After the revolution of 24 June 1932, he became one of the small handful of new political leaders who shaped Siam's political direction over the next two decades. While still in his mid-thirties and successively serving as the minister of the interior, foreign affairs, and finance, he introduced many reforms to modernize Siam's economy and polity. He instigated a major revision of the law codes; founded Siam's second university (Thammasat); initiated representative local government; revised the taxation system for greater equity; introduced the first revenue code and the first proper parliamentary scrutiny of the budget; abrogated the unequal treaties with the colonial powers; and laid the groundwork for the establishment of the central bank. Through the Second World War, from his position as regent for the young King Rama VIII, he led the underground Seri Thai movement in opposition to the Japanese occupation. At the end of the war, he and others used the Seri Thai experience to persuade the Allies not to treat Thailand as a defeated ally of the Japanese. He became prime minister for a short time, oversaw passage of a constitution which he believed fulfilled the aspirations of the 1932 revolution, and was awarded by the king the title of "senior statesman" *(ratthaburut awuso).* The title reflected the intensity of his political contribution rather than his age: he was just forty-five.

But this was the high point. From the late 1940s, royalists and generals combined to block the liberal direction of Pridi's politics and to drag Thailand towards dictatorship. They accused Pridi of responsibility for the mysterious death of King Rama VIII in 1946. They took power by coup, tore up Pridi's constitution, and had several of his political allies killed. Pridi opposed them—first in election and debate, and then in the street battles which supplanted parliamentary politics from 1947 onwards. But Pridi could not match their firepower. On 6 August 1949, he escaped from Bangkok on a fishing boat, and never returned to Thailand in his lifetime.

# WRITINGS

This book is a collection of some of Pridi's own words (writings, speeches, interviews) on his life and career, presented in English translation and published on the occasion of the hundredth anniversary of Pridi's birth on 11 May 1900.

It is obvious from the above whirlwind history that Pridi was primarily a man of action. In the seventeen years of his active political career (1932–49), he spent little time writing. The documents in this collection which date from that period include the handbill from the day of the 1932 revolution, Siam's first constitution presented to the king on that day, a letter he wrote to his wife a week later, the economic plan submitted to the government in 1933, three radio speeches from 1934–36, and one of the last speeches of his parliamentary career in 1946.

But before these seventeen years, Pridi had already established himself as a writer—on legal matters. Soon after he travelled to France to study in 1920, and up to the eve of the 1932 revolution, he turned out law collections, commentaries, journal articles, and lecture notes. These were far from being simply academic works or legal treatises. Pridi was recruiting supporters, and campaigning for a very different relationship between citizen and state to that prevailing under absolute monarchy. Two examples of these pieces are included in this collection.

Yet it was in exile that Pridi truly became a man of letters. From 1949 he stayed in China. About this period he has been totally discreet. His book, *Ma vie mouvementée et mes 21 ans d'exil en Chine Populaire* is a history and analysis of the Chinese revolution but has no account of "his years" there at all. On 8 May 1970 he arrived in Paris where he lived until his death in 1983. Through the 1970s and early 1980s, a great deal of his work appeared in print.

These writings (and speeches and interviews) cover a range of topics. First, there are discourses on political philosophy, especially *Khwam pen anitchang khong sangkhom* [The impermanence of society] (1970), an attempt to blend together some elements of Marxist political economy and Buddhist ethics. A second and related group of essays are about words (especially political terminology), their origins, historical meanings, and importance.

The third and by far the largest category includes discourses on democracy, constitutions, and opposition to dictatorship. A fourth category concerns regional affairs and the threats posed by conflicts within Asia. Fifth, there is a large group of writings in which Pridi looked back on his own political experience and tried to draw lessons and learnings for the present. Finally, there are some writings where he replied to critics and accusers, often by reproducing original documents and legal testimony. These categories are not totally separate. Pridi criss-crossed, borrowed, and cross-referenced all the time. Most of the selections included here come from the fifth category of retrospection, but they also contain glimpses of his interest in words, world history, philosophy, and the protection of his own reputation.

The guiding principle of this selection was to include writings (or speeches and interviews) which relate to Pridi's own personal background, and to his political career up to his escape to China in 1949. The selections thus fall into two types: original documents from the time, and later writings in which he recounts and analyses his own political career. These selections have been organized into three parts. The first focuses on his family background and education. The second looks at the overthrow of the absolute monarchy on 24 June 1932. The third traces his career from then until 1949. Each part is introduced with a short biographical sketch of the period covered, a description of the writings in that section, and some prefatory remarks to provide background and highlight themes. Full bibliographic details of all the selections are provided in an appendix.

# IDEAS

Pridi always insisted that the 1932 revolution was not an attack on the institution of monarchy but on the society of privilege and exclusivity which blocked opportunities for Siam to progress. As historians such as Nakharin Mektrairat and Matthew Copeland[1] have shown, Pridi was far from alone in this thinking. In the 1920s, such convictions were very widespread in urban Siam. Throughout Asia, this was a period when new thinkers and leaders argued that "progress" was blocked by colonial rule, outdated traditions, and ancient political structures. Siam's new men of this era were sensitive that their own country was even more "backward" than most of their colonized neighbours. Many summarized the problem of Siam with the word "birth". Allocating political power on grounds of family was simply inefficient. Social privileges institutionalized social inequity. Political privileges were increasingly being turned into economic privileges as Siam's aristocrats grabbed landholdings and entered into business partnerships with new foreign investors. Pridi took little interest in this rhetoric about birth. His approach was shaped more by his legal training and his interest in economics. For him the first problem was that the king was above the law, and that other aristocrats had privileged status in the law. This institutionalized privilege had to be removed by redefining the relations between state and citizen. The three major tools for this work of redefinition were: a constitution, revised legal codes, and an elective parliament. The second problem was the economic structure which made 1 percent of the society rich and left the other 99 percent in poverty. This had to be overcome by government intervention in the economy.

But what made Pridi stand out from many others with similar ideas was his precocious belief that he could do something about them. In his mid-twenties, he gathered six friends together in Paris and laid the first plan to overthrow the absolute monarchy. According to Pridi's own account, his earliest conviction that absolutism could be overthrown was inspired by the Kuomintang and the Chinese revolution of 1911. The Chinese communities in Siam at the time included many political or economic exiles who were fascinated by revolutionary events in China. Pridi's Chinese-Thai family was part of the market community in Ayutthaya. He learnt about the Kuomintang from his school teachers, from market gossip, and from drama performances staged in the market.

But Pridi's conviction that change was possible was undoubtedly also influenced by his experience of Europe. He arrived in Paris in 1920 when the Russian revolution was still struggling for consolidation. He left in 1927 when the first Soviet five-year plan had been launched. These new experiments in political and economic organization were the focus of intellectual fascination throughout Europe at the time. Pridi mentions learning about Russian planning in his economics courses, but he professes no deep enthusiasm about such debate. Partly this may reflect his own later problems with accusations of communism. But in truth he seems to have had little interest in the new model of the party-led state. By contrast, he was much more fascinated by western European models of constitutional monarchy, parliamentary democracy, and social welfare. It was the legal philosophy and legal underpinning of these structures which he carried back to Siam and put into his lectures at the law school in the late 1920s and early 1930s.

In these lectures and in the three political documents he authored in the early 1930s—the People's Party's manifesto, the outline economic plan, and the provisional constitution—we can see the ideas behind his political convictions at the outset of his seventeen-year political career.

The first of these ideas was simply the importance of establishing law based on rights as the foundation of an equitable and efficient society. He grasped onto the power of the idealized roman law in the French republican tradition. In his lectures at the law school on the eve of 1932, he founded administrative law (and public law in general) on human rights and on the French Revolution trinity of liberty, equality, and fraternity. Implicitly, he offered this meaning of law as a challenge to a social and legal order grounded on the supremacy of the ruler's will.

Second, he saw the constitution as the foundation of all other laws, and as the political weapon to fight against the concept of the supremacy of the ruler's will, and against the privileges and exclusions which resulted. Throughout his writing, he liked to use the term *maebot*, literally mother-origin, to refer to the constitution and more specifically to the grant of the first constitutions in 1932. The opening clause of the charter which Pridi and the other People's Party leaders presented to the king after the 1932 revolution ran: "The supreme power in the country belongs to the people."

Third, he believed the bureaucratic state had the potential to be the motor of "progress" in all forms through its ability to contrive a more rational organization of society. In the past this progress had not been realized because of colonial restrictions (the unequal treaties) and because of the absolutist state's dedication to the protection of privilege. The progress which the state could achieve was outlined in the "six principles" which were laid down at the founding meeting of the People's Party in 1927, and which Pridi continued to use as the measure of political achievement throughout his writings. These principles were briefly: national independence; public safety and the reduction of crime; economic well-being and employment; equal rights and equality before the law; civic liberties based on human rights; and education for all.

The outline economic plan was the clearest and most extreme expression of where this faith in the bureaucratic state might lead. The idea of economic planning was obviously influenced by the Russian experiment. But as Nakharin has pointed out, against the background of the economic depression, planning was a very fashionable idea in the early 1930s. Pridi's was not the only economic plan written in Bangkok in 1932–33. There were several others reflecting widely differing political ideas and levels of sophistication.[2] Pridi appears to have been impressed not so much by the Russian model as by the growing importance of state economic management and social welfare in western Europe. The only major economist cited in Pridi's plan is Friedrich List, the German theorist of state-led catch-up industrialization. Pridi positioned the outline plan in the context of a growing state responsibility for social welfare which reflected trends in France and in western Europe generally after the First World War. In the plan, Pridi examined how this state responsibility for economic growth and social welfare could be adapted for a backward, agrarian society.

Fourth, he believed in the importance of an elective parliament. His 1931 article reviewing the councils set up under the absolute monarchy can be read as gentle mockery of attempts to moderate absolutism from the top down. In his constitutional draft for June 1932, almost three-fifths of the length was devoted to the house of representatives. In 1946, he used his brief moment of power to pass a constitution delivering on the People's Party's early promise to create a fully elective and properly sovereign parliament. Much of his later writing was taken up with anger and regret that this constitution was quickly destroyed, and that parliament was subordinated to dictatorship.

Fifth, he had absorbed the Enlightenment belief in the perfectibility of human beings. He believed so strongly in education (which had transported him personally from a houseboat in Ayutthaya to the University of Paris) that he suggested people should be forced into education in contravention of his usual devotion to human liberties. Within less than two years of the revolution, he had founded Thammasat University to cultivate a new sort of human being to populate his benign bureaucracy. At the university's opening he said: "Now that our country is governed by a democratic constitution, it is particularly essential to establish a university which allows the people . . . to develop to their utmost capability."

Finally, Pridi had an overriding belief in the nation. Time and time again, he called on "those who love the nation" to pool their forces. But unlike many other nationalists of the era, Pridi's nation was more practical than mystical. He saw no close connection between nation and race. He described the Thai nation as a mix of ethnic groups. For him, nation-states had simply become the principal form of political organization in the twentieth-century world. The benefits of constitution, equality before the law, economic engineering, and social welfare could only be delivered by the nation-state. Either one's nation was strong and hence able to deliver those benefits, or it was subordinated by great powers or ambitious neighbours.

## LEGACY

Pridi belonged to the same political generation as Jawaharlal Nehru, Soekarno, Ho Chi Minh, Aung San, and other anti-colonial nationalists of the inter-war period. They all emerged in the same political and intellectual context. They shared many of the same ideas on law, constitution, parliament, education, and the potential of the state. But the career and political legacy of Pridi differ from these other figures in an important way. The others were all pitted against colonialism. Colonialism crumbled away. They either became martyrs in the victorious struggle, or founders and builders of a post-colonial future. At around the same time these others were gaining power or immortality, Pridi was escaping into exile. The long remainder of Pridi's life was spent outside the country. He still existed, but he had become peripheral to his country's politics. In these circumstances, his historical significance and his political legacy have been unclear and unsettling.

By the time he escaped in 1949, he was already being demonized. His political enemies pinned two charges on him: communism and regicide.

Pridi was first charged with communism after the publication of the outline economic plan in early 1933. In 1934, the charge was examined by a tribunal and dismissed. Pridi never claimed to espouse communism and many times directly denied it. He was not tempted when left-wing credentials became fashionable in the 1960s and 1970s. The student radicals of that era certainly did not see him as a communist. In his writings, he often drew on the Marxist dialectic as a tool to analyse historical change. But this was one element in an eclectic mix rather than an overriding faith. In later life, he described his creed as "scientific democratic socialism."[3]

On the question of regicide, Pridi challenged the accusations in court, and won every time. The demonization of Pridi for regicide began within days of King Rama VIII's mysterious death by gunshot on 9 June 1946. Three people were especially important in building a public conception that Pridi had somehow been responsible for the young king's death.[4]

The first two who contributed to the public case against Pridi were the Pramoj brothers, Seni and Kukrit. Their family traced back to King Rama II. As great-grandsons of a king, they held royal titles *(momratchawong)*. They were among many royal family members and royalists who seized the opportunity to reassert themselves in the confused period at the end of the war. Seni Pramoj had been ambassador in Washington during the war and a key leader of the Seri Thai movement in the USA. In 1945, he returned to Thailand to play a role in the peace negotiations, and was prime minister for a few months. Many other royalist exiles in Europe had been active in Seri Thai, and also returned at the same period. Kukrit Pramoj had been working as a banker, lecturer, and journalist. With the dissolution of the People's Party which had monopolized political leadership since 1932, the years 1945–46 were a period of intense political organizing. The Pramot brothers were important in the royalist grouping which founded the Progressive Party in 1945, and merged it into the Democrat Party in 1946.

Both Kukrit and Seni wrote in the Bangkok press with insinuations linking Pridi to the regicide. After the 1947 coup, Seni (under the pen-name Malaengwi, "midge") wrote a series of articles claiming that "the majority of Thai people . . . welcomed the political change [i.e. the coup] as a piece of miraculous magic responding to their yearning". He went on:

> Many people in the street said that there should be no reason for Pridi to feel the heat and escape to Singapore . . . Watcharachai who has been accused of regicide escaped with him. This makes ordinary people think that Pridi escaped abroad because of the regicide case.[5]

In 1950, Kukrit founded the *Siam Rath* newspaper and wrote daily columns which often made reference to Pridi and the regicide. In 1954, ukrit wrote a longer piece making clear that he believed the king was murdered, that it was a communist plot, and that Pridi was evidently a communist in the light of the 1933–34 affair and his residence in China:

> It should be no surprise that Pridi sides closely with the communists now, given some of the old stories . . . But communists are not stupid. On the contrary they must be very clever, patient, and full of tricks . . . Before the communists accept someone, they will investigate that person's past behaviour and opinions. Pridi has a lot in his past to make him acceptable to the communists, including the regicide case which is like his certificate . . .[6]

The third architect of Pridi's demonization was Phra Phinitchonkhadi, the police officer who was appointed by the 1947 coup group to lead the investigation of the regicide. As is evident from the court proceedings and all subsequent accounts, the evidence was already very unclear within hours of the event, and could only get murkier in the highly emotional and politicized circumstances following. In his investigation, Phra Phinit concentrated on establishing a *political* motive for the murder. Three palace functionaries were identified, charged, and later executed. Two of them had some association with Pridi. Some believed that these two were dragged into the case in order to create a political link to Pridi.[7] Phra Phinit also issued arrest warrants for Pridi and his aide Watcharachai for plotting the murder, but never brought this case to court. It was revealed much later in 1979 that Phra Phinit had bribed a witness to substantiate the charge of conspiracy against Pridi.[8] Phra Phinit was a brother-in-law of the Pramoj brothers.

Through 1945–50, this royalist grouping joined hands with military leaders (some from the People's Party, some from a later generation) to suppress Pridi and his coalition of followers from the civilian side of the People's Party, the local ranks of Seri Thai, and the navy. The demonization of Pridi was part of this battle. At first, the demonization focused on the accusation of regicide. But by the early 1950s, the US and its cold war against communism in Asia had become a factor in Thai politics. The US became the godfather of this royalist-military alliance.[9] The 1933 charge of communism against Pridi was now recalled. Pro-militarists claimed the military had to take power by coup in 1947 because Pridi was on the point of raising a communist uprising. The fact that Pridi had fled to China was held up as proof of his true political leanings. After China formed a Thai Autonomous Zone in Sipsongpanna in 1953, the US constructed an image of Pridi spearheading a Chinese invasion of Thailand from Sipsongpanna. This image was part of the US's psychological warfare to persuade Thailand to serve as the US's "anti-communist bastion" in Southeast Asia.[10]

The result was that within a short period of his removal from the scene of

Thai politics, Pridi was also being removed from its history. Over the next twenty years of military dictatorship, Pridi's name was scarcely mentionable in any positive light. In 1964, the publication of a book which doubted Pridi's role in the regicide, provoked a prominent conservative to respond that

> . . . the Pridi regime . . . was a regime of the iron fist. Many innocent people who had the courage to speak out their sincere opinion were liquidated. In Pridi you have a coldblooded fanatic, who has no hesitation to use any means to carry out his plans and ideas. [11]

Conservatives painted Pridi as a monarchy-destroying communist, a demon designed to frighten off anyone who might be tempted by liberal ideas about democracy, social equity, and human rights.

This demonization served the purpose of the military dictators who were engaged in suppressing or distorting the constitution, laws, parliament, and other institutional innovations of Pridi's era. The demonization was also appealing to many old aristocrats who found it difficult to accept that their lineage might no longer convey status and privilege.[12] Many well-born Thais adjusted easily to the new era and some worked closely with the People's Party. Pridi always honoured the fact that King Prajadhipok had favoured reform of absolutism, and had welcomed the transition to constitutional monarchy in 1932 with no apparent hesitation. But others adjusted less well or not at all. Conservatives inside the court had blocked Prajadhipok's aspirations for reform before 1932. Such conservatism lingered. Many simply found it difficult to accept that the social dividing-line between commoner and high-born was being removed. After 1947, the new absolutism of military dictatorship allowed such conservatism to prosper.[13]

Circumstances changed by the early 1970s. Through the previous decade, the alliance of royalists and military dictators had gradually fallen apart. In the international arena, the Sino-Soviet split had made the cold war more complex. Student protests were weakening the US resolve to make a stand in Southeast Asia.

In May 1970, Pridi left Kwangtung and moved to the Paris suburbs. He now became accessible to a new generation of students and intellectuals, who were already leveraging open the cracks in Thailand's military dictatorship, and who would finally bring it crashing down in October 1973. This new generation took interest in Pridi as a figure who stood for opposition to military dictatorship, and who might have suitable left-wing credentials. Journalists and academics travelled to interview him in Paris. Articles about him appeared in the Bangkok press. Meetings of Thai students in Europe invited him to speak. Pro-democracy seminars in Thailand asked him to send speeches. His publications began to appear—the philosophical *Impermanence of Society* in 1970, his account of China in 1972, and then from 1972 to 1976 a flood of pieces in which he tried to draw the links between his own political experience, his studies of world history, and the new politics of Thailand after the 1973 student revolt. Suphot Dantrakun published a short study of Pridi's life and works in 1971.[14] A sympathetic English-language study of Pridi and the 1932 revolution, originally written a decade earlier, was published in 1972.[15] Duan Bunnag wrote a study of Pridi and his outline economic plan in 1974.[16] Several of Pridi's writings were published, particularly by the former 1932 promoter and Seri Thai activist, Pramot Phungsunthon.

But the student movement of the 1970s ultimately decided that Pridi was not the hero it needed. The rhetoric of the student movement was soon dominated by socialism. On inspection, Pridi's ideas were clearly rooted in a European liberal tradition and not in the Marxist framework. The students seized on the historian, linguist, polymath, and martyr, Jit Phumisak, as a much more suitable hero figure.[17] In addition, recruiting 1932 into a revolutionary history of Thailand was difficult. Attempts to dress it up as a popular insurrection or bourgeois revolt were condemned to failure. When the 1973 student leader, Seksan Prasertkul, later went to write his Cornell doctoral thesis about modern Thai history, he almost ignored 1932 altogether. In Seksan's account, the event was simply a coup. The result was only a slight readjustment between the monarchy and the military which enabled these two institutions to retain a domination which went back to the Ayutthaya period. In other words, nothing had really changed.[18] Other writers of this generation echoed this interpretation. The 1932 coup had been a failure. The People's Party had prepared the way for the military dictatorship which dominated Thailand from the 1930s to the 1970s. Laws, constitutions, and parliaments had not turned out to be the foundations of a new social order. Rather they were foreign imports which had failed. They had very easily been converted into instruments of dictatorship.[19]

Ironically, in the late 1960s and 1970s the prospect that Pridi *might* become a new revolutionary figure, and *might* even return to Thailand and stir up the spirits of the past, provoked a second round of demonization. Several of the old royalists were now prominent in the politics of constitution-making and party-building which followed on from the 1973 student uprising. The Pramot brothers were again in the foreground. Seni was briefly prime minister in 1975 and again in 1976. Kukrit held the post for a little longer in-between. Although he did not write directly on Pridi in this period, Kukrit's *Siam Rath* carried many articles inveighing against Pridi, and vehemently opposing any attempts to rehabilitate his memory. Kukrit also instigated others to spread a rumour that Pridi was planning to return to Thailand and set himself up as president.[20] The charges against Pridi were the same: regicide and communism. Shortly after Pridi moved to Paris and was visited by Thais associated with the government, *Siam Rath* cautioned: "if the government invites a former defendant who is an enemy of the throne to return and become someone big in the government, it is as if that government is in rebellion against the throne".[21] With Thailand facing a communist insurgency supported by China, the charge of communism was fine-tuned: Pridi was now portrayed as a willing tool of China's policy to dominate the country.[22] Later in 1979, Pridi successfully sued Kukrit and *Siam Rath*, the historian Rong Sayamanon, and the Education Ministry over publications which associated his name with the regicide.

After the coup and return of the military in 1976, Pridi's memory was not totally suppressed. Despite the return of political reaction, the 1973–76 period had won some intellectual space which would not be totally surrendered. An English-language biography appeared by a relative of Pridi's wife. But it was written in Singapore and privately published.[23]

The renewed demonization, coupled with the reluctance of the student radicals to embrace Pridi and the People's Party, allowed a fundamental rewriting of Thailand's history of constitutions and parliaments. The role of Pridi and the People's Party was carefully painted out. In one of the new versions, King Prajadhipok had been on the point of granting a constitution in 1932, but the People's Party had sprung the coup to preempt him and claim the credit.[24] In 1976, this history was codified in a textbook.[25] In another version, the events of June 1932 were simply forgotten: the king alone granted the constitution and was the sole progenitor of Thailand's parliamentary tradition. Pridi and the People's Party simply did not figure. In 1980, the erection of King Prajadhipok's statue outside the new parliament building put this history in solid form.[26] The establishment of the King Prajadhipok Institute (dedicated to political education) in 1994 gave further confirmation.[27]

Pridi died in Paris on 2 May 1983. His ashes were brought back to Thailand. But the reconciliation was more muted than in the case of other exiles, and the official response less enthusiastic than usual for past premiers. But over the years following, efforts to rebuild his memory continued. A Pridi Banomyong Foundation (1983) and Institute (1995) were created to host academic and cultural events. Thammasat University erected a statue on 3 July 1984, and arranged part of the campus' most prominent building as a museum in Pridi's memory. Pridi's *Concise Autobiography* was printed. Thammasat University published a collection of his legal writings.[28] Over the late 1980s and early 1990s, several of Pridi's writings were republished in more accessible collections. The novel, *The King of the White Elephant,* which Pridi wrote during the war, was republished. The film which Pridi made from the novel was rediscovered and shown. "The Revolutionist", a Brechtian play about Pridi and 1932, was first staged in 1987.

Pridi was no longer unmentionable. Yet the demonization still threw a long shadow. Pridi's historical legacy was still unsettled and difficult. The revival of interest tended to focus on Pridi as a writer, thinker, and educator. It emphasized his founding of Thammasat University, his long list of publications, and the thinking of the outline economic plan. It skirted carefully round his political career and his contribution to founding Thailand's democracy.

Pridi had gone into lifelong exile in the wake of the 1947 coup. His disciple, Puey Ungphakorn, suffered a similar fate after the coup of 1976. Both men had played hugely creative roles in shaping twentieth-century Thailand. But the effect of their long exile was that they tended to be remembered as old, powerless, and remote. Their creative contribution was blotted out by reminders of their later impotence. Their memory was defanged.

The best-known quote from Pridi, given in one of his last major interviews in 1979,[29] unfortunately confirms this impression:

> In 1925, when we began to organize the nucleus of a revolutionary party in Paris I was only 25 years old. Very young. Too young. Inexperienced . . . Without experience, I applied theory sometimes dogmatically. I did not take into account the realities in our country. I did not have enough contact with the people. All my knowledge was book knowledge. I did not take into account human elements as much as I should have. In 1932, I was 32 years old. We had a revolution but I was inexperienced. When I had power, I had no experience and when I had more experience, I had no power.

The quote highlights the powerlessness and frustration of his later life, and helps to undermine the achievements of his early years.

The approach of Pridi's birth centennial has seen the first moves towards a more full-hearted reconciliation and reclamation of Pridi's historical legacy. This signifies a lot more than nostalgia. The 1990s have been an intense period of political debate in Thailand, focused first around the coup of 1991 and its popular overthrow in 1992, and then around the political fall-out of the 1997 economic crisis. This debate has centred on constitutional reform, extension of the rule of law, strengthening of parliament, bureaucratic reform, educational reform, human rights, decentralization, social welfare, economic policy—all issues which were part of Pridi's vision of Thailand's progress sixty years earlier.

Further, in the transition from the 1980s to the 1990s, Thailand has passed imperceptibly from an era in which political leaders needed the extra magic provided by a title, whether traditional or military, to an era in which such top-dressing seems almost an impediment. However imperfect Thai democracy may still be, this transition indicates an important sea-change of popular attitude. Chuan Leekphai, who has fronted this transition, is in many ways a total contrast to Pridi—one determinedly cautious and self-effacing, the other brilliantly adventurous and mercurial. But the two share some interesting parallels. Both are descendants of mixed Thai-Chinese families which earned their living selling food in the market of a provincial town. The ascent of Chuan provides some retrospective legitimacy for what Pridi stood for as political sociology. The energies devoted to the constitutional reform of 1997 provide some retrospective legitimacy for what Pridi stood for as political ideology.

The approach of the centennial has occasioned a programme of republishing Pridi's writings; a new staging of "The Revolutionist" in Thailand and Europe; publication of a detailed Thai-language history of the Seri Thai movement by the author of the earlier biography;[30] calls for several commemorative measures; and a revived academic interest in his writing, especially the outline economic plan.[31] Sulak Sivaraksa reissued a confessional memoir, tracing his conversion from conservative demonizer to one of Pridi's most enthusiastic promoters.[32] Charnvit Kasetsiri (on behalf of Thammasat University) commissioned a song on "Young Pridi"—hoping to find a way to reach back beyond the memory of impotence, and back beyond the history of demonization.

The celebration or Pridi's centennial has also seen efforts to undo the efforts at demonization. The committee to organize the centennial is headed by the prime minister.[33] Besides liberal academics and veterans of Seri Thai, the committee is leavened with representatives of some great lineages. At the inaugural ceremony for the centennial project, Dr Prawase Wasi, whose prominence is a result of his own social commitment and his known closeness to the monarchy, delivered a speech entitled "The Monarchy and Senior Statesman Pridi Banomyong". Prawase argued that the introduction of a constitution in 1932 had not weakened the Thai monarchy but enabled it to survive and strengthen. He went on:

> There have been people intent on creating an image that he [Pridi] was an enemy of the monarchy. But researching the various documentary records shows that the truth was quite the opposite. He was someone who tried to uphold the monarchy both through changing the system of government at the time he had political power and at the time when he no longer had power through to the very end of his life. If intellectuals study the documentary records they will discover this truth—a truth which is the opposite of hearsay, in the same way that the earth going round the sun is the opposite of the sun going round the earth . . . Thai society should get

over the kind of thinking, which is child-like rather than adult, that to love one person means not loving another person. Thinking that divides people into sides, into groups *(phuak)* has already done too much damage to Thai society.[34]

Chris Baker
Pasuk Phongpaichit

# NOTES

1. Nakharin Mektrairat, *Kanpatiwat sayam pho. so. 2475* [The 1932 Revolution in Siam], Bangkok: Munnithi khrongkan tamra sangkhomsat lae manutsayasat, 1992; Matthew Copeland, "Contested Nationalism and the 1932 Overthrow of the Absolute Monarchy in Siam", Ph.D. thesis, Australian National University, 1993.

2. Nakharin Mektrairat, "Khao khrong sethakit khong nai Mangkon Samsen mua pi pho. so. 2475" [Mangkon Samsen's economic plan of 1932], and the summarized proceedings of the seminar on Pridi's plan at Thammasat University on 11 May 1999, both in Narong Petchprasoet (ed.), *Pridi Phanomyong*, Bangkok: Political Economy Centre and Pridi Banomyong Institute, 1999.

3. See fn. 1.

4. This section draws heavily on Morakot Jewachinda, "Phap lak Pridi Phanomyong kap kan muarg Thai 2475–2526" [The images of Pridi Banomyong and Thai politics 1932–83], M.A. thesis, Chulalongkorn University, 1994, especially ch. 3.

5. Seni Pramot, "Bung lang prawatisat" [Historical background], in *Chumnum wannakhadi thang kanmuang* [Collected political writings], Bangkok, 1968, 52, 61. The police tried to link Lt. Watcharachai, a naval officer who served as Pridi's aide for many years, to the regicide case without success.

6. Kukrit Pramot, "Khian tam khao" [Written according to the news], in *Kep lek phasom noi* [Bits and pieces], Bangkok: Thaimit, 1959, 470.

7. Morakot, "*Phap lak*", 81, 111; R. Kruger, *The Devil's Discus*, London: Cassell, 1964.

8. Pridi was supposed to have learnt that the king planned to abdicate the throne in favour of his brother and then to stand for parliament. As the story went, Pridi had thus resolved on the regicide because the king's strategy would block Pridi's parliamentary ambitions. Morakot, "*Phap lak*", 117–8.

9. Daniel Fineman, *A Special Relationship: The United States and Military Government in Thailand, 1947–1958*, Honolulu: University of Hawaii Press, 1997.

10. The US approach worked. Thanom Kittikhachorn described Sipsongpanna as "China's lackey to invade Thailand"; see his foreword to Bunchuai Sisawat, *Lu: khon Thai nai prathet Chin* [Lu: The Thai in China], Bangkok, 1955. But at the Bandung Conference in April 1954, Zhou Enlai told the leading Thai delegate, Momchao Wan-waithayakon, that Pridi was in Beijing not Sipsongpanna, the US was playing games, and Thailand should send a delegation to China to verify. Zhou and Wan dined together and exchanged presents. Phibun subsequently began building relations with Beijing, and even floated the possibility that Pridi might return to Thailand. But the 1957–58 coups by pro-US Sarit cut off this possibility, and revived the demonization of Pridi. See Fineman,

*A Special Relationship*, 172–73, 213, 225–26. The result was that the Chinese leaders refused to allow Pridi to visit the Tai areas in southern China.

11. In 1964, copies of Rayne Kruger, *The Devil's Discus,* circulated in Bangkok. An "official who has been close to the events" wrote a note on the book for the government. The passage quoted here comes from that note, which was printed (with no attribution of authorship) in *Bangkok Post* of 21 July 1964. It also appeared in the cremation volume of Phraya Siwisanwacha at Wat Thepsirin in 1968. In 1933, Siwisanwacha had been one of the fiercest critics of Pridi's economic plan, describing it as "pure socialism".

12. Writing in 1972, Pridi commented pointedly about two nineteenth-century commoners who criticized absolute monarchy: "It is as if people of the old order do not like to mention K. S. R. Kulap or Thianwan, who in their youth over a hundred years ago openly called for change in the absolute monarchy." See in this volume, "Some Aspects of the Establishment of the People's Party and Democracy."

13. See Sulak Sivaraksa's confession of his youthful enthusiasm for demonizing Pridi in his *Powers That Be: Pridi Banomyong through the Rise and Fall of Thai Democracy,* Bangkok: Committee on the Centennial Anniversary of Pridi Banomyong, 1999.

14. Suphot Dantrakun, *Chiwit lae ngan khong Dr. Pridi Phanomyong* [Life and works of Pridi Banomyong], Bangkok: Prachak, 1971. In 1973 alone, Suphot published no fewer than nine other titles on Pridi. He has kept going since. Morakot's bibliography cites forty works by Suphot, all on Pridi or closely related subjects.

15. Thawatt Mokarapong, *History of the Thai Revolution: A Study in Political Behaviour,* Bangkok: Thai Watana Panich, 1972.

16. Duan Bunnag, *Than Pridi ratthaburut awuso phu wang phaen sethakit Thai khon raek* [Senior statesman Pridi, compiler of Thailand's first economic plan], Bangkok: Samakkitham, 1974.

17. Craig J. Reynolds, *Thai Radical Discourse: The Real Face of Thai Feudalism Today,* Ithaca: Cornell University, 1987.

18. Seksan Prasertkul, "The Transformation of the Thai State and Economic Change (1855–1945)", Ph. D. thesis, Cornell University, 1989, especially 302.

19. Perhaps the most elegant version of this argument is in Nidhi Eosiwong, "Ratthathammanun chabap watthanatham thai" [The Thai cultural constitution], originally in *Silpawatthanatham,* 13(1), November 1992, reprinted in Nidhi, *Chat Thai, muang Thai, baep rian lae anusawari* [Thai nation, Thailand, school texts, and monuments], Bangkok: Silpa Watthanatham, 1995.

20. Sulak, *Powers That Be,* 55.

21. *Siam Rath,* 1 August 1930. When Puey Ungphakorn, former follower of Pridi and leading technocrat, visited Pridi in Paris, *Siam Rath Sapdawichan* (30 August 1970) cautioned Puey by describing Pridi as "defendant in the case of conspiracy to murder King Ananda Mahidol". *Siam Rath* was a victim of believing its own rumours. Pridi had never been defendant in such a case and these two articles gave Pridi cause for a successful suit against Kukrit and the paper. See Morakot, "Phap lak", 185–6; *Chiwaprawat yo khong nai Pridi Phanomyong,* 71–2.

22. Morakot, "*Phap lak*", 181–7.

23. Vichitvong na Pombhejara, *Pridi Banomyong and the Making of Thailand's Modern History,* Singapore, 1979 (privately published).

24. The king himself gave this account a few days after the 1932 takeover: "People's Party and I have been working towards the same aim namely Constitution for our Country, but without knowing each others plans. My plans have met with much

opposition of ultra-conservatives and even foreign advisers deemed radical change unwise. The people became naturally impatient and took matters into their own hands." King Prajadhipok's telegram to Mr and Mrs Ogden Reid, 30 June 1932, quoted in Benjamin A. Batson, *The End of the Absolute Monarchy in Siam*, Singapore: Oxford University Press, 1984, 237.

25. Sonthi Techanan, comp., *Phaen phatthana kanmuang pai su kan pokkhrong rabop prachathipatai tam naew phraratchadamri khong phrabatsomdet Phrapokklao chaoyuhua* [Plans for political development towards democracy according to the ideas of King Rama VII], Bangkok: Thai Kasem, 1976, cited in Thongchai Winichakul, "Thai Democracy in Public Memory: Monuments and Their Narratives", keynote speech, 7th International Conference on Thai Studies, Amsterdam, 1999, fn. 29.

26. Thongchai, "Thai Democracy".

27. A recent article extolling the institute describes how King Prajadhipok granted the first constitution without any other human agency and subsequently abdicated. The article comments: "Many historians have given their opinion that the reason why he decided to abdicate was that he was the most democratic person of all in the realm at that time." Thongthong Chantharangsu, "Phrapokklao-phrapokchat", *Matichon Sutsapda*, 1 June 1999, 26.

28. *Prachum kotmai mahachon lae ekachon khong Pridi Phanomyong* [Collection of public and private law of Pridi Banomyong], Bangkok: Thammasat University, 1983. This volume also has a superb bibliography of writings by and about Pridi.

29. "Pridi through a Looking Glass", interview by Anthony Paul in *Asiaweek*, 4 January 1980.

30. Vichitvong na Pombhejara, *Seri Thai: wirakam ku chat* [Seri Thai: heroism to save the nation], Bangkok: Saengdao, 1999.

31. See Narong, Pridi; and the reprinting of Luang Praditmanutham (Pridi Banomyong), *Khao khrongkan sethakit* [Outline economic plan], Bangkok: Committee on the Centennial Anniversary of Pridi Banomyong, 1999.

32. Sulak, *Powers That Be*.

33. When the committee was formed, the prime minister was Chavalit Yongchaiyudh who warmly supported the project. By ironic chance, he was soon succeeded by Chuan Leekpai, head of the Democrat Party which had been founded in 1946 specifically to oppose Pridi, his allies, and his ideas. Chuan strongly supported the applications of both Pridi and the late Princess Mother to be included in UNESCO's list of Great Personalities and Historic Events for the year 2000.

34. The speech is printed as a special appendix in *Khao khrongkan sethakit* (see fn. 31), 5, 7.

# NOTE ON THE TRANSLATIONS

Where Pridi used an English or French word, this has been italicized in the translation, e.g. *ultra-royalist*. In several cases, these foreign words are misspelt in the original, probably by the printer. We have corrected them.

At some points where we feel some readers might like to know what the Thai original was, we have included a transliteration. This is always italicized and enclosed in curved brackets, e.g. *(prachathipatai)*.

At some points, we have inserted material which does not appear in the original. These are always enclosed [in square brackets]. Mostly these insertions are brief background material. Sometimes they are suggested additional words which clarify the meaning of the original.

Pridi liked to number paragraphs, as in legal documentation, with complex multiple levels. Often the results are quite labyrinthine. To improve the readability, we have removed many of these numbers, leaving only those which are truly lists. Where appropriate we have inserted a blank line to indicate a new section.

Royal names are left in their official English form (e.g. Prajadhipok). Certain well-known names are left in a conventional English form (e.g. Jayanama, Puey Ungphakorn). Other Thai words and names have been transliterated according to the Royal Institute system. The long *ratchathinnanam* titles that were also used as names have sometimes been broken into two words to improve readability. In the final set of extracts from *Ma vie mouvementée et mes 21 ans d'exil en Chine Populaire (My Chequered Life and My Twenty-One Years of Exile in People's China)*, proper names have been left in the spelling Pridi used in the original French.

Titles have been left as in the original, with some culling when repetition overloads a sentence. With the exception of "king", all royal and commoner titles have been left in transliterated Thai. An explanation of these titles is given in an appendix, based on the work of Thadeus and Chadin Flood. Military ranks have been converted to their English versions using the appendix in Domnern and Sathienpong's Thai-English dictionary.

With the exception of province *(changwat),* all other official territorial divisions (monthon, amphoe, etc.) have been left in transliterated Thai, unitalicized. They are explained in the glossary.

A chronological table of the key events referred to in the writings is provided in an appendix.

# Ayutthaya and Vicinity
## Places mentioned in the text

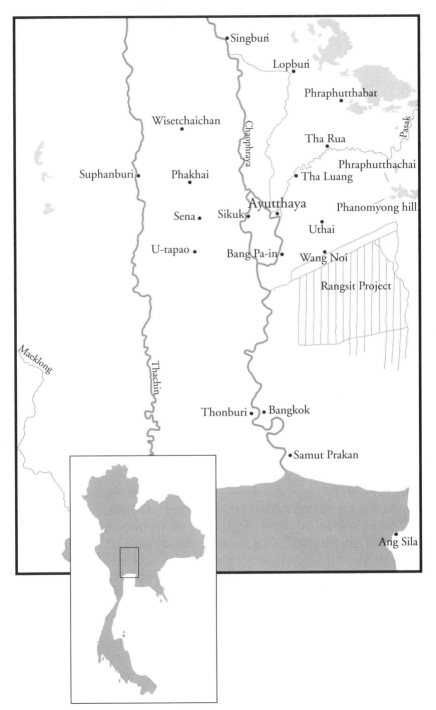

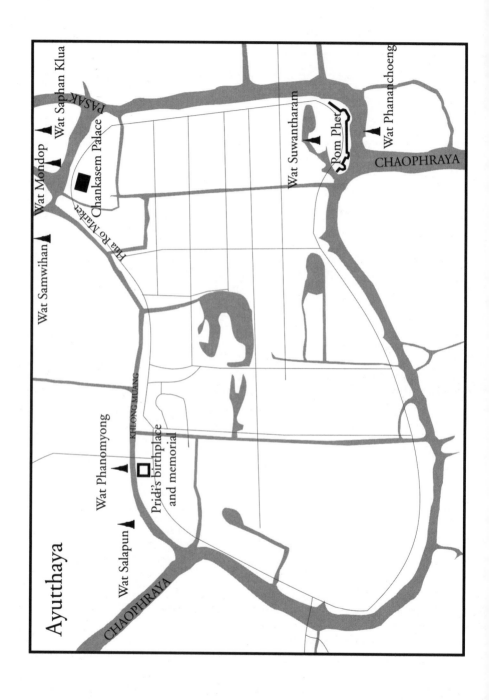

Ayutthaya

Wat Salapun

Wat Phanomyong

Pridi's birthplace and memorial

KHLONG MUANG

CHAOPHRAYA

Wat Samwihan

Hua Ro Market

Wat Mondop

Wat Saphan Klua

PASAK

Chankasem Palace

Wat Suwantharam

Pom Phet

Wat Phananchoeng

CHAOPHRAYA

# PART I: BEFORE THE REVOLUTION

*Marriage of Pridi Banomyong and Phoonsuk na Pombejra, 16 November 1928*

# INTRODUCTION

## LIFE

Pridi Banomyong was born in Ayutthaya on 11 May 1900. He was a brilliant student, completing his secondary schooling two years ahead of time and law school one year before the minimum age (twenty) for induction as a barrister. In 1920, he won a scholarship from the Justice Ministry to study law in France. He topped the class on comparative law. He became a leader within the small Thai student community in Europe, and in 1926 was almost sent home for challenging the Thai ambassador in Paris over the payment of allowances. In 1927, he returned to Siam with a doctorate in law and a diploma in political economy. He entered government service in the Ministry of Justice, had a short spell working in the courts, then transferred to the law-drafting department. Over the next four years he compiled a volume of the civil code, taught at the ministry's law school, and initiated a course on administrative law about constitutions, the role of law, basic political economy, and political rights. He was promoted rapidly and, like all officials of a certain grade, received an official title—Luang Praditmanutham. In 1928, he married Phoonsuk, daughter of the distant uncle who was a leading figure in Ayutthaya and who had been a patron of Pridi's education.

## WRITINGS

The first two pieces in this section—backgrounds on his and his wife's families—were written by Pridi while he was staying in China, and were printed as appendices in the second edition of the *Concise Autobiography* in 1992. The third piece contains excerpts from an interview conducted with Pridi and his wife Phoonsuk by Chatthip Nartsupha and two other Chulalongkorn University lecturers (Kanoksak and Kanchana Kaewthep) in Paris on 10 April 1982. The extracts which Thanphuying Phoonsuk reads during this interview are taken from a longer version of the autobiography which has never been published. The *Concise Autobiography*, from which the extracts in the fourth piece are selected, was published shortly after Pridi's death in 1983. It was written in the style of notes, and that style is here reproduced in the English. The fifth piece is an article on administrative law published in a legal journal just nine months before the 1932 revolution. The last piece is the student handout for Pridi's lectures on administrative law at the Justice Ministry law school. The lectures break off abruptly just three months before the revolution.

## PREFACE

The first three pieces offer a background to Pridi's life and career. They lay out Pridi's lineage with its mix of Thai and Chinese heritage. The maternal (Thai) side contributed a connection to the dynasty (through wet nursing) and a tradition of Buddhist merit-making. The paternal (Chinese) side contributed a migrant flair for enterprise and adventure. The account suggests that such Thai-Chinese blending was commonplace in Ayutthaya—a city which for four centuries had combined roles as the capital of a warrior kingship and as one of the most cosmopolitan and thriving ports of Asia.

In some ways, Pridi constructs his own background as a micro-study of one and a half centuries of Thai history. Both the Thai and Chinese components of Pridi's lineage are introduced during the warfare attending the sack of Ayutthaya in 1767, the year zero of modern Thai history. Both sides of the family joined with King Taksin in the first efforts at reassertion and regeneration. Through the hard times of reconstruction following, the Banomyong family survived and prospered by the manufacture and sale of sweets (the paternal inheritance) and by Buddhist good works and elite official connections (the maternal inheritance). They reached the status of provincial gentry but still lacked any significant degree of economic security. They were sustained by the transfers of money and human resources within the extended family. This insecurity, combined with the adventurous streak in the genes, drew Pridi's father into the expanding rice economy which came to dominate Siam at the close of the nineteenth century. Finally the family made the crucial investments in education when the opportunity opened up at the dawn of the twentieth century.

Through these writings, Pridi presents himself as heir to traditions of immigrant Chinese enterprise, networking in the official elite, and Buddhist merit-making. Onto this he adds his personal experience of the peasant economy, and of the expanding horizons of education in Thailand and overseas in the early years of the twentieth century. Finally he establishes his connections to dissent through the role of his wife's grandfather in the 1885 petition to King Chulalongkorn, and through his youthful fascination with the Kuomintang and the Ro. So. 130 movement of 1912.

The first of Pridi's academic writings on law appeared in June 1921—an article on the study of law in France sent back from Paris. It already showed his interest in the political aspects of law by dealing with legislation concerning the French president and ministers. After his return to Siam in 1927, he turned out a stream of commentaries, collections of laws, and legal articles. The two pieces included here date from shortly before the 1932 revolution and are among the best known. The first article may appear at first sight as a rather dry recitation of existing Thai law on national institutions of government. But the hidden meaning in the article is a rhetorical question: is this it?

The rhetorical answer is found in the following piece, the notes on Pridi's lectures on administrative law. Pridi invented the course—the first given on such a subject in Siam. Into the course, he crammed human rights, comparative government, and a touch of political economy. On the one hand, we see something of the evolution of ideas which Pridi clung to throughout his life—the importance of the state, the primacy of human rights, and the crucial role of law as the guarantee of rights and freedoms. On the other hand, we get some flavour of a course which was part teaching, and part political recruitment.

## NOTE ON THE SPELLING OF NAMES

The first two pieces generate some confusion over the English spelling of names. According to the Royal Institute's system of transliteration, Pridi's last name should be Phanomyong, and this spelling is used below in the first piece when referring to the *wat* from which this last name derived. But Pridi used the form Banomyong, which approximates closer to the pronunciation in spoken English.

Similarly, the place from which his wife's family derived their name transliterates according to the Royal Institute system as Pom (fort) Phet (diamond). But when King Rama VI granted this last name to the family, he wrote "na Pombejra" in English, and the family members have generally retained this form.

# 1. THE BANOMYONG FAMILY

1

On the north bank of Khlong Muang, almost one kilometre to the west of the corner of the ancient palace wall (in Ayutthaya), there is a *wat*. Elders have passed down the story that a wet nurse of one of the kings in the Ayutthaya period was the builder of this *wat*. This wet nurse was named Phrayong (the name of a tree called in Pali, *Piyongku*). At that time, the Ayutthaya townspeople pronounced the word for wet nurse *(phranom)* as *phanom*, dropping the "r"; and wrote it as *phnom*, dropping the vowel. This is similar to the way that *khaphachao* is used instead of *kha phra chao* [a formal version of "I"]. The Ayutthaya townspeople pronounce many words without the "r", and write them without the vowel. As for names with several syllables, the townspeople like to use only the first syllable or the last, for example calling someone named Phrayong as Yong. The wet nurse Phrayong was known among the people of Ayutthaya as Phanomyong. Hence the *wat* was named Phanomyong after the person who built it. The name of the *wat* with this spelling was passed down through several generations. Around 1923, someone spelled the name of the *wat* slightly differently giving a different meaning from the historical name.

When nurse Phrayong or Phanomyong had completed building the *wat*, she went to worship at Phraphutthabat and Phraphutthachai in Saraburi district, and established a *chedi* as an offering to the Buddha on top of a hill about ten kilometres south of Phrachai hill. People call that hill Phanomyong hill (and over the years, some people have written the name this way).

Nurse Phrayong or Phanomyong established a house on the south bank of Khlong Muang, opposite Wat Phanomyong. Her descendants established houses there and in the area close to the *wat*. After some time had passed, her descendants were not always able to trace back the line through several generations, but there was one thing binding them together: these descendants believed Wat Phanomyong was the *wat* of their ancestor. Even those who moved to settle far away came to make merit at the *wat* whenever they had the opportunity.

In particular, the land on which nurse Phrayong's house was built was passed down as inheritance through many generations to Nai Kroen who was born there at the time that the army of the king of Burma invaded Ayutthaya in 1767.

Nai Kroen's father was the head of a unit in the Thai army which opposed the Burmese army at tambon Sikuk. He lost his life fighting there. By the time Nai Kroen's mother heard the news of her husband's death, the army had approached even closer to the city. She took Nai Kroen and some other relatives to board a boat and quickly paddled and poled out in the direction of the Pasak river to a relative's house at tambon Tha Luang in Saraburi district. They reckoned this was far from the city which was the target of the enemy. They stayed there with relatives until King Taksin led the people to drive the Burmese army out of Ayutthaya. Nai Kroen's mother took Nai Kroen back to the home in front of Wat Phanomyong. The home had been destroyed by the soldiers, as had other people's houses and various *wats* in the city.

On the land Nai Kroen's mother built a house of bamboo to occupy temporarily. She made various sweets to sell. The sweets had a delicious taste and became known among the townspeople as "the sweets from the house in front of Wat Phanomyong". Nai Kroen's mother's skill in making sweets was passed down to her descendants who made a living this way for several generations.

The group of families who had lived in the vicinity of Wat Phanomyong before fleeing from the Burmese army came back to their old homes after the army had been driven out, so the area close to the *wat* revived as a market again. Nai Kroen's mother expanded her trade, so that she was able to build a wooden house on the same land. She was a leader in contributing money and inviting close relatives and other people of religious mind to rebuild the destroyed ordination hall (*ubosot*) of Wat Phanomyong on the foundations of the old one, to build a teaching hall (*sala*) and monks' quarters (*kuti*), and to invite monks from other *wat* to come and reside at Wat Phanomyong.

When Nai Kroen was twenty years old, he entered the monkhood at that *wat* for over ten seasons and became the abbot before leaving the monkhood.

After leaving the monkhood, Nai Kroen married Kaew, the daughter of the head of the orchestra of tambon Suan Prik. They had four daughters: Pin, Bunma, Sap, and On.

Pin married Kok sae Tang and had two sons, Koet and Tua. Their descendants moved their domicile out of the old house, and were given various surnames by officials, but one group of descendants had the surname Phanomyong.

Bunma married Phra Phithakthepthani (Duang), the assistant governor (in that time officials still held that Ayutthaya was the "old capital" of the Thais and so called the post of governor of this district "governor of the capital"). Their descendants took the surname "na Pombejra".

Sap married a Chinese man and had two sons, Ruen and Phung (Khun Prasoet), and three daughters, Suk, Phuak, Chan, and others who did not marry.

## 2

Nai Kok sae Tang, who was the paternal ancestor of the Phanomyongs, was born in 1794 in Etang village, Thenghai district (which translates as the sea of peace) in the Shantou region of China. His ancestors had moved from the Hokkien region to establish Etang village, not far from Hai Huang tambon. Nai Kok arrived to "depend on the mercy of the king" of Siam in 1814. The records of the sae Tang ancestors of Etang village state that Kok was son of Seng, Seng was son of Heng, and Heng went to Siam when Seng was still small. Heng's mother was the aunt of Tae Ong—the name which Taechiu Chinese use for King Taksin of Thonburi. Heng died helping Tae Ong to fight the Burmese. Seng sent his son Kok to trade in Siam.

The ancestral memories and historical events concerning Heng, grandfather of Kok, are as follows.

Heng entered Siam in the reign of Suriyamarin [1758–67, the last king of Ayutthaya] and stayed with Chinese relatives of Taksin in the vicinity of Khlong Suanphlu (at that time an area where Chinese resided).

The Burmese king sent an army to invade the kingdom of Siam and was able to destroy and scatter the opposing lines. When he moved his forces up close to the city, the king of Ayutthaya commanded officials responsible to gather many people into the city to defend the city walls. On that occasion, a number of Chinese including Nai Heng volunteered to join with the Thai people in this endeavour. Thai officials placed these Chinese in the army commanded by Phraya Tak [Taksin].

As the Thai side had no defence lines left outside the city wall, the Burmese army could surround the city completely and use big guns to bombard it. Phraya Tak saw that this situation—together with the fact that the king was not behaving according to the "ten ways of a king" and was weak in defending the country—meant that Ayutthaya was in danger. Phraya Tak encouraged the Thai and Chinese soldiers under his command to break through the Burmese cordon, gather up Thai people in the countryside and in the main towns of the east, and establish a new people's army to save the independence of the Thai nation.

The family of Nai Heng in China received no news from Nai Heng for several years, because after the fall of Ayutthaya the passage of junks between the Taechiu region and Siam was interrupted for a time. After Phraya Tak had been raised up by the Thai people as the head of state of the Thai nation, and had moved the capital of the Thai nation to Thonburi, he allowed resumption of sea trade with China. Through a sea captain, Nai Heng's mother sent a letter which honoured the king of Thonburi, expressed happiness that he was king of the Thai nation, and also asked for news of Nai Heng. The king replied that Nai Heng had lost his life in the service of the king fighting the enemies of the Thai nation. He made a grant of bullet money to Nai Heng's family.

Nai Heng had a son called Seng who was born in China only a few months before Nai Heng travelled to Ayutthaya. Nai Heng's mother resolved that once Nai Seng was old enough, she would have him travel to Siam to serve the king of Thonburi. But then there was a change of dynasty in Siam. So Nai Seng did not come to Siam, but made a living as a farmer in China. Nai Seng married and had several children including a son called Kok.

When Nai Kok was twenty years old, his parents' efforts to earn a living were going very badly. Nai Kok's father hence sent Nai Kok to "depend on the grace" of the Thai people. Before he left, Nai Kok's father gave him as a legacy one *tamlung* [= four baht] of the bullet money mentioned earlier, with the instruction that he could use that money only as an investment for making a living. One February day during the Second Reign of Rattanakosin [1809–24], the junk carrying Nai Kok from China reached Bangkok. Nai Kok stayed in Bangkok not long before travelling to Ayutthaya to settle and make a living.

Nai Kok knew how to make flour from fermented rice, Chinese-style sweets, bean curd, and fermented soybean. So he exchanged the one tamlung of bullet money which he brought with him for the silver and cowries used as money at that time, and used this as capital for making fermented rice and fermented-rice flour for sale. Gradually he sold more and more. As he desired to expand his business more widely, he borrowed some money from relatives to add to the money he himself had made. He bought a floating house and moored it in the vicinity of the market close to Wat Phanomyong. He was able to expand his trade further by also making Chinese-style sweets, bean curd, and fermented soybean. Before long Nai Kok was able to repay the loan to his relatives completely and still had money left which he used to lend to others. The status of Nai Kok hence changed from a small capitalist to a medium capitalist in the provincial centre.

Once Nai Kok had the status of a medium capitalist, he married Pin the daughter of Nai Kroen. To the union he brought a bride price, his capital, and his floating house. Nai Kok moved the floating house from its old site and moored it in front of Nai Kroen's house opposite Wat Phanomyong.

Nai Kok and Nang Pin jointly expanded even further the business which both had carried out earlier. They made both Chinese and Thai style sweets and invented several new varieties.

Nai Kok adjusted himself to suit his new situation and the culture of Nang Pin's family while preserving his Chinese lifestyle and culture where this did not conflict with Thai lifestyle and culture. Nai Kok was a religious man. He adhered to Buddhism in the Thai style, and was a monk's attendant in Wat Phanomyong. Besides making merit at Thai festivals, Nai Kok still performed ceremonies to remember his ancestors at Chinese New Year and at the autumn festival.

Nai Kok and Nang Pin had slaves *(that)* as workers, in keeping with the situation of people who had surplus money in those days. But because they believed in Buddhism, they gave many of their male slaves their freedom by having them ordain into the monkhood. This method of liberating slaves was passed down to the sons and grandsons of Nai Kok and Nang Pin during the period that the slave system was still in force.

Nai Kok passed away from old age. Nang Pin arranged the cremation according to Thai custom, and placed the ashes in a graveyard near Nai Kok's house. Not long after, Nang Pin passed away.

Nai Kok and Nang Pin had two sons, Nai Koet and Nai Tua.

Nai Koet married and remained in the house in front of Wat Phanomyong which he received as legacy. When Nai Tua married, he moved to build a house about four hundred metres away from the house in front of Wat Phanomyong.

Nai Koet was born during the Third Reign [1824–51]. When he was still small and had just learnt to crawl, he fell from the floating house into the canal. Both parents together with others in the house helped to dive in and pull him out. Nang Pin, the mother, hence called this son Bunkoet [literally: merit-birth], meaning that merit had helped this child to be born. Nai Kok, the father, approved of this name, but later liked to call this name by only the last syllable, Koet.

Nai Koet studied Thai at the abbot's quarters in Wat Phanomyong. When he was twenty, he went into the monkhood at Wat Phanomyong for one season, and then left the monkhood to help with his parents' business.

Later Nai Koet married Khum, daughter of a trading entrepreneur in tambon Phra Ngam, Wisetchaichan district (now an amphoe).

Nai Koet and Nang Khum inherited the business from Nai Kok and Nang Pin and expanded it even further. They improved the quality of the sweets in many ways, and improved the making of bean curd and fermented soybean by hiring a teacher from China to instruct their children. The improved fermented soybean was called by the townspeople as sweet fermented soybean. The method of manufacturing this Ayutthaya fermented soybean was passed down to some relatives of later generations. Nai Koet and Nang Khum had the status as capitalists and owners of slaves to an even greater extent than their parents.

Nai Koet was interested in music, which was a cultural legacy passed down from his mother's ancestors. He had a string orchestra and one of his sons was trained in music.

Nai Koet passed away in his old age. After the cremation, Nang Khum and the children arranged the building of a small Chinese pavilion beside the wall of the *ubosot* of Wat Phanomyong, and placed the ashes there.

Nai Koet and Nang Khum had eight children, namely

1. Nang Faeng
2. Nai Huat
3. Nai Chun
4. Nangsao Nguai
5. Nai Chai
6. Nai Ho
7. Nai Siang
8. Nang Bunchuai

Some of the sons of Nai Koet and Nang Khum married and separated to set up house in other tambon and provinces. Nai Huat set up house near Wat Choeng. Nai Chun set up house near Wat Samwihan, and later moved in front of Wat Monthop. Nai Chai moved to tambon Paknam, Bang Phutsa, Singburi. Nai Ho moved to Loi island near Wat Saphan Klua.

Nang Faeng and Nang Bunchuai, daughters of Nai Koet and Nang Khum, were married and had floating houses which their husbands brought and moored at the house in front of Wat Phanomyong.

Nai Siang went to do logging and paddy farming in another amphoe but his family stayed in the old house.

Nangsao Nguai did not get married. The siblings agreed that she should inherit the house along with Nai Siang, and should continue the parents' business.

Those who married and established separate households each made a living with the capital shared out from the parents. Some were able to develop their capital. Some were unable to increase their business and hence declined from the status of the parents. Some were rich for a time and then declined. As for the business which Nai Koet and Nang Khum had once done, the children were unable to develop or maintain it. It gradually declined as others offered more competition, as the vicinity of Wat Phanomyong lost its character as a market, and as Khlong Muang became silted up. Later government established the monthon government office at Chankasem palace and the centre of government offices sprang up in that vicinity. Also government established a new market at Hua Ro, and the gambling den moved from its old site beside Wat Phanomyong to the Hua Ro market. This made the vicinity of Wat Phanomyong lose its character as a market. Making a living for those still in the old house thus became gradually more and more difficult.

3

Nai Siang was born in 1866. He studied Thai and Pali at Wat Salapun, wrote several short poems, practised music, and had special skill on the alto fiddle (*so u*), treble fiddle (*so duang*), and harmonica.

When he was twenty, he entered the monkhood at Wat Phanomyong for three seasons.

After he had left the monkhood, he married Lukchan, daughter of Luang Phanitphatthanakon (Bek) and Nang Phanitphatthanakon (Lek Kitchathon).

After marriage, someone advised Nai Siang to join government service because he had quite a basis of book learning. But Nai Siang liked a free life, so he studied vaccination against smallpox at the office of Dr Adamson (who later received the rank as Phra Bambatsappharok). He passed the certificate, and administered vaccinations to many people. Later he went to do logging in the vicinity of Phraphutthabat, which at that time was infested with malaria. Nai Siang could not ward off this disease, and so had to give up the forest business at great financial loss.

Later Nai Siang and Nang Lukchan went to do paddy farming at tambon Tha Luang. But because there was drought for two years running, there was no output and he became a debtor of others. So he quit paddy farming.

Nai Siang then cleared some empty land at tambon U-tapao at a time when the grasslands in that vicinity had wild elephants. This was before government established amphoe Uthai Noi (now amphoe Wang Noi). Nai Siang planted paddy in the cleared area, and had to fight with the elephants which came to create problems by eating the rice plants. The paddy farming was not successful because some years there was drought and some years heavy flooding. Also there were pests which bothered the rice plants. Then the Siam Land, Canals, and Irrigation Company, which had a concession from the government to dig canals, dug a canal to the area where Nai Siang had cleared his land. Nai Siang had to pay the company a rate for digging the canal. He had no money of his own so had to borrow from others to pay the company. This brought Nai Siang debts on top of those he had already. Because the paddy farming was not successful, the status of Nai Siang changed from a small capitalist in the city to a peasant with small capital in the countryside who was becoming poorer with increasing debt. Nai Siang had to fight with poverty for several years until the government's South Pasak irrigation project expanded to the area of Nai Siang's paddy fields. This helped Nai Siang to recover to be a peasant with small capital in the countryside.

While he was in the countryside, Nai Siang had another wife called Pui. Nai Siang had six children with Nang Lukchan, namely

1. Nang Tharathonphithak (Kep)
2. Nai Pridi
3. Nai Lui
4. Nang Nitithanpraphat (Chun)
5. Nang Noeng Limpinan
6. Nai Thanom

Nai Siang had two children with Nang Pui, namely

1. Nai Athakittikamchon (Klung)
2. Nang Nom Tamsakun

## 4

In 1913, over thirty years after Nai Koet and Nang Khum had passed away, the law to introduce surnames was enacted. At that time most people in the main provincial towns and the countryside had little interest in applying to register themselves as required. Hence the amphoe officials thought up surnames and registered them according to their own convenience.

Because many sons of Nai Koet had moved away from the old home to other amphoe and provinces, the amphoe officials in the tambon where they had set up house established surnames for them. Some of Nai Koet's grandchildren who were on military service were given surnames by their commanding officers.

Nai Siang was told by the village headman *(phuyaiban)* that officials had thought up a surname for him. He saw that this surname had no connection with his ancestors. So he went to pay his respects to the monastic head of the province of the time, Phra Suwanwimonsin. He asked the monastic head to give him an appropriate name, and to advise one of his pupils, who had the post of thinking up surnames for the amphoe around Ayutthaya (now the amphoe Phranakhon Si Ayutthaya), kindly to amend the name that he had been given before. The provincial monastic head knew the story of Nai Siang's ancestors well. Hence he told Nai Siang that he should use the surname Phanomyong. Then he sent someone to bring his pupil from the amphoe, and told him to advise the amphoe office to give Nai Siang the surname Phanomyong. This man approved and arranged for the amphoe office to give Nai Siang the surname Phanomyong.

# 2. THE ROYAL GRANT OF THE SURNAME NA POMBEJRA

King Vajiravudh granted a surname to Phra Samutburanurak (Kham) (later he was given the ranks progressively as Phraya Warunritthi Sisamutprakan, Phraya Phetchada, Phraya Chaiwichit Wisitthammathada) while he was residing at a royal pavilion in Ang Sila in Chonburi province between June and July 1913. Later, officials gathered together several surnames granted by the king and published them as the third round of royally granted surnames in the Royal Gazette on 14 July 1913.

The Chaokhun who received this grant of a surname told me that at the time when the king came to reside in Ang Sila, he was the muang governor (later changed to provincial governor) of Samut Prakan which is adjacent to Chonburi. He had an audience with the king. He had not thought of requesting a surname, because he had not yet consulted his relatives descended from the same ancestors on this matter. But when he entered the audience, the king said: "Perhaps you have come to ask for a surname?" (At the time the king was enjoying thinking up surnames for close royal retainers). Thus the Chaokhun took the opportunity to respond to the king's suggestion.

Then the king said in front of many people attending the audience, for instance Phraya Boranratchathanin, the monthon commissioner *(samuha thesaphiban)* of monthon Krung Kao (later Ayutthaya), that he knew the history of the ancestors of Phra Samut (Kham). The king was familiar with Phraya Chaiwichit Sitthisattra (Nak), previously governor of Ayutthaya, the father of Phra Samut. The king, as heir to the throne, had gone to beg for alms at his house at the time the king entered the monkhood at Wat Bowonniwet. The king was also familiar with Thanphuying Yommarat (Talap Sukhum), the elder sister of Phra Samut, from the time the king was studying in Britain. The king stated that an ancestor of Phra Samut had been in the household of Somdet Phrapathom (the father of King Rama I). This ancestor had set up house in the vicinity of Pom Phet [Fort Diamond]. King Rama I donated most of the land of this house to build Wat Suwanthararam, and later gave the remainder to "old royal retainers" *(khaluang doem)* to settle around Pomphet. The king set up some of their descendants as assistants to the garrison commander of the city, and some as garrison commanders in later times for many generations. Then the king said: "it is not possible to grant 'na Ayutthaya' because 'Ayutthaya' is mine". The king was alluding to the fact that he himself had previously held the title of Kromluang Thepthawarawadi Siayutthaya. It should be noticed that initially after the Surname Act of 1913, the king allowed descendants of the royal family to append the words "na Krungthep", but later on 24 March 1924 the king changed this to "na Ayutthaya" to be used from Mahachakri day, 6 April 1925. Then the king commanded the royal secretary in attendance to write out a card, which the king signed as "Vajiravudh Po. Ro." [Po. Ro. is the equivalent of "rex"], to grant to Phra Samutburanurak (Kham) the surname na Pomphet, written in roman characters as "na Pombejra".

Phra Samut thus informed relatives descended from this ancestor that those who wished could use this surname. But there were some lines which received royal grant of other surnames.

Later around April–May of 1919, when the king was residing at the Bang Pa-in palace, it was announced that the king would go to stay at Pom Phet. The officials of monthon Krung Kao built a royal pavilion to receive the king at Pom Phet. The king stayed there one night, and invited those with the surname na Pombejra to attend in audience. He maintained they were descendants of "old royal retainers" and granted an insignia with "Vajira-vudh Po. Ro." to those attending in audience according to their status.

It should be remarked that at that time people used the word "na" in front of a surname without royal permission. Hence a royal command was issued, which thereafter was considered part of the Surname Act of 1913, as follows:

> By this royal command of 15 December 1915, "na" shall not be used as prefix of a surname. Those who have used it before this announcement, must remove the "na". Anyone who wishes to use it, must first request royal permission.

Because the Chaokhun had many titles, and today's new generation might be interested in the grant of titles in the old times, let me explain further about them. Previously it was stated in the Three Seals Law concerning military and civilian sakdina, that anyone who held a government post received a title associated with that post. But the king had the power to invent new titles for specific persons who had done good deeds which attracted royal favour. After the government service had expanded greatly, from the Fifth Reign [1868–1910] onwards, the titles under the old rules were not sufficient, so the king granted many new titles for the expansion in posts.

According to the old rules, a provincial governor who had sufficient royal favour was promoted from Phra to Phraya. Hence, the title for the post of governor of Samut Prakan would be Phraya Samutburanurak. But Phra Samut (Kham) was specially given a new title by King Vajiravudh as Phraya Warunritthi Sisamutprakan. I have written about this once already in the preface of the book distributed at the funeral of Chaokhun Chaiwichit (Kham). The essence as I can remember from what the Chaokhun told me, was that around 1914 King Vajiravudh came to reside in a pavilion at Samut Prakan (at that time there were no resorts at Hua Hin, Bang Saen, Pattaya, and so on). By chance there was a heavy storm. Phra Samut, along with officials from that place, directed operations through the storm to prevent rain getting into the royal pavilion. King Vajiravudh saw how Phra Samut worked hard throughout which pleased him a great deal. In the morning the king summoned Phra Samut to be granted a new title which the king invented outside the old rules. Phraya Warunritthi Sisamutprakan means a person who has power like rain and who is auspicious to Samut Prakan. From then on, this title has been granted to governors of Samut Prakan.

When Phraya Warun (Kham) moved to the post of director-general of the penitentiary department, he received a new title as Phraya Phetchada, which was a title under the old rules for the Department of the Capital in old times. The father of Phraya Wichit (Kham) once held this title before he became Phraya Chaiwichit Sitthisattra, governor of Ayutthaya.

When the penitentiary department moved out of the Ministry of the Capital to be under the Justice Ministry, a new title was conferred, taking the title of Chaokhun's father and adding a title appropriate for the Justice Ministry on the end.

*Facsimile of the royal grant*

*Vajiravudh Po. Ro.*
*I grant to Phra Samutburanurak (Kham) as requested the surname "na Pomphet",*
*written in roman characters as na Pombejra. This is an auspicious name.*
*May the na Pomphet family progress, flourish, and endure in Thailand for ever.*

*Ang Sila*
*2 July 1913*

# THE BANOMYONG FAMILY'S CONNECTION WITH THE NA POMBEJRA FAMILY

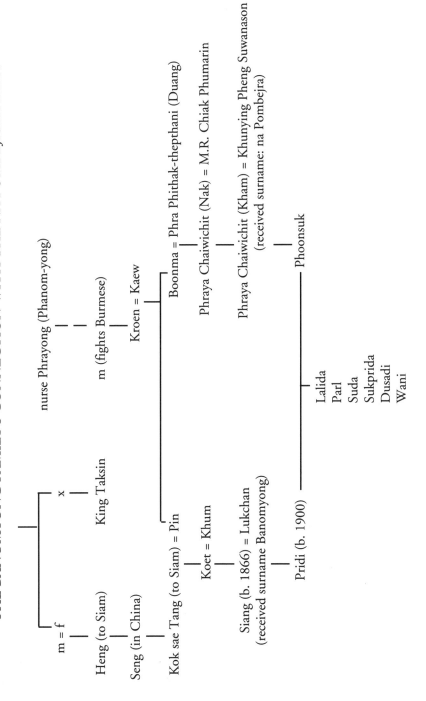

# 3. EXCERPTS FROM:
## *SOME EXPERIENCES AND OPINIONS OF SENIOR STATESMAN PRIDI BANOMYONG* (1981)

[Interview of Pridi and Phoonsuk by Chatthip Nartsupha, Kanoksak Kaewthep, Kanchana Kaewthep, 10 April 1982]

PRIDI: Chaophraya Yommarat, who wrote that piece [an excerpt from the cremation volume of Nai Siang, Pridi's father] and whose old name was Pan, came from Suphanburi. He went into the monkhood as a novice and monk at Wat Hong (Thonburi). He studied Pali and passed the theological exam then left the monkhood. He entered government service as a teacher of Thai language at the Suan Kulap school, which was attended by several sons of King Rama V. King Rama V conferred on him the title of Khun Wichitworasan. Later he sent four of his sons to study in England, namely Phraongchao Kittiyakonworalak (Kromphra Chanthaburi Narunat), Phraongchao Raphiphatthanasak (Kromluang Ratchaburi Direkrit), Phraongchao Prawitwatanodom (Kromluang Prachin Kittibodi) and Phraongchao Chiraprawatworadet (Kromluang Nakhonchaisi Suradet). The king commanded Khun Wichitworasan to accompany them in the post of their Thai teacher.

Later Khun Wichitworasan moved to become secretary at the Thai embassy in London, and advanced his rank in stages until he became chargé d'affaires. Then he returned to Siam to work in the Ministry of the Interior as monthon commissioner *(samuha thesaphiban)* of Nakhon Si Thammarat and was granted the title of Phraya Sukhumnaiwinit. Subsequently he was appointed minister of public works, and then minister of the capital, with the title Chaophraya Yommarat. Later in the Sixth Reign [1910–25] the Ministry of the Capital was merged with the Ministry of the Interior and he was appointed minister of the interior. He asked to resign at the start of the Seventh Reign. Later King Rama VII abdicated the throne and the Assembly passed a resolution for the government to invite Phraongchao Ananda Mahidol to ascend the throne in succession. But as he was still in his minority, the Assembly passed a resolution to appoint a Regency Council of three persons of which one was Chaophraya Yommarat.

As Chaophraya Yommarat has written, the paternal grandmother of Nai Siang was also my great-grandmother, and had the same mother and father as the paternal grandmother of Phraya Chaiwichit (Kham na Pombejra). Let me explain that Phraya Chaiwichit (Kham) was the father of Phoonsuk, my wife. My wife and I are thus related. We are descended from the same great-great-grandparents.

My great-great-grandparents had a daughter Pin who was my paternal great-grandmother. She married Nai Kok, a Chinese merchant from the Tang (Tan) lineage (sae). They had several children including my paternal grandfather, Koet. He and his wife had several children including my father, Siang.

My great-great-grandparents had a second daughter called Bunma who was the paternal grandmother of Phoonsuk. She married Phra Phithak-thepthani, previously called Duang, who held the post of assistant governor of Ayutthaya. Together they had several children including Phraya Chai-wichit Sitthisattra (Nak) who was the paternal grandfather of Phoonsuk. He and his wife had several children including Phraya Chaiwichit Wisit-thammathada (Kham), Phoonsuk's father.

Phraya Chaiwichit Sitthisattra, previously called Nak, was Phoonsuk's paternal grandfather. At the time he held the rank of Luang Wisetsali, he was posted as attaché at the Siamese embassy in London. On 8 January 1885, he joined with three brothers of the king, a prince, an official of the London embassy, and six from the Paris embassy—in total eleven people—to petition King Rama V to change the absolute monarchy to a form which they called a "constitutional monarchy", transliterated from English. At that time, nobody had thought up the Thai word to translate *constitution.* In the petition they referred to a monarchy whose power is limited by the term "limited monarchy", transliterated from English.

King Rama V did not agree to change the system of government as they petitioned. Yet when Luang Wisetsali returned to Siam, he explained to his close family members that, according to what he had seen, the governmental system with a parliament was beneficial for the people. My father was one of those who heard this account, and he related it to me in outline at the time I was an elementary student. After Luang Wisetsali returned to Siam, he served in the Ministry of the Capital, and was promoted in rank and position until he became Phraya Chaiwichit Sitthisattra and governor of Ayutthaya.

From the time I first have memories, the domestic situation of the family descended from my paternal grandfather was what today would be called "comfortable". It could be compared to the class which modern academics call "middle bourgeois". But my paternal grandparents were not modern capitalists. Rather, they were part of a feudal mode of production of a type called gentry [*kahabodi*—literally, a man of property] according to the social divisions of the feudal time (see my book, *The Impermanence of Society*).

My paternal grandparents had several sons and daughters who shared the inheritance. Some preserved their status as gentry. Some lost their capital and became petty capitalists. My father chose to become a paddy farmer and suffered the fate of paddy farmers. This had an impact on the family. I saw that my parents were not well-off. And when I went to live with my father, I saw the neediness of farmers in general.

Whatever the economic status of my parents' family, it was a family that acted strictly according to Buddhist teaching. I was aware of this from the time I have memories.

Later I went through all the levels of the school system and went on to study in France, where I experienced bit by bit the economic and political situation of both Thailand and foreign countries.

Ask what else you want to know.

CHATTHIP: Have you even done paddy farming?

PRIDI: Yes. It's better if you first know the background. Let my wife read something.

PHOONSUK (reading): Nai Siang, Pridi's father, did not want to enter government service because he liked adventure. So after he had married Pridi's mother and had a first child, Nai Siang went to do logging around Phraphutthabat, an area where forest fever was common. At that time, logging was not worth it because of the fever, so he switched to planting rice at Tha Luang, where one uncle called Phung (Khun Prasoet) had already settled. At that time there was no irrigation.

PRIDI: Have you ever been to Tha Luang?

CHATTHIP: Tha Luang where there are factories?

PRIDI: Back then, there was no cement factory, no dams. The place was called Tha Luang [royal landing] because it means the landing for the king. From old times there was a road cut from Tha Luang direct to Phraphutthabat, a distance of one *yot* [sixteen kilometres]. When I was still tiny it was called the road of the foreigner with two pipes. The tambon was called Tha Luang. Later, when kings went to Phraphutthabat, they went from the place now called Tha Rua [boat landing]. Previously there was a road there which Sunthorn Phu wrote about. But most went up to Phraphutthabat by elephant. Later that road disappeared. Kromphra Nara secured a concession to build a small railway from Tha Rua to Phraphutthabat.

PHOONSUK (reading): At that time there was no irrigation. The rains failed two years in a row, and there was no output from paddy farming. Nai Siang went to tell his troubles to Chaokhun Chaiwichit (Nak) to have him find some work to feed his family. Chaokhun had already resigned from government service for several years. He advised that if Nai Siang liked adventure, he should go to clear new land around amphoe Uthai which then was a grassland for elephants. He suggested to get Nai Ho, Siang's elder brother, to go along too. And he would allow his own youthful son, Khun Daeng (who later entered government service as Luang Pranityothakit), to go and clear land and chase away the elephants too. The three would share the cleared land among them. The three agreed with Chaokhun's advice. After they had cleared the land and battled elephants until the herd withdrew from the area, they divided up the land. Khun Daeng staked his claim around Lamdaeng, Nai Ho and Nai Siang around Lamchamaek. But the elephants still gave them constant trouble, especially when the rice shoots were growing well. Whole herds of elephants came to eat the rice that had been planted. Later government established amphoe Wang Noi, and the area of Lamdaeng and Lamchamaek, which had been under amphoe Uthai, was transferred to amphoe Wang Noi. Later the Siam Land, Canals, and Irrigation Company dug a canal to the area which Daeng, Ho, and Siang had cleared and claimed. The concession which the government gave the company included a provision that in any area where the company dug a canal, the company could claim forty *sen* [*sen* = forty metres] of the land on each bank. But where people had already staked claims to this land, the company allowed them to retain the right in return for paying a fee of four baht per *rai* to cover the cost of digging the canal. To retain property rights over the land that Daeng, Sun, Ho, and Siang had staked, Chaokhun Krung (Phraya Chaiwichit, Nak) paid the company on their behalf for about two hundred *rai* each. Nai Siang had many ideas about improving the method of paddy cultivation. Whenever he had an idea, he went to Bangkok to consult Chaophraya Yommarat. As the latter stated in the history of Nai Siang, Nai Siang was a person with interests. Pridi got to know various ideas which his father had about paddy cultivation.

PRIDI: Let me tell you about the basis of the Siam Land, Canals, and Irrigation Company. At that time, in the areas of the Chaophraya river valley which were distant from the river, there was still vacant waste land. King Rama V granted concessions for digging canals to various capitalists besides the Siam Land, Canals, and Irrigation Company. One who took a concession was

Phraya Banlu. When the canal was dug, the land thirty or forty *sen* wide on each bank belonged to the owner of the company digging the canal. The whole Rangsit plain, which is now prosperous, was really a grassland with elephants. In 1920 when I received a government scholarship to study in France, before leaving Siam I went to the house in Ayutthaya and still observed elephants among the paddy fields. I can remember their silhouette, and mostly I saw them in pairs. When the rice grain was forming, many of them would come. The Siam Land, Canals, and Irrigation Company had three main shareholders: Phraongchao Saisanitwong; his eldest son, M.R. Suwaphan; and Phra Patipat Ratchaprasong, who was a German [actually Austrian] called Müller. But whoever had already staked a claim, like my father and uncles, had to chase away the elephants. I was still young but it was like this. To claim land lying vacant you had to battle the elephants. When the company had dug the canals, the land on both sides became the company land. Prior claimants paid a "land registry fee" of four baht a *rai*. That was the story. My father already had land there, but cultivating two hundred *rai* alone was too much. So in some years he rented out. At first he cultivated it by himself. He had five or six water buffaloes. I can remember they were all stolen. Paddy farmers had lots of problems including buffalo theft.

CHATTHIP: Please tell about the situation of paddy farmers you saw in the central region.

PRIDI: The term "central region" must be more specific. The central region is really very extensive. You must know the distribution of good and poor land. After you have listened to me, you must go and investigate again. In the old times, in order to know whether the paddy land was good or bad, and how poor the people were in any tambon, you looked at what type of land tax was collected, whether it was *kuko* or *fangloi*. *Kuko* land meant that however much land you owned, for instance ten *rai*, they collected land tax from you for the full ten *rai*. For *fangloi*, they collected according to measurement [of the extent cultivated] at the time. The *kamnan* had the duty of *sena*, of measuring how much land each owner had each year. *Kuko* was divided into grades one, two, three, and *fangloi* into grades one, two, three, four, and five. I recall that for grade five usually you paid one *salung* [= 1/4 baht] for each *rai* measured. For land not cultivated there was no payment. In Wang Noi, the tambon where my father was, he paid at grade five because the land was not very good. If you dug a well, the soil was very acid. So to collect water for the dry season, you had to dig a well just half-deep. The water was brackish. The paddy land in the amphoe around Ayutthaya was *kuko*, because in the rainy season water from the north flowed down and flooded it. The land was not damaged except in a really bad flood. Another thing you needed to know about was rice strains. Paddy farmers used strains which rose with the water.

❖❖❖

PHOONSUK (reading): Before Pridi went to study in France, there gradually arose in him the knowledge and consciousness that it was appropriate to change the system of government in which the king was above the law to one in which the king was within the law. This consciousness arose in stages as follows.

While Pridi was studying in elementary level, he once heard his father talking with farmers who were complaining about their difficulties in making a living. His father told the farmers how he had heard Chaokhun relate that in England there was a parliament, that is, an assembly, for which the people chose the representatives. Whoever had any serious problem could assign his representative to appeal to the government. At that time Pridi was still a very small child and so had no interest in such things. Only later could he recall this.

Later when Pridi had entered secondary school and had to study geography somewhat more broadly, together with the history of the world in outline, the teacher taught that governmental systems could be divided into three types, namely

1. king above the law, known as "absolutism"
2. king within the law of the land
3. leaders elected by the people, known as a "republic" (at that time, translated into Thai as *prachathipatai*; later after 1932 the word "republic" was translated into Thai as *satharanarat*). A council of ministers governed the country with the approval of parliament.

Pridi came to know about methods of government from these outline headings.

Then in Ro. So. 130, or 1912, there were two important events which made Pridi interested in changing the system of government in which the king was above the law.

First, the newspapers constantly ran exciting news stories about the war in China between the Kuomintang (Kek Meng, in the Taechiu dialect) under the leadership of Sun Yat Sen and the Manchu imperial court. Some progressive teachers followed this news and analysed for the students which side was winning or losing each day. This made Pridi and other interested students enjoy this news. In Ayutthaya, Chinese of the Kuomintang made publicity by renting a room in the Hua Ro market as a reading room, and by distributing pictures of the fighting to those interested. The Chinese opera which was performed regularly by Chinese artistes at Wat Choeng (Wat

Phananchoeng) changed its plays to suit the times by being about the Kuomintang and the imperial armies. The audience enjoyed this. Not long after, the Manchu imperial side had to concede defeat. A progressive teacher told Pridi casually that absolutism was already finished in China, leaving only Russia and Thailand. The teacher did not know in which of these two countries absolutism would come to an end first.

Second, at the end of 1912, news reached Pridi's house in Ayutthaya that some military officers along with some civilians had been preparing to change the absolute monarchy to a form in which the king is within the law. But before they launched the attempt, the government arrested them, tried them before a special court, and found them guilty of a serious crime. Pridi took a great interest in this news, because he saw that Siam had the Ro. So. 130 group who were patriotic and courageous enough to attempt to end the absolute monarchy, but just one person in the group had betrayed them to the government. Pridi tried to enquire from knowledgeable people about the Ro. So. 130 group with great sympathy.

Later in 1915–16, Pridi went to help his father with paddy farming before he entered the law school of the Justice Ministry. As noted in the second chapter, Pridi experienced the realities of life.

PRIDI: That is, I had finished secondary school. Usually one could study anywhere. But I was only fifteen. I could not enter the public administration school. So I went off to the fields for a time to be of some use. Once I was seventeen or eighteen, I entered the law school.

PHOONSUK (reading): This was a lesson to teach Pridi about the difficulties and deprivation of the peasants.

In an area of about one million *rai* of rice fields under the Siam Land, Canals, and Irrigation Company, 60 percent of the peasants were tenants. This was different from other localities where tenants were fewer, and different from localities where people cleared waste land and staked claims to ownership.

PRIDI: In the amphoes Sena, Bakhai, Rop Krung, Bang Pa-in near to any rivers and canals, we can see many houses built of wood.

PHOONSUK (reading): Whether farmers owned their land or rented from someone else, they all had to face the deprivations noted in the next paragraph below. But the farmers who rented were saddled with the burden of paying rent to the owner in the form of money or rice. Many landowners exploited them.

In the dry season, farmers who were far away from canals which had water all year round lacked drinking water for people and animals. In the rainy season, farmers experienced risks such as too little rain for planting, too much rain ruining the rice plants, enemies of the young rice plants such as those the farmers call *plia* [aphids] which eat and destroy many plants, and death in epidemics of the water buffaloes which are an important source of draught power. The farmers could not help themselves. Their output did not match the labour they put in. At the start of the next season, they had to borrow money from those who had some to invest. They had to pay a high rate of interest, and if they faced the same events in the following year, the debts piled up. Government could not help.

Robbers were everywhere. There were people who made a living from stealing farmers' buffaloes to claim ransom. Farmers had to borrow to pay the ransom, which increased their debts. Government could not help.

In any year when the farmers had enough rice, they still had to sell the paddy to a merchant who took advantage of them in weighing, measuring, and pricing.

If they sent the rice to a rice mill, the mills had a trick to fool the farmers. They did not charge a fee to mill the rice but instead took the husk, chaff, and broken rice. Most farmers were happy not to have to pay a milling fee. But in reality the mills took advantage of the farmers by setting the machines to increase the amount of chaff which went to the mill, so that the mill made a large profit.

In any year many farmers died from epidemics.

Farmers faced many other kinds of deprivation which showed that farmers received no help from government. Yet farmers had the burden of paying poll tax. If they had no money, they had to do corvée for fifteen to thirty days a year. They also had to pay land tax. Hence Pridi told the farmers that the officials, who claimed that farmers were the backbone of the nation, spoke without seeing that the farmers' backbone was already broken. This was what Pridi had experienced by mixing closely with the farmers. He recalled the lesson of his teacher and the events noted above: that if Siam had a parliament—that is, an assembly of representatives elected by the people to appeal to the government to solve the problems and improve the lot of the people—it would overcome the people's difficulties.

PRIDI: This was my experience. Next I will talk about what I found when studying at the law school.

KANOKSAK: May I ask an an additional question? In the written history about how you saw that the farmers were cheated by the rice mills, did you hear it from the farmers or see it yourself?

PRIDI: In my account above, I did not use the words "the farmers were cheated by the rice mills". Rather I conveyed the meaning "the rice mills had many ways to take advantage of the farmers". The farmers knew this but they went along with it because of the convenience. I saw it for myself. Once I went with my step-mother to take two measures *(krabung)* of paddy to mill. The mill owner did not want to offend and so returned two measures of milled rice. But this was special. The mill owner had added rice of his own to make up the two measures. But ordinary farmers would get only one and a half. The farmers knew about this, but the consciousness had not yet awakened in them. As I have said, and they themselves said, milling rice uses up time, so let the mill do it. The mills made a lot by exploiting lots of people just a little bit. You must understand. Milling rice yourself takes a lot of time. Hence I like the way Mao Zedong told the students that if they did not work with their hands themselves, they would not know the life of the farmers. It's the truth. If you don't take the paddy to the mill, when you want to eat rice, you have to mill the paddy yourself and then process it further before it is rice you can eat. Alternatively, big farmers have special mortars to mill the rice. Farmers eat a lot of rice. If they have to mill their own rice, it takes a lot of time. Better to give it to the mill, because it is more convenient. I've read some articles written by some people after 6 October [1976] who picture life in the jungle as very easy and convenient. I think this is different from how I experienced it before I had to leave Thailand because of the coup of 8 November 1947. However, let me repeat that my answers about the situation of Thai farmers were based on my own experience which created a consciousness in me before the time I went to study in France. As to whether Thai farmers today are being exploited by the rice mills or not, I have not had the opportunity to see for myself.

PHOONSUK (reading): In 1917 Pridi became a student at the law school in the Justice Ministry. At that time, the law school taught civil and criminal law which were mostly private law. But in courses on judicial procedure and on civil and criminal court proceedings, the teachers had to talk about people who had special rights outside the power of the courts of justice for the people in general, namely:

1. If royal relatives from the level of Momchao upwards committed a criminal offence, the court had the power to send the case to be considered by the Ministry of the Palace and to be judged by the king. This differed from the people in general who came under the criminal court. If the king found a royal relative guilty of a criminal charge, he would be imprisoned in a place belonging to the Ministry of the Palace known as *sanom*—not the jail. He would not be put in irons, but the officers would just leave the fetters on a pedestal inside the cell. In addition, even though the criminal law

code of 1908 nullified many old criminal laws, it did not nullify the old law under which a male commoner having sexual relations with a noble lady of level Momchaoying and above, was held to be a criminal offence liable to imprisonment not exceeding seven years.

2. Nationals under the jurisdiction of countries which had unequal treaties with Siam had special rights in criminal and civil law. If they committed a civil or criminal offence the courts of justice did not have the power to try them. The plaintiffs or prosecutors had to sue them in the consular court of that foreign national. Apart from Europeans and Japanese, Asians from the colonial territories of the West and Japan had the same special rights. Many Chinese understood this and sought the benefit of coming under the jurisdiction of a foreign power, because some countries' consuls sheltered them when they broke Thai law. If the Thai police made an arrest, the consuls made the prosecutor lodge the case at the consular court, and often decided in favour of those under their jurisdiction.

PRIDI: My teacher, even though he was an upcountry teacher from Ayutthaya not Bangkok, was a progressive type. I suspect he may have been influenced by the Ro. So. 130 group.

CHATTHIP: Do you think your teacher got his thinking from the Ro. So. 130 group more than from the Kuomintang group?

PRIDI: The Ro. So. 130 had the nickname of "Thai Kuomintang" *(Thai meng)*. But before that group could exist you had to have people return from overseas who had been persuaded to think about changing the government.

❖❖❖

## ADDITIONAL EXPLANATION ABOUT THE THINKING BEHIND THE ECONOMIC PLAN FOR SIAM

[Pridi often insisted on his right to insert extra material into transcripts of interviews which were to be published. In the following insertion, he clearly wanted to clarify the connections between his personal experience, his education, and the outline economic plan which appears in part 2.]

My thinking that Siam should have an economic plan did not arise suddenly and was not based on guesswork without any economic theory.

I have already referred to the state of Thai society and how I found from my own experience that the people faced economic deprivation, lacked political rights and freedoms, and were under the power and influence of several capitalist countries. Before I went to study in France I had the idea to study and research further on how to improve the situation of the people.

When I had the government scholarship to study law in France, although I was already a barrister in Siam, I was only twenty years old. So my teacher advised me to study at the university from the beginning level like French students following the curriculum of the law faculty *(Faculté de Droit)*. The curriculum was different from that in Siam and in the Anglo-Saxon countries. At the time of the French Third Republic *(3e Republique,* 1870), French law faculties taught only private law and constitutional law like many Anglo-Saxon countries. But later the government of the French Third Republic expanded the curriculum of the law faculty. On top of private law they added economics on grounds it was the foundation of society. They also added several departments of public law on grounds these were the superstructure of society.

So I studied Economics 1 in the first year and Economics 2 in the second year of the law degree course. In the third year for the Licence degree I studied fiscal law and labour law as well.

As I was interested in economics, once I had passed the examination for the doctorate of law in jurisprudence, I took a further examination for the advanced diploma in political economy *(Diplôme d'Etudes Supérieures d'Economie Politique)* which included advanced economics, history of economic theory, law and science of public finance, law and science of labour. So I studied many parts of the economic system including the socialist economic system about economic planning.

So the consciousness arose in me that Siam should have an economic plan which followed the science of socialist theory and which took into account the local situation and contemporary state of Siam as I had experienced it and as it was changing further during the time I was studying.

Hence I drafted the economic plan and presented it to the friends who joined together to create the People's Party in Paris.

# 4. EXCERPTS FROM: *CONCISE AUTOBIOGRAPHY OF NAI PRIDI BANOMYONG* (1983)

[N.B. This autobiography was written in the style of notes, and that style is here reproduced in the English.]

## 3. EDUCATION IN THAILAND

Began studying at the house of teacher Seng in tambon Tha Wasukri, then moved to the house of Luang Prani (Piam) in amphoe Tha Rua.

Once could read and write, entered the school of Wat Ruak which at that time was the government school for amphoe Tha Rua. Passed the first grade at level 1 (in the Education Ministry's curriculum of that time which divided primary education into three levels and four grades; the division into *mun, prathom, mathayom* did not yet exist).

Later when the Education Ministry set a new curriculum divided into *mun, prathom, mathayom,* moved to study at the school of Wat Sala Pun, amphoe Krung Kao. Passed *prathom* exams under the new curriculum, then moved to study lower secondary *(mathayom triam)* at Wat Benchamabophit [in Bangkok], and then to the monthon Ayutthaya demonstration school until passed *mathayom* 6 (which was the highest level available in a provincial town). Went to study further at Suan Kulap school [in Bangkok] for six months, then quit to go back to help father with paddy farming. Acquired much practical knowledge from the farmers.

In 1917, entered the law school of the Justice Ministry, and studied French language at the Bar Association under the teacher, E. Ladeker, who was advisor to the foreign court.

In 1919, passed the bar exams, but under the limitations of that time was unable to become a barrister as not yet aged twenty. Had to wait until attained the age of twenty in 1920, and then became an ordinary member of the bar.

*M.C. Dilokrit Kridakon, Pridi, and Amrung Sunthonwon*

# 4. SPECIAL ACTIVITIES AND GOVERNMENT SERVICE DURING TIME AS A LAW STUDENT

In 1917–18, clerk in the law office of Phra Wichitmontri (Sut Kunthon-chinda), former chief judge of monthon Chumphon and former assistant head of the department of military procedure.

In 1919–20, second-grade clerk in the penitentiary department.

Received special permission to act as counsel in some cases.

# 5. STUDY IN FRANCE

In August 1920, selected by the Justice Ministry for a scholarship to study law in France.

Studied French language and general knowledge at the Lycée in Caen, with special tuition from M. Lebonnois, secretary of the Institut Pédagogique International.

Studied law at the University of Caen, passed the Bachelier de Droit and the Licencié de Droit.

Studied further at the University of Paris, passed the Docteur en Droit in Sciences Juridiques, and also the Diplôme d'Etudes Supérieures d'Economie Politique.

# 8. GOVERNMENT SERVICE PRIOR TO THE REVOLUTION OF 24 JUNE

Judge attached to the Ministry of Justice: trained as a prosecutor in the foreign court and the foreign cases court for six months; took records of cases filed in the High Court for six months

Promoted as assistant secretary in the law-drafting department.

Taught at the law school of the Ministry of Justice: compiled third volume of the civil code on partnerships, companies, and associations; taught private international law; was the first person to teach administrative law.

*The future King Prajadhipok with Thai students in France, 1924.*
*Pridi is third from right in the second row.*

# 9. SPECIAL ACTIVITIES PRIOR TO THE REVOLUTION OF 24 JUNE

Taught at the law school in a way to arouse, by stages, the consciousness of students to be interested in the necessity of changing the absolute monarchy to a form of monarchy under a democratic constitution.

At the Silom house, began training and critique of law with no teaching fee for law students to foster even closer relations with students, such that many law students joined as type-1 members of the People's Party, and as type-2 and type-3 supporters of the People's Party.

# 5. COMMENTARY ON ADMINISTRATIVE LAW: DURING THE CURRENT REIGN (1931)

[N.B. This is part of a series first published in the law journal. Cross-references are to other articles in the series by other authors.]

In the current reign, there are three councils for affairs of the realm, namely

1. the Supreme Council of State *(aphiratthamontri sapha)*
2. the Council of Ministers *(senabodi sapha)*
3. the Committee of the Privy Council *(sapha kammakan ongkhamontri)*

## CHAPTER 1: THE SUPREME COUNCIL OF STATE

This council was established on 28 November 1925 (see the royal decree to establish the Supreme Council of State in the Royal Gazette, volume 42, p. 2168).

1. Duties of the council. The decree states "for the king to take counsel on all matters of state regularly in order to contribute to decisions on all state matters".

2. Members.
    i. Total members of this council number five.
    ii. Qualifications of supreme councillors. Those receiving royal appointment as supreme councillors must have qualifications as laid down in the royal decree as follows: "those fitting to be members must have considerable prior experience and expertise of government affairs, and must have the reputation as well as ability worthy of the trust of the king and of the people as a whole".

3. Chairman of meetings. For meetings of this council, the king himself acts as chairman or deputes to a regent in his stead (see the duties of the regent examined above).

## CHAPTER 2: THE COUNCIL OF MINISTERS

The Council of Ministers has existed since the Fifth Reign. Ministers have duties not only of executing laws and carrying out administration, but also of offering advice to the king on matters concerning the administration of the realm.

This chapter deals with the Council of Ministers as a council of the realm. As for the ministers in their capacity of executing laws, this will be considered below.

1. Duties of the Council of Ministers as a council of the realm.

i. General duties. It appears in the decree on the appointment of the Supreme Council that: "the Council of Ministers who oversee the work of various ministries totalling less than twenty, offer advice to the king on official matters which are specified as the duty of those ministries". By this it is understood that although any official matter is the duty of a specific ministry, it may be considered in the Council of Ministers if the king wishes.

ii. Special duties on certain matters. By the royal household law on the succession, the ministers have certain duties, for instance to invite the successor to ascend the throne in accordance with the order of succession, which has been examined already. Or to invite senior royal family members *(chao nai)* to serve as regent in the case of a royal minority, as has been examined already in section 3. In this respect there is a problem: does "ministers" here mean the Council of Ministers or not?

2. Membership. The members of the Council of Ministers are ministers, supreme councillors, and royal secretaries with position equal to ministers.

3. Chairman of meetings. The king or regent acts as chairman of meetings.

## CHAPTER 3. THE COMMITTEE OF THE PRIVY COUNCIL

This Committee is descended from the Privy Council *(priwi khaonsiw)* which was established in the Fifth Reign and later renamed as *sapha ongkhamontri.*

The number of privy councillors is not limited, and is expanding all the time. When the present king ascended the throne, he reappointed the privy councillors who had been appointed by Rama VI.

In 1927, the king had the Royal Secretariat issue a statement that the king wished to hear opinions of the Privy Council on the national flag. In the

Sixth Reign, the elephant flag had been changed into the tricolour. In the present reign, the king asked five cases to be considered:

1. use the elephant flag in place of the tricolour; or
2. use the elephant flag as the royal standard and the tricolour as the national flag; or
3. use the elephant flag as both the royal standard and national flag, with the tricolour as the national colours used for decorating locations on festive days; or
4. use the tricolour and red elephant combined into a single flag; or
5. continue as at present.

The privy councillors offered the king varying advice. Later on 25 May of that year, a royal decision was issued on the national flag as follows: "the advice offered by the privy councillors on the national flag varies a great deal. There is no clear weight on any one side. Thus the decision is to remain as before." (Royal Gazette, volume 44, p. 607)

The king was unable to take advice from the Privy Council on this matter. It may be that some of the privy councillors agreed with King Rama VI that the elephant flag is difficult to make, and is not made in many places. Countries which make it do not know the elephant, and make the shape unattractive, such that if those using the flag are not careful they may fly it upside down which is awful and embarassing. Others may have had very different opinions, to the point where the opinions had no clear weight on any side. Since there were five possible options, there may well have been five different opinions offered.

## THE PRIVY COUNCIL ACT OF 1927

Subsequently in September 1927, the king had a new act drafted on the Privy Council, superceding the act of 1874.

1. Concerning privy councillors. Under the provisions of the new act, it should be observed, the existing privy councillors remained as privy councillors, but had no right to sit on the Committee of the Privy Council. Those with such a right had to be "Members of the Committee of the Privy Council" who were appointed from among the privy councillors. Hence the status of the privy councillors changed somewhat.

i. Qualifications: those considered by the king to have the qualifications, recognized ability, and moral integrity suitable for royal trust should be appointed as privy councillors (clause 4).

ii. Appointment is by issue of a royal command *(sanyabat)*, supplemented by drinking the water of allegiance (clause 5).

iii. Expressing opinions: may offer any opinion directly to the king (clause 6).

iv. By clause 7, anyone who has served as privy councillor for ten years and receives salary *(biawat)* and pension of not more than 1,600 baht a year, the king will provide financial support for the whole time he is a privy councillor including living allowance and other money of not less than 1,600 baht a year, rising to 2,400 baht if that person has been a member of the Committee of the Privy Council under clause 12.

v. Relinquishing the position. At the end of the reign. Under clause 8, anyone who has been a privy councillor shall remain in the position until the end of the reign and may be retained for six months beyond. If the successor wishes that person to remain as privy councillor, he must reappoint.

By removal (see clause 9). Besides this, relinquishment may come about through death. There is a problem that when a privy councillor loses ability or appears to lose ability, must he relinquish the position or not?

2. Concerning the Committee of the Privy Council.

i. Qualifications and appointment. The king appoints from among the privy councillors (see clause 12).

ii. Expressing opinions: (a) to discuss, debate and agree on matters which the king himself asks to be considered; (b) in addition, if no fewer than five members of the Committee of the Privy Council together write a petition to the head of the Council that there is an important issue concerning the welfare of the country and people, on which they should meet to discuss and offer an opinion to the king, the head of the council may request permission from the king to proceed with such a meeting.

iii. Prerogative in expressing opinions. Under clause 14, members of the Committee of the Privy Council need bear no liability for any words spoken or expressed as opinions, or for any vote made in its meetings. If anyone wishes to complain against, sue, or accuse a privy councillor for that reason, it is not permitted.

In addition, persons whom the Council invites to give explanation or opinion shall receive the same exemption.

iv. Living allowance. See clause 7 on the living allowance of the privy councillors above; that is, if a privy councillor becomes a member of the Committee of the Privy Council, then the rate is increased up to 2,400 baht.

v. Relinquishing the position. (a) End of term. Appointments to the

Committee are for three years renewable by royal appointment (see clause 15). By clause 16, if any member of the Committee of the Privy Council must quit the post for any reason other than end of the normal term, the king shall appoint another privy councillor in his place to complete the number, but this replacement shall hold the position only for the remainder of the term of the member who has quit. (b) By resignation (see clause 17). (c) By the Council petitioning the king for removal, Under clause 18, if the behaviour of any member of the Committee of the Privy Council is not appropriate for this position, the committee shall meet and submit advice for the king to remove that person from the post, but must give opportunity to that committee member to provide justification before the advice is forwarded to the king. (d) By relinquishment of privy councillorship, for instance at the end of the reign of the king who made the appointment, and for other reasons for relinquishment of term as privy councillor detailed above.

3. Meetings of the Committee of the Privy Council

i. Number of members. Forty persons. The Committee elects a president and vice-president who must be approved by the king before assuming office (see clause 12). To help them compile their advice, the committee may invite any person to offer explanations and opinions to their meetings (see clause 13, paragraph 3). Non-committee members invited to meetings have no right to vote.

ii. Duties of the Committee. To meet and discuss government issues which the king has forwarded for discussion (see clause 11). The king may forward such matters himself (see clause 13, paragraph 1), or five committee members may make a petition to the president that there is an issue concerning the welfare of the country and people on which there should be discussion and opinion. Such a matter can be discussed after the president of the Committee has requested and received the king's permission (see clause 13, paragraph 2).

iii. Officers of the committee: (a) president; (b) vice-president; both are elected by the committee members but must receive royal approval (see clauses 12, 19, 20); (c) secretary; an official from the royal secretariat shall be appointed by the king to serve as registrar and secretary of meetings (see clauses 10, 23, 27).

iv. Meetings: (a) the quorum is not less than fifteen members (see clause 25); (b) the president shall call meetings (see clause 22); (c) rules: any matter for consideration must be noted in the agenda (clause 23); meetings must proceed according to rules and agenda as laid down, unless the meeting agrees otherwise (clause 24).

v. Chairman of meetings: the president shall be chairman; if absent, the vice-chairman; if both absent, the members may elect a temporary chairman (see clause 21).

vi. Resolutions shall be by majority vote, with each member having one vote, and in the event of a tie, the chairman having an additional casting vote (see clause 26).

vii. Presenting advice to the king; the president has the duty to present the advice of the Committee of the Privy Council to the king at the king's wish (see clause 28).

viii. Reports of meetings: the secretary must take minutes, and propose them for approval at the following meeting (see clause 27).

ix. Sub-committees: by clause 29, the Committee of the Privy Council has the power to establish sub-committees for any purpose or for examining any issues to propose to the full meeting for further discussion and agreement; if the chairman of a sub-committee is not appointed by the Committee, the sub-committee members may select themselves.

Sub-committees have the power to invite heads of ministries, other officers, and outsiders as prescribed for the Committee in clause 13.

Sub-committees and those they invite to give explanations and opinions also have the benefit of clause 14.

By clause 30, the quorum for meetings of sub-committees is three persons, except in cases where the sub-committee has only three members, when the quorum shall be two.


[Translators' explanatory note: King Prajadhipok established the Supreme Council three days after ascending the throne in 1925, and filled the Council with five senior royal princes (Damrong, Narit, Boriphat, Phanurangsi, Chanthaburi). Prajadhipok's predecessor had tended to bypass the senior princes, hence this move was a deliberate attempt to signal a return to a stricter policy of royal seniority in official positions. The press heavily criticized this exclusivity. Thus in 1927, Prajadhipok considered reviving the moribund Privy Council as a public display of a marginally more open policy. The issue of the flag which Pridi describes ended any notion that this existing Privy Council could serve such a purpose. Hence the king consulted his close advisers about constituting a new body with fewer members (the Privy Council had ballooned to several hundred) but a slightly broader social base for discussing national issues. Several senior princes were horrified, but the balance was in favour of such a move. The king talked of including some commoners. However, eventually all the forty appointees to the new Committee of the Privy Council were either members of the royal family or senior officials. The king noted that "if reforms are gradually introduced in this way, a democratic form of government could possibly be introduced without too much harm". The Committee of the Privy Council was in existence for four years, dealt only with minor administrative affairs, and was abolished (along with the Supreme Council of State) after the 1932 revolution. See Benjamin A. Batson, *The End of the Absolute Monarchy in Siam* (Singapore: Oxford University Press, 1984), ch. 5.]

# 6. LECTURES ON ADMINISTRATIVE LAW (1932)

## PRELIMINARY MATTERS

### 1. WHAT ADMINISTRATIVE LAW IS

It is difficult to interpret the phrase "administrative law" with exactness and certainty. However, the title of this course is comprised of two words, "law" and "administrative". So as a guide at this preliminary stage, it should first be understood what these two words mean.

The word "law" can be interpreted in two ways.

First, in a narrow sense, the word law means the commands or orders laid down as laws for people to follow by the person who holds the supreme power in the realm (which depends on what is laid down by the constitution or the customs for ruling the country; for example, in Siam it is the king).

Second, in a broad sense, the word "law" means the principles which people must follow, which they may be forced to follow, and for which, if they refuse, they may be charged with a civil, criminal, or administrative offence. Thus law may be commands or orders which the person with the supreme power in the realm lays down, such as ministerial decrees; or rules enforced by officials; or other principles of conduct, such as customs and general legal principles, which may not be written down but which have the same result when they are infringed.

The Civil and Commercial Code of 1923 has followed the first interpretation, that is, law must be written law. But this code is no longer in force because a new version has come out to replace it. In the new version, there is no direct interpretation of the word, but clause 4 tends towards a broad meaning which is different from textual law. The law which we study here must have the broad meaning since the written law on administration is inadequate, and we must refer also to custom, comparative law, and general legal principles.

The word "administration" or "government" (*kan pokkhrong*) is understood differently by different people. Sometimes it means the business of the Interior Ministry. Sometimes it has a broad meaning as the collective supreme powers of the country.

The dictionary of the Education Ministry interprets the word somewhat neutrally as: protecting, taking care of, looking after, controlling.

This protecting, taking care of, looking after, and controlling may take place among private individuals, or in the family where parents govern children and husband governs wife, or in the protection and care of people who are incapacitated or appear to be. These examples of government are part of civil law which is outside the law we shall study.

When many human beings associate together as a country, they need to protect, take care of, look after, control. The course we shall study here will focus on the administration of human beings who have associated together as a country. The protecting, taking care of, looking after, and controlling which are the elements of this course may be considered a branch of the supreme power in the country.

This supreme power in the country can be divided into three:

1. the power to make laws or the legislative power;
2. the power of enforcing laws or the executive or administrative power;
3. the power to adjudicate laws or the judicial power.

That is, when human beings associate together as a country and agree to have laws to control behaviour, there must be some people with the power to write those laws, to enforce them, to take care that people act in accordance with them, and to adjudicate effectively on problems which arise with the law or its enforcement.

According to French legal theory, the legislative power and the judicial power should be separate from the executive power or administrative power, because if they are combined it may lead to injustice. In other words, those adjudicating are adjudicating on laws which they themselves legislated.

The administration under study here comes within the executive or administrative branch, that is, the power to enforce laws or to adjudicate on laws. Therefore, administrative law may be briefly defined as the principles and rules concerned with the regulations and practices of officials in the executive or administrative branch, and concerned with relations between private individuals and officialdom.

There is another consideration. Administrative law is different from the constitution of the realm. The constitution is a law which lays down rules concerning all the supreme powers in the realm and the general practice of those powers. In other words, constitutional law lays down the general principles of the supreme powers in the country, while administrative law codifies the regulations and procedures of the executive or administrative powers in detail, and deals with the use of these powers. However, both these laws are branches of public law. Hence in certain matters, they cannot be completely separated (on the division of law into departments, see the teaching text on jurisprudence).

## 2. WHY ADMINISTRATIVE LAW IS A SEPARATE BRANCH OF LAW

Administrative law is not a separate branch of law in all countries. This is because the significance of administrative law varies among the legal theories of different peoples.

We may divide the major legal theories into four groups as follows:

1. FRENCH LEGAL THEORY
2. GERMAN LEGAL THEORY
3. ANGLO-SAXON LEGAL THEORY
4. JAPANESE LEGAL THEORY

1. FRENCH LEGAL THEORY. This theory wishes to make a definite separation between administrative law and judicial power. As major principles, this theory upholds that a. in any matter concerning government administration, ordinary law cannot apply; that is, the law used must be a special law, because in government there are special principles different from those of ordinary law; b. judicial courts do not have power to adjudicate cases on government administration; that is, such cases must be decided according to the practice of government in order to maintain the independence of governmental power.

2. GERMAN LEGAL THEORY. Administrative law in Germany is developed from the legal theory of *Rechstaat*. The duty of the state is not simply to control and command us like a policeman. The state must act according to laws, which impose principles which the government must follow. These principles give rise to administrative law which is classified as a branch of public law.

3. ANGLO-SAXON LEGAL THEORY. Dicey stated there is no theory of administrative law in Britain. But Goodenough in Columbia University, New York, stated in a book on comparative government that it is not that there is no principle of administrative law, but only that writers of legal texts have not treated it separately.

That may be so. In England there is no administrative court similar to those which under French law decide cases related to government administration.

4. JAPANESE LEGAL THEORY. According to the exposition on the principles of Japanese administrative law by Professor Ota, Japanese administrative law follows the principles of German law.

The major differences between the various theories described above are over the separation of powers, the limitation of administrative power, and the adjudication of cases on administrative issues. The special principles of government, such as the administrative rules concerning the relations between government power and private individuals, exist in all countries, even in Siam in the same way as other countries. We shall see in future study that there are many enactments which lay down the rules of government power, for example with respect to the power to establish various ministries and offices. Also there are laws which regulate the practices of the administration with respect to policing for maintaining peace and order, with respect to activities for the welfare of the people, or with respect to strengthening the economy. In addition, there are also enactments about administrative cases, for instance about appeals against various orders by officials of the legal administrative department. All these matters are not civil, commercial, or other private law. So they must be organized as another branch of law.

## 3. THE VARIOUS PRINCIPLES OF ADMINISTRATIVE LAW

Administrative law arises because every country has government and so must have this branch of law.

Administrative law may be in the form of written law or unwritten, for instance custom, comparative law, and general legal principles.

Written law is in very widespread use, and we will have a chance to study this in later sections. As for custom, we may refer to it sometimes, but it is difficult to describe completely because it is not written down. As for comparative law, there should be some opportunity to deal with some parts. You should look at the teaching text on jurisprudence.

The other principle of law which we must invoke in the absence of legislative enactments, custom, and comparative law, is general legal principles. These general legal principles refer to the principles of behaviour towards one another which must be followed by human beings who associate together in groups or countries. But the question of how human beings should behave towards one another in order to associate for common happiness depends on the science of social relations as a tool of analysis. This science has many branches, for instance social science, economics, ethics, religion, public administration, law, and so on. These disciplines should be required for the study of government administration, in the same way that they are necessary for the study of law in general.

Among the general legal principles which are embedded in various disciplines, there is one type which must be understood at the preliminary stage, because it is the most necessary in studying administrative law. That is the principle concerning human rights.

Human beings are born with rights and duties. In order to exist and join together in associations, these rights and duties arise from the ordinary condition of humanity. They can be classified into three:

1. *seriphap (liberté)*
2. *samaphap (egalité)*
3. *phraradoraphap (fraternité)* or helping one another as brothers.

But it must be understood here that these rights and duties are not absolute because they arise from the state of nature *(saphap tham)*.

Thus they may be limited by enactments or by the customs of the place and time. These limitations vary across time and across countries. They cannot all be the same. They are dependent on the needs of the country and of the time.

### Liberty

Liberty means the rights of people to do anything without compulsion, as long as it does not inconvenience or infringe upon other people.

We may classify liberties as follows:
1. liberty of person
2. liberty of dwelling
3. liberty in making a living
4. liberty of property
5. liberty of religion
6. liberty of association
7. liberty in expression of opinions
8. liberty of education
9. liberty in appealing against hardship

1. Liberty of person. A person should have freedom in one's person to do anything with respect to one's person. There are three important results of liberty of person:

i. A person must be free *(thai)*; in Siam at present there are no slaves *(that)* (see the Slavery Act of 1905).

ii. A person cannot be arrested at the will of an official. Arrest must proceed according to the forms and conditions laid down by law (see the teaching text on criminal procedure).

iii. Penalties imposed on those who have committed a crime must follow rules according to the law. The court cannot choose to impose a penalty at will (see criminal law, clause 12). Punishments such as whipping and various tortures no longer exist.

2. Liberty of dwelling. A person should have freedom in the building which is one's dwelling. If anyone enters to intrude, it may be an offence. The criminal law has provisions to control such intrusion. Officials who enter to inspect people and buildings must proceed in accordance with the forms and conditions laid down by law. Otherwise the officials themselves may be wrong in a criminal sense.

3. Liberty in making a living. A person has the right to choose how to make a living. That is, one may choose to make something, to sell in some way, or any kind of occupation. But this liberty has limitations for the benefit of humankind as a whole. For instance:

i. Some occupations are forbidden such as the making of obscene materials, see the Act on the Suppression of the Manufacture, Distribution, and Sale of Obscene Materials of 1928, clauses 3–4.

ii. Those following certain kinds of occupation must have adequate qualifications and must be licensed by government, for instance barristers (see the Act on the Legal Profession of 1914) and doctors (see the Act on the Medical Profession of 1923, amended 1929).

iii. Certain kinds of occupations must proceed within conditions as laid down or must receive concessions, such as railways, irrigation, banks, savings banks, credit foncier, highways, and so on (see the Act on the Control of Trade which Affects the Safety and Well-being of the General Public of 1928, and the Act on Highways under Concessions of 1930).

iv. Some occupations are under government monopoly, for instance the sale of liquor.

4. Liberty of property. A person has the right to use, make profit from, sell, or transfer one's property at will. But this liberty should have limitations for the benefit of other people. See the Civil and Commercial Code, book 4, concerning the domain of ownership rights and the exercise of rights. Because a person has liberty of property, forcing someone to relinquish

ownership rights in property can be done only when there is a public benefit. Even then forced purchase can be carried out only when there is a royal decree, such as the decrees on making roads, railways, irrigation works, or other public services.

5. Liberty of religion. A person may choose to observe a religion or none at all. This principle has been adopted in Siam for a long time. It can be seen that Siam has accepted the status of religions other than Buddhism. For instance there is an act concerning the status of the Roman Catholic church in Siam, which has been promulgated and amended since 1909.

In France at the time of Louis XIV the freedom of people to adhere to Protestantism was taken away. The unfortunate consequence was that those adhering to this religion migrated to other countries which resulted in France losing many important people.

6. Liberty of association. A person is not born to be alone. A person is born to associate together with other people. Therefore a person has liberty of association with other people.

This association in Siam has limitations. Thus we should divide the study of human association into two points.

i. Temporary association for conversation and the expression of opinions, not the establishment of an organization. For instance, ten law students arrange to meet at a certain location on 1 July of this year to discuss legal problems. Associating like this does not amount to an organization. Therefore man should have the liberty to do this, except when the purpose of the association is against the criminal law on robbery and secret societies (*angyi*) (clauses 177–182) or is a basis for fomenting public disorder (clauses 183–184).

ii. Associating to establish an organization. See the Civil and Commercial Code (1274–1297). This means an association with any objective which will be on a continuous basis. Here liberty is limited by legal enactment, that is organizations must be registered, otherwise it is an offence under the criminal law clause 367 (see my teaching text from 1927–29 on the Civil and Commercial Code, book 3, clauses 1012–1297).

7. Liberty in expression of opinions. A person has liberty in one's person, hence a person should have liberty to use one's brain to express one's opinions for public benefit. But this liberty is limited by the criminal law clauses 103–104. In addition, the expression of opinion through books and documents is limited by the Books and Documents Act of 1927.

8. Liberty of education. A person has liberty to choose to study any discipline according to preference, and cannot be forced to study this discipline or not to study that discipline. But this liberty is confined to the choice of study. It does not mean the liberty not to study at all. Education is something of importance for the benefit of a person himself or herself. Hence there is the Elementary Education Act of 1921 to force Thai citizens to study.

People have liberty in the provision of education, but must act within the conditions laid down in the Public Schools Act of 1917.

9. Liberty in appealing against wrongs. When a person is unjustly mistreated by other people, or by officials of any department, that person should have the liberty to appeal against the wrong in order to undo the injustice. This appeal against wrong may be through a case in the courts of justice using the law, or by appeal to someone with high authority, or by appeal to the king (see part 4 of the commentary on administrative cases).

In some countries such as France, there is an administrative court which has the power to decide on administrative cases. In these countries, when people have suffered damage at the hands of an official or department, they have the right to sue. There is only the question whether such cases come under the authority of the courts of justice or the administrative court. Government departments cannot simply deny and refuse to be defendants.

*Equality*

When a person has liberty as described, that person may use that liberty the same as other people. Equality here means equality before the law, that is, equality in rights and duties. It does not mean equality in material things. For instance, it does not mean that people must have equal amounts of money, which is a genuine misunderstanding. There is no theory which makes such a claim, except by supposition.

Equality before the law may be equality both in rights and in duties or burdens.

i. A person has the right to be covered by the same laws as others, with the exception of special persons such as royalty, the army, or navy who have special laws.

ii. A person has the right to call on the same courts to adjudicate, with the exception of special persons who come under the palace courts, army court, or naval court.

iii. A person has the same right to enter government service when that person has the qualifications laid down by law; see the Civilian Bureaucracy Act of 1928 and Judiciary Act of 1928.

Equality in duties and burdens. Examples of equality in duties and burdens are:

i. The duty to pay tax. On this matter we should recall Rama VI who issued a letter to the minister of the capital of which this is a copy:

No 3/49
15 April 1913

To Chaophraya Yommarat

In past collection of tax on land and shops, the king's treasury has never paid tax to the officials of the revenue department. Now I examine matters and find that all of my property which is private is equivalent to the property of an ordinary person. But why do I have advantage over people in general, which seems not fitting? They collect from other people. But my property is treated differently. When it comes to the time for officials to collect tax, any ordinary person in general who has property as land or shops must pay the tax to the officials according to the amount of property he has. Beyond my official position, I hold that I am an ordinary person. The property which I have is considerable. If the government shares some of the benefit which I have from this property in total, I am totally happy to contribute to the support of the nation and country in the same way as a commoner. Therefore henceforth, Chaophraya Yommarat should collect the tax on land and shops which are counted as my private property in the same way as they are collected from other people in general.

Sayamin

Subsequently in the present reign, an announcement about financial difficulties appeared on 2 June 1932 in the Royal Gazette, volume 49, page 152, with the following passage: "even the king has surrendered his own money which was previously used for personal expenditure, in order to assist the realm in large measure, and has agreed to collection of tax on his property at the same rate as all of the people".

ii. A person has the same duty to enter government service. See the Military Conscription Act of 1917, clause 4, which states that all males who are Thai under the Nationality Act of 1913, clause 3, have the duty to enter military service.

*Fraternity*

A person is born to be in society as stated. People must help one another. In a country, if one person must suffer wrong, other people must also suffer wrong, either directly or indirectly, either in a small or large measure.

Therefore, having only liberty and equality is not enough for uniting together. People must help one another directly, or they must help by carrying out their duty to the central state which in turn redistributes those contributions to private individuals. Thus mutual assistance as referred to here can be divided up for study as:

> i. the duty of private individuals to the state;
> ii. the duty of the state to private individuals.

*The duty of private individuals to the state*
The duties of private individuals to the state must be studied with reference to the doctrine practised by each country. For Siam we can see that the important duties of private individuals to the state include:

> i. Private individuals have the duty to respect the family because the family is the foundation of associating together as a country.
> ii. Private individuals have the duty to respect the law, otherwise there will be no freedom, liberty, and equality.
> iii. Private individuals have the duty to make a living which is a way of sharing the burden of bringing about the progress of the country. Idleness and vagrancy may be charged under the criminal law, clause 30, and by the Act to Reform Vagrants of 1909, clause 1.
> iv. Private individuals have the duty to pay taxes (see under equality above).
> v. Private individuals have the duty to enter military service (see under equality above)

*The duty of the state to private individuals*
Study of the duty of the state to private individuals touches on the important question of what kind of duties the state has to private individuals in return for what the state takes from private individuals. On this matter, experts on politics are not in agreement. There are many theories which we may classify into two views.

According to the first view, the state has the duty to perform only those actions which are necessary to protect and maintain peace and order, for instance, maintaining peace and order within the realm, protecting the realm, and looking after state property. As for economic affairs, development activities, or increasing the well-being of the people, these should be left to free private enterprise case by case. Therefore according to this view, the duty of the state is limited. Any state which upholds this theory has been given the title of a police state *(Etat-Gendarme)*.

According to the second view, besides the duties cited under the first view, the state also has the duty to assist the people to have well-being in economic matters and social affairs. The government must intervene in certain aspects of the economy, or must own and manage them itself. Leaving things to private free enterprise may give rise to conflict, with the final result that whoever has the most power of property will triumph over the poor. People have called states which uphold this theory as welfare states (*Etat-Providence*).

I believe that every day now it can be said that in almost every country, the state has entered into some role in the economy. Whether that role is large or small depends on the preference of that country. Even in Siam it can be seen that there are factories or some types of business which the government runs itself or where it has intervened. Therefore the duty of the state to the private individual should be divided under two types as follows.

 i. Duties which the state must perform as necessity to protect and maintain peace and order.

 ii. Duties which the state must perform to help improve the status, existence, and well-being of the people.

Duties under point i which the state must perform as necessity to protect and maintain peace and order include for example: a. maintaining peace and order within the realm; b. protecting the realm; c. looking after state property.

Duties under point ii which the state must perform to help improve the status, existence, and well-being of the people, can be divided under two major branches.

 a. In the economy. Government must help intervene in activities related to the economy, for example: i. Manufacture, meaning the manufacture of articles, or can be called the manufacture of goods, which is related to industry, including the provision or improvement of various things which are factors of manufacture such as labour, land, and capital. ii. Exchange, which means the movement or circulation of economic goods, for instance, transport and trade. iii. Distribution, which means determining the division of economic goods such as fixing salaries or wages between employer and worker, or dividing property ownership in the country, as for example in the royal decree of 1930 on the division of land to people in amphoe Bang Bo and Bang Phli of Samut Prakan province and Bang Pakong of Chachoengsao province. iv. Consumption, which means the usage of economic goods which have been manufactured, whether food or non-food, and saving which is related to economizing on goods.

 b. In social matters. In truth social matters may be part of the economy, but some problems concerning man and society should be raised here. Examples of such matters are: i. public health; ii. assistance for the destitute and incapable; iii. providing employment for citizens; iv. forecasting, such as for pensions for the old and disabled; v. providing for citizens to receive education.

### The consequences of infringement of human rights

The human rights cited above are held to be important principles which various officials and offices must respect. Infringement may have the following consequences: i. legal consequences; ii. administrative consequences; iii. moral consequences.

i. Legal consequences. Some human rights are protected by legislation. Those who infringe may be charged, for instance in the matter of liberties of person and dwelling as cited above.

ii. Administrative consequences. Anyone who infringes human rights, if the infringement has not come within the scope of a case in the courts of justice, the person whose rights have been infringed may appeal to the government, as stated above concerning the liberty to appeal against wrongs. If the infringer is an official, there may be an administrative charge such as the charge of indiscipline as stated in the Civilian Administration Act of 1928.

iii. Moral consequences. Any infringement of human rights which is not against the law and which is not known to the administration, still has a moral implication. That is, the infringement may make the person dissatisfied, and if that feeling grows, there may be bad consequences. Alternatively, the person who committed the infringement may become ashamed because what he did was against human rights.

## PLAN OF STUDY OF ADMINISTRATIVE LAW

Part 1. Rules of administration
Part 2. Administrative work
Part 3. Country's finances
Part 4. Administrative cases

## PART 1. RULES OF ADMINISTRATION

### Section 1. General matters

I have stated already in the preliminary remarks that people who associate together as a country must have a government. Before we can study the rules of administration, we should understand first general matters related to the conditions under which people associate together as a country.

1: Country, realm, state *(State-Etat)*. When people associate together as a country and have a government to administer them, it is held in international law that this association has the status of a juristic person. This means the association has rights and duties in the same way as an ordinary person, for instance, rights to property, rights to enter into agreements with other countries under the name of the country, and duties to respect international agreements or customs (see my commentary on international law on individual cases, at the law school in 1929–30).

There are several words used for a juristic person of this sort, for instance: country, realm, state. But we still cannot be definite on which word is more correct for the Thai case. Moreover, the thinking about allowing the group of people who have associated together like this to be a juristic person, has only just arisen not long ago.

The words country, realm, and state mean something different from a group of people who have the same extraction *(chua sai)*, speak the same language, and have the same customs. In French this is called *nation*, which if a translation into Thai is wanted for the time being, it is the word *chat*. This group of people who have the same extraction may not be a juristic person in international law. For instance, in a state which has many nations together, each nation cannot be a juristic person under international law. For instance before the Great War, Austria-Hungary was combined as one state. The Austrian nation and Hungarian nation still existed but were not counted as juristic persons in international law. In a state which has only one nation of people, the difference between state and nation can hardly arise. For such a state composed of people of one nation, we can say equally that the state is a juristic person or that the nation is a juristic person. But the problem becomes complex when one state combines people of several nations.

The various states in this world have several types, and may be divided for study under several headings.

*1: Simple state and complex state*

1. Simple state *(Etat simple)* means a state in which the supreme authority both internal and external is combined in one place without division. Examples are Siam, Japan, France.

2. Complex state *(Etat composé)* means a combination of several states where the supreme authority is divided up in some way. We should remark that such complex states may have many types.

    a. The head of [several] countries or states is the same person. This means each state has its own supreme authority both internal and external with no subordination of one state to the other, but there is one supreme head of state, for instance, a king. An example is Belgium and the Congo between 1885 and 1895 when King Leopold II was king of Belgium and of the Congo also, with the Congo not being a dependency of Belgium (but currently the Congo is a dependency of Belgium).

b. External authority combined and internal authority separate. An example is Norway and Sweden before they separated as independent.

c. States which have allied together and entrusted external authority to the alliance between the countries to be exercised in the name of the various countries, but each state is still fully independent *(Conféderation des Etats)*. An example is Germany before it was established as an empire.

States of this sort are similar to states known as "federated states" but are different in that each state still claims to have external authority but has entrusted it to the central alliance, which is not a central government exercising power on their behalf.

d. Federated states *(Etat fedéral)*. Many states which have combined to establish a central government to hold and exercise on their behalf external authority, for instance over foreign affairs, and some internal authority, for instance over military, postal, and so on. As for internal authority, each state has full authority. Current examples are the United States of America and the German Federation.

*States with and without full independence*

To study states with and without full independence, we may divide states into two types, namely: 1. states with full independence; 2. states without full independence.

1. States with full independence. States of this type are states which can exercise authority both internal and external without heeding the command of another state. For instance, in Asia there are Japan, Siam, China, Persia, and Turkey. There may still be some deference *(kreng chai)* between countries, but when it is not openly apparent that a state must heed the command of another state, then that state can be considered to have full independence.

2. States without full independence. States which do not have full independence may be of many situations, for example:

a. Protectorate. Such a state is still a juristic person but authority both internal and external for the most part falls to the state which is the protector, for instance Cambodia which is under the protection of France.

In addition it should be noted that the state which falls under a protectorate is different from a territory which is a direct colony of any one country. The protectorate still has the status as a juristic person, but a territory which is a direct colony has lost that status.

b. States which have to send tribute to another state. There were many such states in Asia in old times, and currently there are still some in Europe such as Andorra which is between Spain and France and which has to pay tribute to France.

c. States whose external authority has fallen under another state, where some external authority is still managed independently, and where there is full internal authority. This refers to states which are called *dominions* within the British Empire. Examples of these states are Canada, South Africa, Australia, and New Zealand. It can be seen that these states may exercise external authority in some ways, such as by being members of the League of Nations.

d. States which are mandated territories of the League of Nations. States which formerly were subject to Germany or Turkey were placed by the Allies under the League of Nations after the Great War, and the League entrusted the management to certain countries on its behalf. The mandate of the League of Nations has three types (see my exposition in *Nangsu bot bandit* [Graduate text], volume 6, part 4, November 1930).

Apart from those above, there may be other examples of states without full independence which should be studied in detail in the international law on state affairs.

## Section 2. State

It is understood that people associating together as a country have the status as a juristic person. But a juristic person in itself is not in a position to do anything. There must be persons or groups of people to manage. These persons or groups are called government. Like an association which is a juristic person, a country must have a committee to manage the association (see the Civil and Commercial Code, clauses 1274–1297).

The classification of governments into various types must be carried out in accordance with the meaning of government itself. This in turn depends on whether government is studied in a broad or narrow sense, or according to the meaning in economics.

1. *Government in the broad sense.* In a broad sense, government is persons or groups who have been entrusted to wield all three forms of the supreme power of the country, that is, legislative, executive, judicial. In this broad meaning, we may divide governments into four types:

i. governments where the people wield the supreme power directly themselves;

ii. governments where the people wield the supreme power through representatives who cannot be removed until the end of their term of appointment;

iii. governments where the people wield the supreme power through representatives which the people can remove at will;

iv. governments where the king has full power to wield the supreme power of the state.

i. Governments where the people wield the supreme power directly themselves. This form of administration may exist in small countries with few citizens. But in large countries, the people cannot conveniently wield authority themselves in all forms. Nevertheless, in the Roman era at the time Rome was newly built, the number of citizens was still small. The people wielded the supreme authority directly but only in legislation. That is, they gathered to pass resolutions on laws to be enacted. As for other forms of supreme authority such as enforcing the law or the executive power, and adjudicating on law, which are day-to-day matters, they had to be entrusted to people or groups which had been elected, and which acted as representatives. If the people had done everything directly, they would have had no time for making a living. But legislation is not something which has to be done every day. Hence the people are able to wield that supreme power directly.

Currently in Switzerland, some legislation has to be approved by the people, such as any amendment to the constitution. For other laws, if just thirty thousand people or eight cantons make a petition, the law must be submitted to the people to take a vote.

In the German empire, the president has the power to submit a law to the people to take a vote.

But Switzerland and Germany should be seen as a combination of the first type and the second type which is described next.

ii. Governments where the people wield the supreme power through representatives who cannot be removed until the end of their term of appointment. In this form of administration, representatives are appointed to wield power and these representatives hold the post for a term which is fixed. The people cannot remove them. This method is very widespread in the world such as in Britain, France, and Japan.

iii. Governments where the people wield the supreme power through representatives which the people can remove at will. In this form of administration, people appoint representatives to wield power on their behalf, but in certain instances the people may withdraw that power, for instance, by proroguing the Assembly by a resolution of the people in Switzerland, or removing representatives in the USA. In this type of administration, the people have not entrusted power to the representatives absolutely. In the German empire currently, some laws have to be approved by a vote of the people. For instance the president has the power to submit a law which has been passed by the National Assembly but not yet promulgated to the people for vote (see the constitution of the German empire, clause 73).

iv. Governments where the king has full power to wield the supreme power of the state. An example of administration by this method is the administration of Siam, which will be studied further in future.

2. *Government in the narrow sense.* When referred to in the narrow sense, government means the persons or groups who have been entrusted to wield the supreme authority in the executive form, sometimes together with the judicial power also, but not the power to legislate laws. Therefore to classify governments into types according to the narrow sense used here, we have to look at what sort of person is the head of state holding the executive power. If it is any person other than a king, then it is called a republican government.

1. Monarchic government. According to this theory, the role of head of state with executive power falls to one person who is called the monarch or king, and this power is passed down by inheritance to members of the royal family in the same dynasty.
Monarchic government can be divided into five types.

i. Monarchic government with unlimited power, as is called in common language, government in which the king is above the law. In this type of government the king has power to do anything without limitation, such as in the government of Siam.

ii. Monarchic government with limited power, in which the king has no powers in ruling the realm except the power to preside over ceremonies, the power to affix his signature on various legal enactments, and the power to allow his name to be cited in various matters where the king does not wield power himself. The true executive power resides with the cabinet of ministers, such as in Britain. Because the king cannot do anything himself, there is an English saying that the king can do no wrong which can be expressed in another way as, when the king cannot do anything, he cannot do anything wrong.

iii. Monarchic government with specific limitations on the power of the king, but with the chief minister having almost full power in executive matters, except having to consult the national assembly in some cases. An example is the administration in Italy at present (see the Italian law dated 24 December 1925 concerning the duties and privileges of the head of government who is the chief minister and secretary of state).

iv. Monarchic government in which the king has power together with the chief minister who is from the military. An example is the government of Spain at the time of General De Rivera. The chief minister had the power to propose decrees to the king which immediately had the effect of law once they had received the royal approval (see the royal decree of the king of Spain dated 15 September 1923). But this system has already come to an end.

v. Monarchic government in which the king has power to act on his own, must consult the council of ministers on some affairs, but has no need to consult a parliament. Royal decrees must have the signature of the chief minister, the justice minister, and the minister with the duty of implementation. This is a safeguard on the king's use of power. An example is the administration of Yugoslavia by the law dated 9 January 1929, but this system has already been revoked.

(Teaching ends here. From here onwards see the lectures of Phra Sarasat-praphan who will teach in my place.)

# PART II: THE REVOLUTION

*New men studying in France. From left: Khuang Aphaiwong; Pridi Banomyong; Thaep Aphaiwong; Luang Wichitwathakan*

# INTRODUCTION

## LIFE

In 1927, Pridi and six friends met in Paris to form the People's Party with the aim of replacing the absolute monarchy with a constitution. Pridi became the party's first leader. In 1931, leadership passed to a military group which provided the firepower. On 24 June 1932, Pridi wrote the "announcement" which served as the manifesto, but military efficiency rather than mass public support was the basis of the fast and bloodless victory. Pridi, however, was interested in two documents which, since the resolutions at the first meeting in 1927, he had seen as basic to any significant change in Siam. The first was a constitution. Pridi drafted the constitution which the king accepted three days after the revolution, but whose title the king amended by adding the word "provisional". Pridi also had a major role in drafting the "permanent" constitution completed in December. Second was an economic plan. Pridi presented a draft in early February 1933. Two months of stormy controversy followed. The king wrote a commentary which was longer than the plan (and which disagreed with Pridi on every point except the introduction of a lottery). The Assembly debate on the document grew heated after some members carried weapons into the chamber. Immediately after this debate (1 April), the king dissolved parliament. On the day after that, a new cabinet enacted an anti-communist law. On the 13th, Pridi boarded a boat for France.

## WRITINGS

This section presents six documents in two very different groups. The first group consists of four original documents dating from 1932–33 and penned by Pridi. The "Announcement of the People's Party No. 1", which is sometimes referred to as the party's manifesto, was read to the soldiers, distributed in handbill form, and broadcast repeatedly on radio on the morning of 24 June 1932. The "Provisional Constitution" was presented to the king on the same day. The letter from Pridi to Phoonsuk dates from a week after the event. The "Outline Economic Plan" was presented to the government nine months later in March 1933.

The second group consists of two pieces which Pridi wrote about the 1932 revolution many years after the event. *Some Aspects of the Establishment of the People's Party and Democracy* was written for the fortieth anniversary and first printed by Pramot Phungsunthon in 1972. "The People's Party and the Democratic Revolution of 24 June" was sent to be delivered as a speech at a seminar in Bangkok to commemorate the fiftieth anniversary in 1982.

# PREFACE

In the speeches and writings of Pridi which appeared after his exit from China to Paris in 1970, the phrase which appears possibly more often than any other is "the change of government on 24 June 1932".

Yet this overthrow of the absolute monarchy has had a difficult fate in Thailand's modern history. Even at the time, the status of the event was uncertain. The bland entitling of the event as "the change of government" suggests something less than confident revolutionary fervour. The argument that the Thai language had not yet invented a word for "revolution" is a poor and partial explanation. It was after all an unusually efficient and dull event. The *Bangkok Daily Mail* of that afternoon reported that "there was not the slightest excitement . . . mail collections and deliveries were as usual . . . there was no hysteria, no bad feeling anywhere". This calm was deceptive. Royalist forces discussed an immediate countermove, but resolved instead to adopt a long-term strategy. The events of 24 June began a long period of bitter struggle between the old order and the new men. But with the renewed strengthening of the monarchy from the 1960s onwards, the historical importance of 1932 has been significantly down-played. The date of 24 June was removed from the list of national holidays in 1960.

For the radical tradition, also, the event has been a problem. Attempts to interpret it as a bourgeois revolution or as a Kuomintang-style blow against an imperial tradition run into obvious problems. The fact that the event was followed, within six years, by the development of militarism and eventually of military dictatorship, prejudices its utility in any radical historical tradition. Perhaps for this reason there has been only one serious academic thesis published on 1932 by a modern Thai historian (Nakharin Mektrairat).

The announcement, the provisional constitution, and the outline economic plan are original documents, but their significance for understanding the 1932 revolution is slightly oblique. All three had a short life. When the king returned to Bangkok two days after the "change of government", Pridi and other members of the People's Party made a formal apology for the contents of the announcement, and all copies were suppressed. The rhetoric found in the announcement does not resurface anywhere else in the subsequent history of the People's Party. The provisional constitution was replaced in December 1932, though much of its content was carried forward in the new charter. The outline economic plan, as Pridi later noted, "was not a proper economic plan . . . Rather, it was a preparatory project . . . the outline or proposition on which a plan should be based" (*Asiaweek*, 4 January 1980). Controversy over the plan provoked a crisis within the ranks of the party, and sent Pridi into temporary exile from April to September 1933. The plan was not discussed thereafter and not openly published at this point. When Pridi later had responsibility for economic policies, his actions did not closely reflect the thinking and the prescriptions of the plan. Yet he never disowned the plan, and in later life spoke wistfully about his failure to win sufficient support for it.

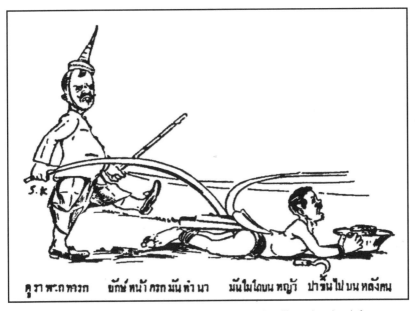

ดูรา พะ:ภ หาวก    ยักษ์ หน้า ภรก มัน ทำ นา    มัน ไม่ไถบน หญ้า    ปา ฉัน ไป บน หลังคน

*"Cruel-faced giants don't plough on the grass. Instead they lift up the plough for use on human backs."* Si Krung, *4 August 1931*

Even so, the announcement, provisional constitution, and plan are important guides to contemporary thinking in the early 1930s. As Nakharin has pointed out, the plan is not really a plan and was clearly written in a great hurry. Like the announcement, it is perhaps best read as a tirade against the old order. A series of themes run through the trio of documents. First, there is the strong dislike, not of monarchy itself, but of the power, privileges, and pride of a parasitic aristocracy of royal blood. As Matthew Copeland has shown, this strong dislike had become gradually more powerful and more widespread in urban society over the previous two decades. The resonant phrase about "farming on the backs of the people" was not Pridi's coining, but was in more general use (see cartoon reproduced from Copeland's doctoral thesis). A second theme of these three documents is a strong faith in the power of a new national state, armed with a constitution and law codes, to transform both economy and society. Third, there is an over-riding concern for the rural poor which made up the mass of Siam's population. Fourth, there is sensitivity to the outside world. This sensitivity emerges on the one hand as a wish to emulate the West's level of " civilization", and on the other as a desire to avoid becoming entangled in the last adventures of Western colonialism. Fifth, there is the conviction that Siam needed a vision of a perfect society as a trigger for change. In both the announcement and plan, Pridi presented this conviction through the concept of *(phra) si-ariya*, the future Buddha who heralds a utopian age.

Nakharin and Copeland have shown that such ideas were widespread among urban Siamese in the five years before 1932. But, as the suppression of the plan and announcement anticipated, these ideas would not guide the governments which descended from 1932. Why this was not so is the major theme of Pridi's retrospective writings.

The two reflections on 1932 written by Pridi at a much later date are both less and more than records and reminiscences. They were written (or at least, first presented) forty and fifty years, respectively, after the event. Both appeared at times when military dictatorship was strong. In 1972, the generals had conducted a coup against their own government, sacked parliament, and were engaged in writing a new constitution to institutionalize their rule. In 1982 the military was still in the ascendant following the coup and massacre of 1976, and was engaged in broadening its penetration of the Thai economy, polity, and society by infiltration, internal espionage, vigilante groups, and outright suppression. Against these backgrounds, Pridi's tortured concern in both these retrospective pieces was to identify why the 1932 movement and his vision of a society based on a democratic constitution and economic planning, on law and equity, seemed to have been so conclusively defeated.

The two pieces must also be read as part of Pridi's connection to a new radical generation. Once he had moved to Paris in May 1970, Pridi became accessible both as an icon and a source of learning and inspiration. Many academics, intellectuals, and journalists made the pilgrimage to Paris to see him. The extracts from *Some Experiences and Opinions of Senior Statesman Pridi Banomyong* in part 1 are the result of one such pilgrimage. Thai student groups in Europe began to ask him for speeches, articles, and messages. Both of the retrospective pieces in this section originate from such invitations. Pridi was very happy to accept. His concern with tracing the history and legacy of 1932 was far from morbid. He was intent on passing on the learnings to a new radical generation. This theme is clear in both these pieces, and also in "Uphold the Aim for Full Democracy of the Heroes of 14 October" included in part 3, and in many other pieces where he set Siam's experience in the context of the revolutions of the modern world.

## NOTE ON THE TRANSLATION

The outline economic plan already exists in an English translation in an appendix of Kenneth Landon's *Siam in Transition* published in 1940. Originally we had not intended to include the plan in this collection because this translation exists. However several people dissuaded us from that course on grounds that Landon is not easily available, the plan is too important to ignore, and a new translation might be enlightening. We decided to complete our translation before checking it against that of Landon. If anyone now cares to compare the two translations, they may be shocked how different they are.

We are not suggesting that Landon's translation is seriously inaccurate, although we think there are several slips. The big difference arises for three main reasons.

First, it is not possible to make a literal translation between Thai and English because the structure of the two languages is so different. Some recasting is always necessary. Landon recast quite liberally. We have been much more conservative. As a result, Landon reads more smoothly as English. But at some points we feel he strays quite far from the original sense.

Second, as Nakharin has noted, the plan was written in great haste. In places, it seems Pridi's mind was racing faster than his pen. Occasionally Landon has been tempted to guess the missing bits, and to embroider quite liberally to help the reader. We have tried to resist this temptation, to approximate the translation to Pridi's compressed and elided form, and occasionally to insert a few words in square brackets which are not present in the original but which help to improve the sense.

Third, Pridi was writing before much of the modern Thai terminology for economics had been invented. For some important concepts, he had to invent new phrases by stringing together ordinary Thai words and expressions. Some of these concepts are of major importance in the plan, and the translation is not at all straightforward.

For example, one basic concept is: *ekachon tang khon tang tham*. Literally it means: private/each person/does differently. We have translated this throughout as: private free enterprise. Landon is less consistent. He varies the translation to suit the context. Often he too has "private enterprise". But he also has other forms such as "individualism", "individualist enterprise", "each doing as he likes", and so on.

Even more vexed is the phrase *ratthaban prakop sethakit eng* which is fundamental to the whole document. Literally it means: government/composes or undertakes/economy/itself. This is the opposite of private free enterprise. It describes government management or control of the economy. Again Landon varies the translation according to the context. He starts out with "government must administer a national economic policy", but later uses forms such as "when the government administers the whole economic system", "the government controls the whole economic system", "the administration of the whole economic system", and so on.

For consistency, we wanted to use a single phrase for this term throughout. However, the choice of term is not simple. Nowadays our interpretation of all terms related to state control over the economy is affected by half a century's experience of communist and socialist governments. Yet Pridi was writing in 1932 (or before; he claims to have presented the "principles" of the plan shortly after foundation of the People's Party in 1927). Stalin's first five-year plan was not yet complete. Some of Pridi's ideas may have originated from the international discussion provoked by that first essay in state socialist planning. But Pridi's whole conceptualization of the state's economic role did not have the benefit of the huge subsequent learning, debate, and literature on this issue. If we adopt a modern term for this crucial phrase—such as "state economic management"—we will risk conjuring up in the reader's mind some ideas and constructs which were not available to Pridi and whose meaning is shaped by later history. Hence we have adopted a quasi-literal translation and used it throughout: "the government runs the (whole) economy itself". Occasionally Pridi used slight variations, such as replacing the verb with *chat tham* or *chat kan*, and we translate such instances as "manages". The result is rather clum-sy in places. But this seems better than trapping the reader into an interpretation which may significantly distort Pridi's original intention.

In the retrospective pieces written from 1970s onwards, Pridi made constant use of the term *thatsana* or *thatsana sangkhom*. The dictionary definition of *thatsana* is standpoint, view, or point of view. *Sangkhom* is society. Pridi used this term to describe the ideas or mental outlook of any society, also the ideas behind any movement to change a society. In modern usage, "ideology" might be a suitable translation, but Pridi was not using any of the modern Thai terms for ideology, some of which were available to him at the time of writing.

It is tempting to vary the English translation to suit the context. At different points, words such as outlook, idea, ideology, culture all fit very well. However, as Pridi used the term very often and very prominently, we wanted to find a single word to signal his usage. Suphot Dantrakun has translated the term as "culture", but again Pridi's term is not the modern Thai translation for culture, and this translation does not work well in all contexts. We have adopted "vision" and "social vision". This translation captures the visual metaphor which is the root of the original word. In some cases, the resulting English is a bit odd. But overall we prefer the consistency.

# 7. ANNOUNCEMENT OF THE PEOPLE'S PARTY NO. 1
# (1932)

*All the people*

When this king succeeded his elder brother, people at first hoped that he would govern protectively. But matters have not turned out as they hoped. The king maintains his power above the law as before. He appoints court relatives and toadies without merit or knowledge to important positions, without listening to the voice of the people. He allows officials to use the power of their office dishonestly, taking bribes in government construction and purchasing, and seeking profits from changes in the price of money, which squanders the wealth of the country. He elevates those of royal blood *(phuak chao)* to have special rights more than the people. He governs without principle. The country's affairs are left to the mercy of fate, as can be seen from the depression of the economy and the hardships of making a living—something the people know all about already.

The government of the king above the law is unable to find solutions and bring about recovery. This inability is because the government of the king has not governed the country for the people, as other governments have done. The government of the king has treated the people as slaves (some called *phrai,* some *kha*) and as animals. It has not considered them as human beings. Therefore, instead of helping the people, rather it farms on the backs of the people. It can be seen that from the taxes that are squeezed from the people, the king carries off many millions for personal use each year. As for the people, they have to sweat blood in order to find just a little money. At the time for paying government tax or personal tax, if they have no money, the government seizes their property or puts them on public works. But those of royal blood are still sleeping and eating happily. There is no country in the world that gives its royalty so much money as this, except the Tsar and the German Kaiser, whose nations have already overthrown their thrones.

The king's government has governed in ways that are deceiving and not straightforward with the people. For example, it said it would improve livelihood in this way and that, but time has passed, people have waited, and nothing has happened. It has never done anything seriously. Further than that, it has insulted the people—those with the grace to pay taxes for royalty to use—that the people don't know as much as those of royal blood. But this is not because the people are stupid, but because they lack the education which is reserved for royalty. They have not allowed the people to study fully, because they fear that if the people have education, they will know the evil that they do and may not let them farm on their backs.

You, all of the people, should know that our country belongs to the people—not to the king, as has been deceitfully claimed. It was the ancestors of the people who protected the independence of the country from enemy armies. Those of royal blood just reap where they have not sown and sweep up wealth and property worth many hundred millions. Where did all this money come from? It came from the people because of that method of farming on the backs of the people! The country is experiencing hardships. Farmers and soldiers' parents have to give up their paddy fields because cultivating them brings no benefit. The government does not help. The government is discharging people in floods. Students who have completed their study and soldiers released from the reserves have no employment. They have to go hungry according to fate. These things are the result of the government of the king above the law. It oppresses the minor government officials. Ordinary soldiers and clerks are discharged from employment, and no pension is given. In truth, government should use the money that has been amassed to manage the country to provide employment. This would be fitting to pay back the people who have been paying taxes to make royalty rich for a long time. But those of royal blood do nothing. They go on sucking blood. Whatever money they have they deposit overseas and prepare to flee while the country decays and people are left to go hungry. All this is certainly evil.

Therefore the people, government officials, soldiers, and citizens who know about these evil actions of the government, have joined together to establish the People's Party and have seized power from the king's government. The People's Party sees that to correct this evil it must establish government by an assembly, so that many minds can debate and contribute, which is better than just one mind. As for the head of state of the country, the People's Party has no wish to snatch the throne. Hence it invites this king to retain the position. But he must be under the law of the constitution for governing the country, and cannot do anything independently without the approval of the assembly of people's representatives. The People's Party has already informed the king of this view and at the present time is waiting for a response. If the king replies with a refusal or does not reply within the time set, for the selfish reason that his power will be reduced, it will be regarded as treason to the nation, and it will be necessary for the country to have a republican form of government, that is, the head of state will be an ordinary person appointed by parliament to hold the position for a fixed term. By this method the people can hope to be looked after in the best way. Everyone will have employment, because our country is a country which has very abundant conditions. When we have seized the money which those of royal blood amass from farming on the backs of the people, and use these many hundreds of millions for nurturing the country, the country will certainly flourish. The government which the People's Party will set up will draw up projects based on principle, and not act like a blind man as the government which has the king above the law has done. The major principles which the People's Party has laid out are:

1. must maintain securely the independence of the country in all forms including political, judicial, and economic, etc.;

2. must maintain public safety within the country and greatly reduce crime;

3. must improve the economic well-being of the people by the new government finding employment for all, and drawing up a national economic plan, not leaving the people to go hungry;

4. must provide the people with equal rights (so that those of royal blood do not have more rights than the people as at present);

5. must provide the people with liberty and freedom, as far as this does not conflict with the above four principles;

6. must provide the people with full education.

All the people should be ready to help the People's Party successfully to carry out its work which will last forever. The People's Party asks everyone who did not participate in seizing power from the government of the king above the law to remain peaceful and keep working for their living. Do not do anything to obstruct the People's Party. By doing so, the people will help the country, the people, and their own children, grandchildren, and great-grandchildren. The country will have complete independence. People will have safety. Everyone must have employment and need not starve. Everyone will have equal rights and freedom from being serfs *(phrai)* and slaves *(kha, that)* of royalty. The time has ended when those of royal blood farm on the backs of the people. The things which everyone desires, the greatest happiness and progress which can be called *si-ariya,* will arise for everyone.

People's Party
24 June 1932

# 8. PROVISIONAL CONSTITUTION OF THE KINGDOM OF SIAM, 1932

King Prajadhipok issues a royal command as follows. As the People's Party has called for him to be under the constitution of the kingdom of Siam so that the country may progress, and as he has welcomed the call of the People's Party, he graciously enacts a law with the following clauses.

### SECTION 1: GENERAL MATTERS

Clause 1. The supreme power in the country belongs to the people.

Clause 2. The persons and groups mentioned below will execute power on behalf of the people as specified in the constitution that follows:
1. The king *(kasat)*
2. The Assembly of Representatives of the People
3. The Committee of the People
4. The courts

### SECTION 2. THE KING

Clause 3. The king is the supreme head of state. Legislative acts, court decisions, and other matters as specified by law must be made in the name of the king.

Clause 4. The person who is king of the country is King Prajadhipok. The succession will proceed in accordance with the Royal Household Law on the Succession of 1924 and with the approval of the Assembly.

Clause 5. If there is any reason that the king is unable temporarily to carry out his duties, or is not in the capital, the Committee of the People will execute the right on his behalf.

Clause 6. The king cannot be charged in a criminal court. The responsibility for a judgement rests with the Assembly.

Clause 7. Any action of the king must have the signature of any one member of the Committee of the People that it has been approved by the Assembly, otherwise it is void.

### SECTION 3. THE ASSEMBLY OF THE REPRESENTATIVES OF THE PEOPLE

Part 1. Powers and duties.

Clause 8. The Assembly has the power to pass all legislation. Such legislation comes into force once promulgated by the king.

If the king does not promulgate within seven days counted from the day of passage in the Assembly and shows reason for not agreeing to affix his signature, he has the power to return the legislation to the Assembly for reconsideration. If the Assembly passes a resolution the same as before, and the king does not concur, the Assembly has the power to promulgate that legislation to have the force of law.

Clause 9. The Assembly has the power to take care of the affairs of the country, and has the power to call a meeting to dismiss a member of the Committee of the People or any official of the government.

Part 2. Representatives of the people

Clause 10. Members of the Assembly of Representatives of the People will be by time period as follows.

*Period 1.* From the time this constitution is enforced until the time when members of the second period take office, the People's Party which has a military force protecting the capital, has the power to appoint seventy persons as provisional members of the Assembly.

*Period 2.* Within six months, or when the country has been made normal and orderly, there will be two types of Members of the Assembly working jointly, namely:

Type 1. Persons elected by the people, one per province, or for provinces with over 100,000 persons, one member for every 100,000 inhabitants, and a further one if the remainder is more than half that number.

Type 2. Members from period 1 up to the same number as members of type 1. If the number is in excess, they shall choose among themselves who shall remain members. If the number falls short, those remaining shall choose any persons to make up the number.

*Period 3.* When the number of people throughout the kingdom who have passed elementary education exceeds half the total, or at the latest within ten years of the implementation of the constitution, members of the Assembly must all be persons elected by the people. Type-2 members will no longer exist.

Clause 11. The qualifications for those standing for election as type-1 members are:

i. passed a political course in accordance with a syllabus which the Assembly will establish;

ii. aged twenty years and above;

iii. not incapable or seemingly incapable;

iv. not deprived of the right to vote by a court of law;

v. of Thai nationality by law;

vi. those standing for election as type-1 members in period 2 must be approved by members during period 1 that they are not people likely to cause disorder.

Clause 12. Election of type-1 members in period 2 shall take place as follows.

i. inhabitants of a village elect a representative for electing a tambon representative;

ii. the village representatives elect a tambon representative;

iii. the tambon representatives elect the members of the Assembly.

For Assembly election in period 3, a law will be passed subsequently on the procedure for direct election of members of the Assembly.

Clause 13. Type-1 members will serve for terms of four years counted from the day of assuming office. But when period 3 is reached, members from period 2, even if they have not yet been in the position for four years, must relinquish the position from the day that the period-3 members assume office.

If a member's position falls vacant for reasons other than the end of the term, the members shall elect another to fill the vacancy, but the new member shall hold the post only for the remainder of the term of the member who is replaced.

Clause 14. Persons of whatever sex who meet the following qualifications have the right to cast their vote to choose village representatives:

    i. aged twenty years and above;
    ii. not incapable or seemingly incapable;
    iii. not deprived of the right to vote by a court of law;
    iv. of Thai nationality by law.
The qualifications for representatives of the village and of the tambon are the same as those laid down in clause 11.

Clause 15. The election of representatives shall be by simple majority. If votes are tied, a second election shall be held. If votes are tied on the second occasion, a neutral person shall be appointed to give a casting vote. The candidates shall appoint the neutral person.

Clause 16. Apart from relinquishment at end of term, members must relinquish office if they fail to meet the qualification in clause 11, if they pass away, or if the Assembly decides that the member has caused damage to the Assembly.

Clause 17. Criminal charges against a member of the Assembly must be sanctioned by the Assembly before the court may adopt the case.

Part 3: Regulations for meetings.

Clause 18. Members of the Assembly shall select one person as chairman to conduct the affairs of the Assembly, and one vice-chairman to act on the chairman's behalf when the chairman has temporary reasons for not fulfilling his duty.

Clause 19. When the chairman is absent or unable to attend, the vice-chairman will maintain the orderliness of the Assembly on his behalf and will manage the deliberations according to regulations.

Clause 20. If both the chairman and vice-chairman are not in the meeting, the members attending shall elect a temporary chairman.

Clause 21. Arrangements for ordinary meetings are the responsibility of the Assembly. A special meeting may be held when requested by no fewer than fifteen members, or by the Committee of the People. The chairman or his substitute shall call the meeting.

Clause 22. Every meeting must be attended by no fewer than half of the total number of members to have a quorum.

Clause 23. Motions on any subject shall be decided by simple majority with each member casting one vote. If the vote is tied, the chairman shall have an additional casting vote.

Clause 24. Members shall not be held liable for any statement or opinion made, and shall not be sued for any matter arising from a vote cast in the meetings.

Clause 25. In every meeting, the chairman must command the Assembly's officials to keep a record; submit it for the members to check, amend, and approve; and the chairman of the meeting must affix his signature.

Clause 26. The Assembly has the power to appoint sub-committees to perform any task, or to examine and report on any matter to the Assembly for further decision. If the Assembly does not appoint the chairman of a sub-committee, the members of the sub-committee shall elect their own.

A sub-committee has the power to invite others to offer explanations and opinions. The sub-committee members and such invitees shall be covered by the provisions of clause 24.

Meetings of sub-committees must be attended by no fewer than three persons to achieve a quorum, except in the case of sub-committees which have only three members, in which case two persons shall constitute a quorum.

Clause 27. The Assembly has the power to establish rules of procedure in accordance with this constitution (at the initial stage, the rules of the Committee of the Privy Council may be adapted, but only those that are not in conflict with this constitution).

SECTION 4: THE COMMITTEE OF THE PEOPLE

Part 1: Powers and duties

Clause 28. The Committee of the People has the powers and duties to act in accordance with the wishes of the Assembly.

Clause 29. If there is any urgent matter over which the Committee cannot call a meeting of the Assembly in time, and if the Committee sees it fitting to issue a law appropriate to that urgent matter, it can do so but must quickly submit that law for the approval of the Assembly.

Clause 30. The Committee of the People has the power to grant pardon but must first seek royal approval.

Clause 31. The ministers of various ministries are responsible to the Committee of the People on all matters.

Anything which infringes an order or regulation of the Committee of the People or is done without the sanction of the constitution, shall be considered void.

Part 2. Members of the Committee of the People and regular officials

Clause 32. Membership of the Committee of the People consists of one Chairman and fourteen other members, totalling fifteen.

Clause 33. The Assembly shall elect one of its members as the Chairman of the Committee, and that Chairman shall select fourteen other members of the Assembly to be members of the Committee. When this selection has been approved by the Assembly, it shall be held that those selected are committee members of the Assembly. If the Assembly considers that a committee member has not conducted affairs according to the policy of the Assembly, the Assembly has the power to invite that committee member to relinquish his duty and to select a new member as above.

Clause 34. If any Committee member for any reason lacks the qualifications laid down for members of the Assembly in clause 10, or has died, the Assembly shall select a replacement.

If the Assembly has selected Committee members, and if that Assembly comes to the end of its term, the Committee shall also be considered to have come to the end of its term.

Clause 35. The appointment and removal of ministers is in the power of the king. This power shall be used only on the advice of the Committee of the People.

Clause 36. Political negotiations with overseas countries are the duty of the Committee of the People and the Committee may appoint a representative for this.

The Committee must report negotiations on any point to the king.

Ratification of any international treaty is in the power of the king, but that power shall be used on the advice of the Committee of the People.

Clause 37. Declaration of war is in the power of the king, but that power shall be used on the advice of the Committee of the People.

Part 3. Regulations of meetings

Clause 38. Regulations of the meetings of the Committee of the People shall be adapted as in section 3.

### Section 5: Courts

Clause 39. The revocation of a judgement shall proceed according to the law in current use.

Promulgated on 27 June 1932 and in force henceforth.

(signed) Prajadhipok
Ananta Samakhom Hall
3 July 1932

# 9. LETTER FROM PRIDI TO PHOONSUK, 3 JULY 1932

Dear Phoonsuk,

So sorry for not speaking the truth that day, and telling you I was going to Ayutthaya. Because if I told you the truth, I feared I would not be able to leave the house. And bad things would definitely have happened. That is, the officers would have captured me the next day at ten o'clock, as we now know. What I have done this time was for the nation and for the majority of the people. I thought we are born only once, and when there is a chance to do something, we should do it. I should not behave like the scum of the earth (*nak lok*). I did not tell you from the beginning because I feared you would be frightened and if the news of your fright leaked out it would spoil all we had planned. I had thought about everything before taking action. I had made plans so that if I died there would still be enough money to support you and the children. I have life insurance and cash in the bank which I transferred to you two to three days before the event. About the printing press, I must ask you to help look after it. What I ordered does not mean you have to take the seal for anything else. The seal is for receiving and sending C.O.D. The money will be brought to you. Besides the money and the C.O.D., I was prepared to transfer as much as 15,000 baht. Apart from that, I have asked for all my salary to be given to you without deduction. Wichit said the cost of sending C.O.D. would be about 300 baht. I asked him not to bother you. I asked Wichit to take it from Luang Prakop, and if that was not enough, to advance his own money. Whatever is left will be given to you. Please do not misunderstand. Please understand that from now you must look after the printing press and make all the decisions. I did not tell you from the beginning because I simply did not have time. There was so much work that I could not finish everything. Right now it happens I'm less busy so I have some spare time to write you a letter. I miss you and the children. I determined to come home, but I thought that at this time it is better to stay here with the soldiers. Please think as if I had gone into the monkhood. Before we made the attempt, I had asked what you would say if I went into the monkhood for six months. You replied that you agreed. What I have done this time is more than going into the monkhood. We did good works *(kuson)*. The merit we did for the nation should pass down to children and grandchildren. The wife will also have a part. In truth, I complained every day to the military head that you must be unhappy. But what could be done? We are acting for the nation. Many millions of other people do not have such an opportunity in their life. Not long now, when things are settled, we will live together as normal again. Please think of the nation and the people a great deal. I had started on all these things since Paris. Once I had decided to take this step, I could not possibly sacrifice my honour. Politics is politics. Personal is personal. Whenever anyone from home arrives or when someone returns from a visit, I always ask after you. I also miss Nu and Parl all the time. It's not that I'm calm and composed.

About the printing press, you must agree to take charge.

Thinking of you always,

Pridi

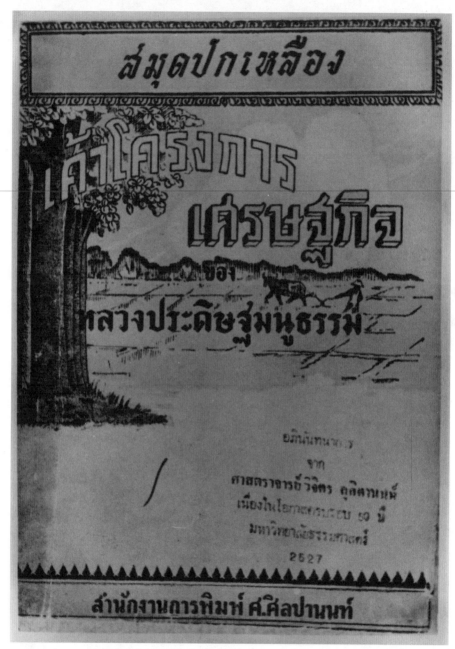

Cover of the 1948 publication of the outline economic plan

# 10. OUTLINE ECONOMIC PLAN (1933)

## PREFACE
### POINTS TO BE TAKEN INTO ACCOUNT IN READING THIS EXPOSITION

In thinking how to promote the well-being of the people, I have carefully studied the true situation, including the habits and disposition of the majority of the people. There is only one way to promote the well-being of the people— the government must manage the economy itself by dividing the economy into different cooperatives.

*Dividing the economy into cooperatives*

My thinking is not because I have an attachment to any doctrine. I have picked up good parts of various doctrines that I believe are appropriate for Siam, and I have adapted them into the outline economic plan.

But there is a point to bear in mind. There are many and varied doctrines about improving the economic well-being of the people. But those who adhere to different theories still cannot agree. Professor Deschamps of the University of Paris made three points about this.

*The reason for bias*

1. All the people do not know all the various doctrines. In this case, ignorance is unintentional. For example, those who have not studied or read the genuine texts of various doctrines are not in any position to come to an agreement.

*Unintentional ignorance*

2. Intentional ignorance. For instance, people listen to the market gossip that one doctrine supports people to kill one another, expropriate the property of the rich, share it out equally among the poor, and make women into common property. They wrongly believe this market gossip. They cling faithfully to this malicious talk. They do no research or follow up to find out whether this doctrine has

*Intentional ignorance*

or has not urged people to kill, expropriate property, share it out equally, and make women into common property.

*Personal benefit*

3. Personal benefit. Some people know various doctrines and their good elements, but pretend not to know and do not act accordingly, because they have a personal benefit which prevents them adopting these ideologies. For instance, socialist doctrine wishes the government to engage in industry for the benefit of the people as a whole. Industrial entrepreneurs cannot support socialist doctrine because they fear the benefit which they get from industry will be taken away. In other cases, people hate the government for personal reasons. They know various doctrines and can see a doctrine is good, but when the government acts according to that doctrine, they resolve to be hostile to the government and pretend to uphold another doctrine. People like this are the worst evil in the world (*ubat kali lok*) because in the main they pursue personal benefit, not the benefit of the people in general.

*Obstinacy*

In Siam, according to my observation, there is yet another reason. That is obstinacy. I have read writings by some learned people in Siam who argue there are dangers in one particular doctrine. I asked one of them whether he had read this from books opposed to the doctrine or got it from hearsay. I received the answer that he had got it from hearsay. I advised him to read a book by someone neutral. He read, and saw that in truth what had been said was false. But to preserve his own reputation, he obstinately pretended to speak in the same old way. Even while admitting to me that he was wrong, he had to stick to his story. Learned men such as this are the worst evil in the world, along with those who pursue personal benefit in the main.

*Resolve to be neutral*

So, readers of this explanatory note, please resolve to be neutral and avoid the above evils. Judge whether or not the draft plan, as I have conceived it here, can help the people as the People's Party announced. If you get stuck or have doubts on any point, please come and ask me. If you hear anyone arguing against it for any reason at all, please ask that person whether he is objecting for his own reasons or because of some market gossip. Also enquire about any original documents the critic has found and read, and please let me know about them.

To read this exposition and come to a judgement, it is not necessary to have a degree. If those with no degree really research, follow things up, and disbelieve hearsay, they can judge better than those who do no real research or follow up.

## PART 1: THE ANNOUNCEMENT OF THE PEOPLE'S PARTY

On 24 June 1932, the People's Party announced its objectives to the people as six principles. The principle which concerns the economy of the country has this content: to improve the economic well-being of the people by the new government finding employment for all and drawing up a national economic plan, not leaving the people to go hungry

*The third principle of the People's Party*

This point must be imprinted in the mind of the whole population, and will be recorded in the history of the change of government. I will always insist on this point. I believe that if the government draws up an appropriate national economic plan, the government will be able to find employment for all and will not leave the people to go hungry. It is not beyond possibility. Improving the well-being of the people is one of my major objectives in changing the government. I had no desire to change from one king to many—which is a democratic system but only its outer husk. I am focused on the important point: "improve the well-being of the people". I hold that the constitution is comparable to a key which opens a door for the people to have a part and a voice in government, to arrange things according to their needs. When the door blocking that route is opened, the government must lead the people through the door to the summit *(chaiyaphum)* of well-being, not lead the people to walk backwards into a *khlong* [i.e. to regress]. For these reasons, the duty of the government which accepts the six principles of the People's Party is to implement this objective of the People's Party.

*Government can do it, it is not beyond possibility*

## PART 2: THE UNCERTAINTY OF THE ECONOMY
## AT PRESENT

*The
deprivation of
the people*

Those with a humane heart and compassion for their fellow man, when they see the condition of the farmers in the countryside, or the poor and destitute in the capital, will immediately feel pity. You may see how poor and inadequate are the food, clothing, shelter, and so on which are the means of existence of these people. Although they may have food to eat today, they cannot know whether or not they will have it tomorrow and beyond. The future is uncertain. Consider further that a person's life must move towards sickness and old age. Will these people, who already face privation when they are strong and healthy, still have food to eat when they reach the stage of sickness and old age?

*Wealthy,
middle class,
poor may be
deprived*

Uncertainty of existence is not only the case among the poor. Both the rich and the middle class must also face uncertainty in every shape and form. Please consider whether you will be able to hold onto the money which you can earn now until your death? Will it last for the use of your children, grandchildren, and great-grandchildren? There are many examples that you may have met of someone who was rich at one time and who became poor at another time; or of an inheritance which passed down to a son and which disappeared completely, not lasting the whole of the son's life, so that the son of a rich man fell into poverty. Similarly you can see that money is not something certain which can act as an insurance for your existence. Do you know for sure that your body and soul will be robust enough to work all through your life? If you become sick or disabled in any way, you cannot work. You must use the money that you have. This money will ultimately be used up also. Where will you find food to eat when you are sick or disabled and cannot work? Try to think how you will feel if you fall into such a condition.

## PART 3: INSURING THE WELL-BEING OF THE PEOPLE

Such is the uncertainty of the economy, that there are learned people who think about solutions by which the government insures the well-being of the people *(assurance sociale)*. That is, people receive insurance from the government from birth to death. Whether they are children, invalid, disabled, or aged, and unable to work, the people have food, clothing, shelter, and so on—the means of existence. When the government provides such insurance, every person will sleep soundly because he does not need to worry that he will be hungry when he is sick, disabled, or aged. If he has a child, he need not be concerned whether the child will go hungry or be able to earn after he has passed away, because government will provide insurance. This insurance will be superior even to saving money, because such money itself is something uncertain, as I have already described.

*Every person should receive insurance from the government*

Such insurance is beyond the ability of a private company. If a company could do it, the people would have to pay a high insurance premium, and where would they get the money? Such insurance can only be done by government, because government does not have to collect an insurance premium directly from the people. The government can seek ways other than an insurance premium, such as increasing the productivity of people's labour, and collecting tax indirectly in small quantities per person per day which the people do not feel.

*A private company cannot do this*

In other countries, the idea that government should provide such insurance to people has become progressively stronger. To implement the provision of such government insurance for the people, an act must be passed on the insurance of the well-being of the people, making it a duty for the government to pay money to everyone in amounts adequate for them to exchange for the means of existence such as food, clothing, shelter, and so on, according to each person's situation (see the draft act appended).

*Legislation on insurance for the well-being of the people*

Paying a monthly salary to everyone appears to accord truly well with the disposition of the Thai people because, as is well known, everyone likes to work in government service and likes to have a monthly salary. Yet there are still

*Thai people like to be government servants*

some government servants who go around objecting and opposing people being government servants, even though they themselves are government servants on monthly salaries.

When government has to pay a monthly salary to the people in this way, where will the government get the money from?

*Money is something used for exchange*

Before dealing with this subject, let us be warned to keep in mind that money is not something you can eat, that money is something which is used to exchange for the means of existence such as food, clothing, shelter, and so on.

Paying money is equivalent to giving food, clothing, shelter, and so on. Please bear in mind what you do with the money you earn. You exchange it for the means of existence. Therefore, it is not wrong to compare money to points. Paying a monthly salary is equivalent to giving the people points which they can exchange for the means of existence according to their needs.

The ultimate results which people get are the means of existence such as food, clothing, shelter, and so on.

*Government does not have to expropriate the property of the wealthy*

To pay a monthly salary to people, government does not have to seize the property of the wealthy. The government may provide the means of existence by setting up comprehensive cooperatives to exchange the monthly salary which government pays to people and to act as a clearing system.

*Clearing system*

For example, a person has a monthly salary of twenty baht, and needs food, clothing and so on for the amount of this twenty baht. The money government has paid to this person returns to the government again. Money remains with the person only when his needs for food, clothing, and so on cost less than the amount received. Only for this amount which remains in the hands of the person, the government must have a reserve fund such as in gold or silver according to international practice.

*National bank*

Alternatively, if the government does not want to issue many currency notes which require a high reserve fund, government may set up a trustworthy national bank where the people can deposit money, use checks for payment, and have a clearing system *(compensation)*. By this means, the notes in circulation need not be a very large quantity.

Hence, having the government insure the well-being of the people by paying them a monthly salary, makes it also necessary for the government to set up cooperatives to produce and sell the means of existence. If the government does not set up cooperatives to make and sell the means of existence itself, or does not oversee it, how can the government insure the well-being of the people? Where will the government find the money to pay the people monthly salaries?

*The government runs the economy itself*

Running any economic activity requires: 1. land, including property attached to land both above and below ground; 2. labour; 3. capital.

At the present time, does every person have enough land and capital? We can see that 99 percent of people do not have sufficient land and capital to engage in economic activity properly on their own. Each person has his own labour, but what can he do with this labour when he has insufficient land and capital?

*The people do not have enough land and capital*

But if you consider the land, labour, and capital of the people in total, you can see that in Siam there is over 500,000 sq km of land (over 320 million *rai*), full of trees and crops above ground, full of ores and minerals of many kinds under the earth. Siam has a population of over 11 million. As for capital, although we do not yet have a lot, Siam is definitely not a wild jungle. The assets and reputation which the country has gained may provide a route to find capital through fiscal policies which do not cause difficulties for the people.

*Land, labour, and capital of the country*

## PART 4: LABOUR THAT IS WASTED AND SOCIAL PARASITES

It is disappointing that our fertile land has not yet been used profitably, because up to now running the economy in the style of private free enterprise (*ekkachon tang khon tang tham*) has resulted in wastage of labour or excessive use of labour, and a lack of machinery to increase labour productivity. There are also some *parasite social* as I shall relate below.

## Chapter 1: The waste of labour through under-utilization

*Forty percent of labour is wasted*

It can be seen that the farmers who are the majority of the population of Siam work on paddy farming no more than six months of the year per person (including ploughing, planting, harvesting, etc.). There remain another six months which are wasted. If people had a way to use this remaining six months in productive economic activity, the well-being of the people would increase. I am happy to receive explanations from those interested in the economy on how a solution can successfully be found, within the system of leaving everything to private free enterprise, that makes people put this remaining idle labour to productive use. I see that the only way is for the government to lay down a national economic plan so that people put this remaining six months to productive use.

## Chapter 2: Labour is wasted because the economy is not managed appropriately

*Labour is wasted by fragmentation*

Although labour is used in economic activity for these six months, this labour is still wasted without reason because of private free enterprise. For example, the farmers all work separately and individually. More labour is required than if they worked jointly. Each individual farmer looks after his own cattle, ploughs himself, plants and harvests himself (except on some occasions when there is *long khaek*, communal exchange labour), and seeks his own living. But if farmers worked together, they might be able to economize on labour. For instance, farmers who work separately must each look after one head of cattle. But if many farmers with many cattle work together, they may be able to look after the cattle jointly and jointly use the same cattle-keeper. That is one way to economize on labour. Apart from this, household work such as the preparation of food could be done jointly such as through a club or shop to sell food. On any one day, many people would come to eat, while it should be possible to use only one or two people to prepare the food. In this way, when farmers work jointly they can economize on labour for food making, cattle raising, and so on, and use the remaining labour productively on economic activities which we still lack. If we leave it to private free enterprise like this for ever, there will be no economizing on labour.

Chapter 3: Labour that is wasted by not using machinery

This matter is well known. Our paddy farming uses methods of ploughing, planting, harvesting, and so on with human labour and animal draught power. In truth, these methods using human labour and animal draught power were totally necessary in primitive times and in the period before machines were invented. But suppose we had machinery experts to adapt machinery to be appropriate for our geographic conditions (which is feasible because there is no science in this world which could not do such a thing unless there was no interest to do so). It is usual in an economy that when there is mechanization, labour can be greatly increased.

*Waste of labour through primitive methods*

From current experiments with ploughing, it can be clearly seen that one mechanized plough which requires two people may plough many thousand *rai* in one season. Thais have small bodies and are not as strong as Chinese or westerners. In any economic activity which uses human strength, we cannot compete with the Chinese or westerners. But we will be able to compete if we use machinery. The question concerning the introduction of machinery is whether each rice farmer can afford to have a machine. In other words, do farmers have enough capital to buy? It is true that some private individuals could afford it, because they have capital and do not need to rely on the government. But be aware that machinery has enormous benefit but can also cause great damage. In overseas countries, is it not the case that unemployment has increased nowadays because of more machines replacing human labour? When machinery increases, it follows that unemployment must increase.

*The good effects of machinery*

Suppose a weaving factory, which in the past had used a thousand hand labourers, changes to use machinery and needs only a hundred people. The other nine hundred people must leave the factory and become unemployed. But you cannot blame the machinery for this. A machine is something which helps humans to avoid suffering *(tora-man)*. The unemployment which arises because a factory changes to machinery is a result of private free enterprise. This is a common matter. When a factory needs a hundred people, why should the factory owner waste money paying

*The impact of machinery*

the remaining nine hundred people? But where will these nine hundred go to find work? If various factories or agriculturists already use machinery, there will be many unemployed. Ultimately, there will be a disaster. But if the government engages in economic activity itself, there will be only good results from adopting machinery.

*Under government enterprise there will be only good results from machinery*

Suppose that weaving factory which changed to machinery in the previous example has to dispense with nine hundred workers. The government may take them into another newly established factory, for instance a silk factory, a sugar factory, or road construction work, clearing the forest for cultivation, and so on. And suppose that there are already enough factories and various economic activities with no need for further expansion, it can reduce the working hours of the workers. For instance, when machinery increases, working time decreases from the previous eight hours to seven, six, five, four, three, two, one hour a day without reducing the monthly pay of the workers. By this method, there will be a good effect from machinery, that is a reduction in the suffering of human bodies. In truth, private owners of private factories may reduce the working hours, but they will want to reduce the pay also. More than that, if the number with no work is more than the work available, the wage rate normally declines as a law of economics. The ill effect falls on the people, and machinery becomes something which kills people. If you do not want to kill, then you must not use machinery. When you do not use machinery, backwardness persists.

*Providing capital is easier than providing machinery*

If the government runs the whole economy itself by organizing cooperatives, this will not only solve the problem of labour, but it will also be easier than under private enterprise to provide capital, because the government may draw up fiscal policies such as indirect taxes *(impôt indirect)* collected from the people in small daily amounts which the people do not feel as a heavy burden, but which accumulate over a year into a large amount.

*Indirect tax*

For instance, if there is some indirect tax which collects one *satang* per day per person from the population of 11 million, in one year the yield will be over 40 million baht. Apart from this, the government may still borrow money using the reputation and assets of the government which are better collateral than the private sector has. Alternatively, government may make agreements with foreign countries to buy machinery in large quantities at a low price and with payment by instalment. Some countries have already done so to good effect.

Chapter 4: Labour is wasted because of people born as social parasites

In Siam there is no small number of people born as social parasites who live off others. That is, they engage in no economic activity or anything appropriate to their labour. They depend on others for food, clothing, and shelter. Sometimes they work just a little bit. For example, in Bangkok and other major towns, we can observe large numbers of people living in the houses of the middle class or wealthy. This group of people, apart from being social parasites, are also a cause of price rises. For example, suppose in one country there are one hundred people working making rice, each producing one ton of rice, giving a total of one hundred tons. But there are fifty people who live and eat in the country who do nothing. Hence if these social parasites worked along with the other hundred, there would be another fifty tons of rice. The price will increase [this should be decrease] because the amount of rice increases. If this group of people is left to remain as at present, they will become idlers. Leaving things to private free enterprise, and leaving idle people to depend on others like this, the economic ouput of the country will be reduced. There is no way better than the government running the economy itself, and finding a route to force this type of people to work so that the labour of the social parasites may be of some benefit to the country.

*Social parasites hold back progress*

## PART 5: HOW GOVERNMENT WILL PROVIDE LAND, LABOUR, AND CAPITAL

The important principle that should be born in mind is that the government must adopt conciliatory methods— that is, must rely on cooperation between rich and poor. Government must not murder the rich.

Chapter 1: Providing land

At present landowners do not receive sufficient return from the land

At present cultivable land is in private hands. Beyond that is forest which has to be cleared. On land in private hands at present, the return is almost not worth the outlay plus tax or interest, because farmers at present—you can almost say 99 percent—are debtors who have pledged their land, or placed it as collateral with creditors, and the creditors cannot collect the interest or the principal. People who have land for rent, such as in the Rangsit tract, instead of being able to collect rents, have to pay the land tax out of their own pockets. Losses are incurred with disastrous effect on both the rich and the poor. The majority of landowners want to sell their land even at some loss. The creditors who have lent to the farmers want their money back. In mortgage enforcement and distress sales at present, the land price has fallen low. All this has been the result of government allowing private free enterprise to be the principle of economic activity.

*Buying up land*

If things are like this, and if government buys up this land, I believe that the farmers, landowners, and creditors should all be happy in no small measure. Because if they retain the property right in the land, or seize land which has been pledged, they will face only loss. Buying up the land in this way is a different method from the expropriation of the communists.

*Where will government get the money to buy land?*

At present the government does not have sufficient money to buy land. But the government can issue bonds to the landowners according to the price of their land. On these bonds, the government will fix the interest rate according to the loan rate at the time of the sale, which will not be more than 15 percent, the highest rate by law. For example, for land worth a thousand baht, the owner will receive a bond for a thousand baht; and suppose that the interest rate at the time is 7 percent, the landowner will receive seventy baht a year as interest. Thus, this yield is more certain than renting or cultivating oneself. It is as if the landowner, instead of holding a title *(chanot)* or document stating the amount of land, holds a bond which states the amount of money the government owes him.

The land which the government must buy is that which can be used for economic activity, for example land for paddy or cash crops. It is not necessary for the government to buy dwelling houses except when the owner wishes to sell in exchange for a bond. When compared to the total area of the country, family dwellings *(homestead)* are not such a large amount that it will obstruct economic management. Hence they can be left as they are, which is not at all strange and surprising.

*What kind of land must the government buy?*

When land has reverted to the government, the government will determine properly how the economic activity on the land will be divided up, what sort of machinery will be used and in what quantities, and what earthworks and bunding are needed to bring water. At present, on land which is divided among various owners, each makes his own channels and bunds. But when the land belongs to government, if the land is the same level, it will greatly economize on cost outlay. For instance making channels and bunds may be reduced. Besides that, machinery such as for ploughing can be used over adjacent areas, thus removing the need to plough one piece here, one piece there, which is slow and time-consuming. Improving the land by technical means can also be carried out conveniently. We can see that nowadays people still believe in ancient methods, and even though agricultural experts teach otherwise, it will take a long time. When the government runs the economy itself, government may set rules which the people as the employees of government must follow.

Writers of economics texts who like the private free enterprise doctrine, and governments of the type which fear being overthrown by people who work together in large numbers and which worry about a threat to themselves, tend to preach that government ownership of land will make people have no feeling of love for the land like that of people who are themselves landowners, and that hence there will be no land improvement. This statement is comparable to someone speaking with eyes closed. Promoting people to love the land as private property, philosophically speaking, results from the idea of self-regard *(egoisme)*, that is, love of self, love of own property. This is the opposite of promoting love of nation, love of other members of the human race *(altruisme)*.

*Love for the land*

*Love of self or love of the nation*

People are always talking about loving the nation. Promoting people to love self and love one's own property—is that not the opposite of loving the nation? I suspect that those who claim to love the nation but also go around preaching self-love like this, are only doing lip-service, and I wonder if in their hearts they truly love the nation. Besides, as stated above, in order not to eliminate the people's feeling of family, government will allow private ownership of dwelling houses. That should be sufficient for loving land of one's own. Please observe how at present in Bangkok there are many people who rent land or rent a house or rowhouse for accommodation. Do these people have land anywhere which they love? And if it is held that someone must have land in order to love the nation, then do those who rent houses not love the nation? I do not believe that these house renters are all people who do not love the nation. In truth, it is people with a lot of land who will be so concerned about their own land that they will be worried about any economic plan at all. Readers please observe, compare carefully, and look all around you on all sides; see whether or not such people who have land love the nation more than those who do not. At best, I've decided that their love of the nation is equal. Hence owning or not owning land is not a cause of loving the nation less or more, as some claim.

As for the point that those who are not landowners will not be determined to improve the land, I believe this cannot be the case. When government buys up the land to be common property (*khong klang*), it is equivalent to the people as a whole being the owners of that land, like a company which has lots of shareholders and which holds this property right. Would such a company not improve its own land at all? We see it as quite the opposite—the company which has the land will improve it even more than private landowners. Currently we have agriculture experts who are government officials who supervise and advise about land improvement. In future when land belongs to government, we may have government servants who are experts in agriculture who can oversee land improvement using their knowledge, expertise, and ability, like the agriculture officials at present. If it is stated that land will not be improved, I think it is improperly insulting to officials who are expert in agriculture.

I see the opposite—that the land will be improved even more. For instance in providing water, preparing the land surface, and planting with seeds and fertilizer, agriculture experts will use their knowledge and ability in full. It will be unlike at present when, no matter how much experts teach, the people may not believe them because they like the old ways and do not open their eyes and ears.

People who lack land for agriculture may still be government officials who can apply to work in agriculture. If not enough agricultural work is available, they can apply to do something else in order to have food to eat, a place to live, and so on. They will not be any worse off than if they had entered agriculture, but will have improved well-being as a result of the government itself managing the economy.

Please compare with officials at present. Mostly their families in the past worked in agriculture. They had to leave their family land in order to enter government service in Bangkok or the main provincial towns. Why did these officials leave their land like this? And do these officials love the nation less than farmers who have land? If that were the case, they should not have left the land. This is an argument which I cannot believe.

As I have analysed, the arguments of those in favour of private ownership of land are based on arguments by people who hold to the doctrine of private free enterprise. They fabricate supporting reasons which induce private individuals to have property. This is like giving bribes by indirect means. The claims come also from governments of the sort which fear that people will leave the land and apply to work in other industries where they will be gathered together in large groups. These governments fear that if people are grouped together in large numbers like this, they will see the government's bad side, or see that the government is weak and incapable of ensuring that the people have economic well-being. They fear that they will lose their positions. All these fears truly retard progress. And these people go around shouting for people to favour their reasoning. People who do not think carefully about things sign on easily and join in the shouting.

*Beware of the deceptive words of some groups*

Chapter 2: Providing employment

*Some officials discriminate against other people being officials*

The disposition of the Thais is to like being government servants. That is, they like to apply to exchange their labour for a government salary. This disposition is very obvious. Even among the sort of people who oppose the government engaging in industry itself, the majority are government servants. At the time they speak in this way, they can see whether they themselves are government servants or not. They oppose others being government servants, even while these others have the disposition to be government servants like themselves. Hence, readers should beware of the rhetoric of this group of people, and should always ask the people who speak like this whether they are government servants or not, and if they are, why they discriminate against others becoming government servants.

*Accepting people as government servants*

As the disposition of the Thai is to like being government servants, it will not be at all difficult to make all Thai into government servants. But government service does not mean only sitting in authority in an office. The economic activities which the government runs are also called government service.

In this matter, the government should lay down that people of a certain age, for instance eighteen to fifty-five, must work according to their qualifications, strength, and ability. People of higher age will receive a pension throughout their life. And those aged below eighteen must study and do a little work according to their strength.

*Working according to ability*

People will receive monthly salaries from government or from a cooperative just as government servants do today. These salaries will vary according to qualifications, strength, and ability so that all government servants will work hard to the utmost of their strength and ability. However, the lowest salary will be enough for that government servant to buy food, clothing, shelter, and so on—the means of existence.

Will the government force all people to become government servants, or will the government not need to force all people to become government servants?

*Exceptions for some private groups who*

Government may exempt some private individuals from becoming government officials and allow them to conduct their own business, provided they can show that they will have enough income from their business alone for their own livelihood even through sickness and old age, and can provide for their children to receive education and to be in a position to look after themselves. As for others who are in a position that is uncertain, they must be government servants because government service is equivalent to expending labour to save up a reserve fund against times of sickness or old age.

*need not become government servants*

But when government runs the whole economy in this way, how will private individuals find a solo occupation?

There are several types of economic activity which the private individuals can productively undertake on their own, such as *professions liberales* including writers, lawyers, painters, teachers in some disciplines, and so on. When a person wants to do such things independently and does not wish to be a government servant, permission may be granted. For other occupations such as private owners of existing factories, if they wish to continue without being government servants, it will be permitted in the same way, except in cases when they wish to sell to the government, receive in return bonds, and earn interest to use for their own consumption. In certain sorts of trade and farming, if private individuals can show that they can get an output sufficient to provide for themselves, it can be permitted as a special case.

*Independent occupations*

There is no ill effect from the majority of people becoming government servants. Instead, the government gets benefits. That is, the people's labour can be utilized productively throughout. For example, people will work throughout the year, except for the days when they must stop and rest. Our concern that farmers have six months idle need no longer be a concern. The government may use the other six months productively. For instance when the farmers are free from paddy farming, they may grow some other crop, or build roads, according to whatever the national economic plan specifies. Apart from this, when people are considered government officials, government can force them to study, to train in any arts or sciences, and to undergo military instruction and training, which will have the added benefit of saving time required to spend on military service.

*The benefits of the majority becoming government servants*

Chapter 3: The provision of capital

There are two types of capital which the government needs to run the economy: (1) capital which the government needs to buy machinery and articles which the government still cannot make itself; (2) capital which the government needs to pay labour costs.

*The circulation of capital*

The second type of capital is money which circulates around and balances out. For instance, people who receive a salary will use the salary to buy food, clothing, and shelter from the government. If the amount is exactly the same, then it balances out. If there is still money left in the hands of the government servant, government must find reserves against this amount. But as I have already stated above, if government establishes a national bank, government servants will bring the money to deposit in this bank. This means the government servant is the creditor of the government for the amount deposited, and does not need to hold banknotes which may risk being lost.

What method will the government use to raise capital of both types? Learned men in Siam say it will have to be expropriated from private individuals, according to the method which is said to be communist. I do not agree with expropriation. Government should raise capital some other way. These are some methods to raise capital.

*Indirect tax*

By the collection of certain taxes such as inheritance tax, income tax, or indirect taxes *(impôt indirect)* which are collected in small daily amounts which do not aggravate people but which accumulate over a year to a large amount. For example, if there is an indirect tax collected at the rate of one *satang* a day per person, the yearly total from 11 million people will be over 40 million baht. Examples of such indirect tax are: tax on salt sold by government (for instance, government buys salt from those with salt fields at an appropriate price, and then sells to consumers), sugar tax, cigarette tax, match tax, and so on.

*Lottery*

By running a lottery, which I do not see is immoral in any way. In truth, a lottery is gambling. Those who buy a lottery ticket agree to take a risk, but for that risk-taking they must pay only a small amount of money.

*Borrowing*

By borrowing internally, in which case government cooperates with people who are presently wealthy. It may be by direct borrowing or by issuing bonds for a specific factory. For example, if the government sets up a sugar factory and needs capital of one million baht, government issues a sugar bond for that amount. The bondholders have the right to earn the interest as specified and also get benefit from any profits the factory makes. Alternatively, borrowing may be done from overseas if foreign countries are happy to lend. In truth, money borrowed from overseas should be used for buying machinery or articles which we cannot yet produce inside the country. It should not be expended inside the country. Once that is agreed upon, if we cannot borrow from overseas, we may decide to buy machinery direct from overseas companies and pay in instalments as some countries have already done.

For our Siam, we should buy from companies in coun- *Raising credit* tries friendly to us—that is Britain and France—except when they do not agree to sell on instalment or when their price is too expensive. In addition, government may make agreements with companies to come and set up factories here, and government may take the factory and its produc- tion as guarantee for the loan to that company until the money is totally repaid. These are the various methods gov- ernment can use at present, because it is known that the world market for machinery is currently flooded. Com- panies need to sell their products even on the instalment method.

## PART 6: BALANCING THE INCOME AND EXPENDITURE OF GOVERNMENT

If government runs the economy itself and pays salaries to people in this way, a question may occur to you readers as to how the government can achieve a balance. Will it not be the case that the government will go bankrupt, and that the value of our currency will fall because government has to print too much money?

Chapter 1: Domestic balance
From the beginning I have already remarked here and *Balancing out* there that the salaries people receive will balance out *the debt* against the goods which people buy from government. For that to be the case, government must make all the goods

which are the means of existence and which the people want. Then when people want anything, they can buy it from government. Even if over a month or over a year, there is some surplus money left with people, they will save this money for future purchases which they must buy from the government. The domestic balance is assured. Besides this, a balance can be achieved by fixing the prices of goods for sale. But this method should not be used. Government should seek a way to increase the supply of goods which people need.

*Human needs*

Human needs for the means of existence vary. And as humans have wider relations and increasing prosperity, their needs also increase. Professor Charles Gide states that what is known as progress means increasing human needs (*Cours d' économie politique* [Paris 1909], vol. 1, page 49). For instance, forest dwellers need only a few pieces of clothing, enough to cover some parts of their bodies. Then when this group of people progresses, they need more pieces of clothing to cover more of their bodies, and so forth.

*Making the means of existence*

By the same token, when the people of Siam progress, their needs will increase proportionately, for instance more cloth or silk for clothing, more housing and utensils, more communications (for instance, cars and travel to other countries), more rest and leisure such as entertainment and sports. If government provides all of these in total, the salaries which government pays will return to the government, resulting in a balance.

Chapter 2: Balance between countries

Government may still need to borrow overseas to buy machinery and articles which the government cannot make itself. Where does government get the money to pay its creditors?

*Increasing a surplus beyond domestic use*

It is necessary for the government to organize production of goods which can be made domestically (for instance rice, teak, tin) to create a surplus above domestic purchase, and to sell these goods as exports to balance out the money which the government borrows.

*Many imports are unnecessary*

In truth, even with private free enterprise at present, Siam has exports of 134 million baht, that is, goods surplus to domestic use. But Siam imports a large volume of goods other than machinery, for example, consumer goods such as sugar and clothing.

If the government can organize production of virtually all goods which can be made locally, then the 134 million baht of exports can be used to exchange for machinery which we cannot make. Then we will see how much progress we can make. Apart from this, idle labour which the government may put to more productive use will give us a larger surplus of goods above domestic use. This will increase further the country's capacity to exchange for goods which we cannot yet make. Thus it is possible to achieve an external balance.

*Only necessities should be imported*

## PART 7: IN ORGANIZING THE ECONOMY, GOVERNMENT MUST BEWARE OF LETTING HUMANS BECOME ANIMALS

Readers who have bad preconceptions tend immediately to jump to the conclusion that government running the economy will make humans become animals. They claim women will all become common property; family life will disappear; people will no longer have the willpower and perseverance to achieve progress. Those who make such arguments may be making accusations without thinking deeply.

In truth as stated already, I hold that people should be government servants, should have the same status as government servants today who earn a salary for their work, and who get compensation in sickness and old age. I have taken care not to allow humans to have the condition of animals. I wish humans to be even more human, free of the mistreatment of one another which arises from economic causes.

*People as government servants will be in the same situation as government servants today*

I still respect the family. Women will not be held in common. The relations between forebears, such as grandparents and parents and their descendants such as children and grandchildren, may still continue. Marriage laws will not be repealed. People may still have the willpower to achieve progress in the same way as government servants today. If people will lose the willpower to support progress, why have not all government servants today lost that willpower?

*Families will exist*

*The search for*
*knowledge*
*will continue*

There may be people who argue further that there will be no scientific research. This statement is too accusatory. Scientists will still research. Government will have prizes to give, and will recognize any patent rights on inventions. It will be no different from government servants today at all. Readers should not misbelieve derogatory claims that [this plan means] we humans must eat rice from a pan and live in a hole. Please ask those who make such claims, from what books they have read these claims, and please let me know. That would be a great favour.

# PART 8: DIVIDING WORK AMONG COOPERATIVES

*The central*
*government*
*cannot oversee*
*everything*

Even though on principle the government will run the economy itself, in an extensive country with over 11 million population such as Siam today, if running the economy comes directly under the central government, the control and supervision will be imperfect. Hence the running of the economy must be divided among various cooperatives.

*Cooperative*
*members will*
*be paid*
*salaries*

In any cooperative, the people who are members will receive salaries from the cooperative according to a scale, and must work according to their strength and ability except when they are sick, disabled, or aged when they will receive a pension.

*Bonuses*

Cooperatives will conduct economic activities according to the national economic plan. For instance, agricultural cooperatives will undertake agriculture such as crop cultivation, animal raising, and so on. If they have spare labour, they will do other business such as constructing highways or houses and other buildings in the cooperative. The people who are members of the cooperatives, apart from receiving their regular salary according to a scale, may also receive special bonuses according to the output which the cooperative makes. In this way, even the poor and destitute may be members of cooperatives. This is different from the cooperatives which government organizes at present where only landowners can become cooperative members. Farmers who have to rent land, of which there are now a large number, have no opportunity to become cooperative members.

The territorial extent and membership numbers of co-operatives will be a matter up to the cooperative members. For example, an industrial cooperative should have members who are workers in that industry and its size will depend on whether the industry is large or small. The size of agricultural cooperative will depend on the appropriate method of dividing up the land for agriculture, on the number of workers needed to look after it, and the suitable technology.

In these cooperatives, the members will jointly under-take the full range of economic activity, that is:

*Various activities undertaken collectively*

1. joint *production* in which the government provides the land and capital, and the cooperative members provide labour;

2. joint transport and sale *(circulation)* in which the cooperative transports and sells its output under the supervision of government;

3. joint provision of consumption goods in which the cooperative sells consumption goods such as food and clothing to its members. It is not necessary for the cooperative to sell cooked food but rather raw food such as rice and fresh meat for the members to buy and prepare ac-cording to their liking. But if the members want the con-venience, they may buy ready-prepared food from the cooperative according to preference.

4. joint construction of dwellings in which the cooperative arranges construction of dwellings under the supervision of government. One member family will have one house, built according to the cooperative's plan for proper sanitation, convenience in administration, and safety.

Once people have joined cooperatives and have houses together in villages, it will be easy to organize adminis-tration as a *municipality* including sanitation and health. For example, the cooperative will arrange to have a doctor issue regulations about health care. Education and training will also be easy, because the members live close together. On any day when work is over, the cooperative may issue instructions to come for study or training. Study may be by book method, by showing or screening pictures, or by other forms of exhibition. The suppression of thieves and criminals will be facilitated. Apart from this, the military

*Municipality, health, education, military service*

may use the cooperatives as a device for giving military training to people before they are conscripted for military service or the reserves *(preparation militaire)*. Conscription and mobilization like this will be convenient in every aspect.

## PART 9: GOVERNMENT WILL ARRANGE WHAT ECONOMIC SECTORS THE COUNTRY HAS

*Preventing the closure of doors for trade* Government must hold to the principle that it should establish all kinds of agriculture and industry so that ultimately the country has no need to depend on foreign countries. This is to prevent the danger which may arise from the closure of doors for trade. When we have totally everything we need inside the country, even if doors for trade are closed it will not cause any difficulty. People wrongly believe in Adam Smith's theory that different countries must have a division of labour, with some countries doing only agriculture and no industry. In truth, it is a good principle in the hands of countries which treat one another honestly and do not close doors for trade or force prices down. But at present this is not the case.

*The view of a German economist* We should proceed according to the principles of a German economist, Friedrich List [1789–1846], who propounded the view that Germany must first become a developed state—that is, with flourishing industry, agriculture, arts, and sciences—and only then could Germany prosper in international competition. Because the whole country accepted this principle, the government was able to achieve good results, such as the railways, for example. At present Germany recognizes that the country does well with government running the economy, and hence has entrusted the government to Hitler who believes in the doctrine of government managing the economy itself. In England, Mr McDonald, and in France, M Daladier are the heads of government. As is well known, they follow the doctrine of cooperation between people and government along with some measure of government insurance *(assurance sociale)*.

## PART 10: PREVENTING DIFFICULTY OVER THE PROBLEM OF EMPLOYERS AND WORKERS

If Siam is to proceed according to the theory which allows private companies to own factories, the supporters of that theory must first appreciate that they themselves will bring turmoil and disaster to the country. Those who have been to study in Europe should know that wage labourers have created disputes and ill-feelings to the point that on some occasions the employers had to close the factory *(lockout)*, and on some occasions the workers stopped work together *(strike)*. The disputes were sometimes about wages, sometimes about working hours, sometimes about time-off, sometimes about workers' insurance. Are these events not a result of private ownership of factories? In Siam, even though factories are few, we already see this problem has arisen, for instance among the tramcar workers. If the country develops and factories increase, then you will see how much turmoil will arise. But if government is the owner of all economic activities, all of the people whether they are workers or government servants of any sort, when they work according to their strength and ability like other workers and government servants of other types, they will receive the same benefits in equal measure according to strength and ability.

*Private ownership of factories creates turmoil*

The government is the representative of the people. So this is equivalent to the people being the owners of the whole economy. When the output of the economy is high, the people as workers and government servants will receive higher salaries in proportion. There is no need for government to set aside a portion for the benefit of anyone, for there is no one to be benefited in such a way. This is different from the case of private factory owners. It is normal for them to set aside a high profit and exploit the labour of the workers for personal benefit.

*Private owners set aside a high profit*

In truth there are people who claim that if the government arranges to run the economy itself, the government will suffer only losses. The people who make such claims introduce bad examples from some countries, claiming that in countries where discipline is lacking, workers do not work fully. But in such cases it will not only be the government running the economy which

*Government can make only profit*

suffers losses. The private sector will suffer also if discipline among the workers in that economy is absent or deficient. The private sector there will suffer losses in the same way. The way to cure discipline in the factory is not a matter of government or private ownership. In truth it depends on the systems of the factory and the supervision of the foremen. On another point, if we study running the economy in total, we will see that government can make only a profit because government can fully and beneficially utilize all labour, can economize on labour, and can increase labour by using machinery. So what can be the cause of the government suffering loss?

## PART 11: THE NATIONAL ECONOMIC PLAN

So that economic activities may proceed smoothly and productively, the government must draw up a national economic plan. The drafting of the national plan must include research and calculation in stages, as follows.

*The conditions of civilized countries*

1. Research and calculation must determine what are the means of existence according to the needs of the people—what is required and so on, and in what amounts to be sufficient for the well-being of the people at an appropriate level of prosperity, not just reckoned at a bare minimum. For example for food it must be reckoned how much rice, meat, salt, vegetables, fruit, sugar, and so on ordinary people (not poor) will need to eat. For clothing, it must be reckoned how much cloth and silk ordinary people (not poor) need to have as, for example, hats, shirt, trousers, socks, shoes, and so on. For shelter, it must be reckoned that each family will have one house, not a hut or shack, but a house where ordinary people can live happily and which is durable to last a long time, such as a brick building. It must be reckoned that the huts or farmhouses which are like those of jungle dwellers in Africa at present must be changed into good brick buildings of a condition equal to civilized countries. As for communications, we must think of land communications such as railways and roads to link together the people in all the cooperatives and tambon in the kingdom; canals and ports for water communications; air communications; including the vehicles which

people in a family or cooperative should have for use, such as cars, for instance. On these matters, we must bring the situation of the Thai people into line with people in advanced countries.

2. When we have made this research and calculation, we must then research and calculate how much land, labour, and capital will be needed to bring all of this about. Take the example of rice cultivation. Suppose that for a population of 11 million we need 2,931 million kilos of rice, and that will require 15 million *rai* of paddy fields and an input of labour which depends on the different methods used— either human labour with animals for draught power or human labour with machinery. In ploughing for example, suppose the normal method covers half a *rai* a day and requires 30 million man-days in total. But if machines are used on half the area at a rate of forty *rai* a day with one driver and one assistant, the human labour requirement will be only 750,000 man-days, with labour-saving many times over. Suppose that raking and sowing with human labour requires 15 million man-days, but with machinery uses only 750,000 man-days (compare as above).

Suppose harvesting with human labour requires 30 million man-days. But if the land can be modified to drain away the water so that harvesting machinery can be used, the requirement will be 750,000 man-days. Suppose haulage from the paddy field to the farmhouse using human labour requires 25 million man-days, but with machinery only 750,000 man-days.

Thus, totalling the labour requirement will be as follows.

a. If human labour is used with animal draught power alone, 90 million man-days.

b. If machinery is used for ploughing, raking, sowing, and haulage while harvesting requires human labour as machines cannot yet be used, 32,250,000 man-days.

c. If machinery is used throughout, only 3 million man-days will be needed, and the capital requirement will be different; for example, machines and petrol must be purchased. Suppose that 15 million *rai* of paddy fields uses 5,000 mechanized ploughs at 3,000 baht each, then the capital required for purchasing the mechanized ploughs will be 15 million baht. The government should be able to

*With labour-saving machinery*

109

buy on instalment. It must also find capital to buy the petrol, or may establish a refinery and prospect for oil, or use another fuel.

3. From the above calculations, we must research and calculate how much land, labour, and capital the government has at present, and how much these can be increased, in order to know the potential capacity for running the economy. For example, we have over 320 million *rai* of land; out of this, 18 million has already become paddy land; a certain amount which is now upland or forest could be cultivated, and a certain amount could remain for forestry; under the ground there are so many minerals that could be mined. Then we can calculate the labour. For example, suppose that out of the population of 11 million, there are 5 million children and aged who cannot work, and 6 million who can work. With eight working hours per day and 280 working days (and eighty-five days off) per year, the total labour available will be 1,680 million man-days. This can be broken down into so much physical labour; so much skilled labour; so much specialized labour such as technicians, doctors, and teachers; and so much supervisory labour such as foremen and public administrators. Also we must calculate the amount of capital which the government can provide by domestic borrowing, by cooperation with wealthy people, and by collecting indirect taxes which do not aggravate people.

When we have calculated thus, we will know what is the surplus of land and labour; what is the deficit of capital; how we can put that land to profitable use; and how we can divide the economy into cooperatives. Finally we can estimate how much time we will need to bring the people to the required well-being, and how much can be achieved in any one year.

*Begin by stages*

Finally we will know in which localities and in which sectors we will first begin using the national economic plan, by stages extending it to the whole kingdom.

*Training experts*

Any activity will be difficult to achieve unless we carefully calculate the capacity first. Once we know what is lacking, we should go and look for it. For instance, we lack specialized experts, hence we must contract foreigners who are specialized experts to use first and to train our people. Thus we must also draw up plans for training.

# PART 12: ACHIEVEMENTS RELATED TO THE SIX PRINCIPLES

The government running the economy itself by dividing the economy among cooperatives will achieve other objectives of the People's Party more effectively than leaving the economy to private free enterprise, as can be seen from the following explanation.

Chapter 1: Independence

The government announced the policy of making comprehensive law codes. There is no need to talk about this as the drafting of the law codes is almost finished at the present time.

*a. Judicial independence*

Once we ourselves can make the consumer goods and necessities of existence, and once government controls the rise and fall of prices which at present is at the will of the private sector, then we will be independent and will not be forced or oppressed by others in economic matters. As long as we have free private enterprise, we will not be able to throw off the yoke of economic oppression.

*b. Economic independence*

When our country has all the consumer goods, the means of existence, and enough weapons to protect the country, and has strengthened education by having teachers to train and educate the workers, and has improved the health of the people, all by relying on the method of having the government manage the economy itself, then opportunities will open up for improving other matters as well. At that point, what country will come to attack us? At present we only mutter about fearing the foreigners and do not dare to do anything. We must organize our country according to the independence that we have; look after our treaties and agreements with the foreigners; not exploit or obstruct the occupations which they have in Siam at present; and continue to exchange goods with them, that is, buying from them goods of the sort we cannot make ourselves, such as more machinery, rather than food which we can produce ourselves. In this case, what foreign country will come to bully us? If we are intent upon fearing that the foreigner will bully us in a wrongful way even though we are in the right, then it would be better not to do anything at all. Even during the change of government,

*c. Political independence*

at the first stage did we not fear that the foreigners would come to bully us? But they were sympathetic enough not to come to bully us at all. The foreigners are truly members of the League of Nations. Even though there are people who denigrate the League of Nations for never acting with serious intent, yet it is still to some extent a device for restraining oppression and unfair bullying. This is different from the past. Please look at the dispute between the British oil company and Persia. Persia has a territory and population roughly the same as ours. The progress in education among their population is roughly the same as ours. But when Persia withdrew the concession from the British company, why did the British not rush to bully them? I think they had enough fairness to bring the matter before the League of Nations rather than taking out an army to make war. When we do not want to bully or oppress foreign countries, but to strengthen our own country, why should they come to oppress and bully us?

Chapter 2: Maintaining internal peace and order

I gave a speech at the Lecturers Association *(sammak-kayachan)* in 1928, saying that there are two reasons why people commit crimes: 1. reasons related to the character of the wrongdoer; 2. reasons arising from the economy, for instance pickpocketing, theft, and robbery. When the government has ensured the well-being of the people with food to eat, clothing to wear, somewhere to live, and so on, how can there still be reasons for crime which arise from the economy? There will still be reasons for criminal action, but only reasons arising from the character of the wrongdoer, which must be overcome by training and education to correct character. And when the teachers, trainers, and educators also have economic well-being, then their training will have an even better effect.

Chapter 3: The economy

When the People's Party announced that the new government would find work for everyone, and would draw up a national economic plan so as not to allow people to go hungry, it was the truth and not just fooling the people. On this point, there are people who misunderstand because they perceive that the government has not done anything yet. But the fact that the government has not done anything yet is because it has not yet proceeded according to my thinking. When it does proceed according to my thinking that the government should run the economy itself, all the people will have work to do, through the government accepting everyone as a government servant, including children, the sick, the disabled, and the aged who cannot work but who will receive a monthly salary from government. The people will not go hungry because the lowest level of government salary will be determined as sufficient to buy or exchange for food, clothing, shelter, and so on in accordance with the needs of the people.

Chapter 4: Equality

Equality will arise in rights and duties, and not just equality on paper, but also equality in entering government service, whether on the administrative side or the economic side. People will have equal rights in not going hungry, but not equality in the sense that if one person has a hundred baht it must be seized and shared equally among a hundred people at one baht apiece—as learned men in Siam claim that the theory of communism would have it. We detest the theory of communism as stated by those learned men in Siam. We will not seize and share out assets as those learned men state.

Chapter 5: Freedom

On this point, people who see only the surface will immediately object that the government accepting all the people as government servants and running the economy itself will reduce freedom. Yes, when the government runs the economy itself, it is a reduction of freedom. But this reduction of freedom is to enable the people to have full well-being. It is implementation of the third principle. The government will not remove freedom in any other way. People will still have freedom of person, of property, of dwelling, of speech, of education and training, of association. When people have contentment in economic matters, then they will have physical contentment. Do people need freedom to the point of not having food to eat? That is not the wish of the people. Even now people must work for a living, except for those born as *parasite social* who live off other people. In any country freedom is limited for the common benefit of the people as a whole. The People's Party has already announced that freedoms will be achieved when they do not conflict with the four principles mentioned above.

Chapter 6: Education

People will have full education. When people have well-being as a result of the government running the economy itself, people will receive education, instead of worrying about their property and the danger of it being lost. Government may force the people who are government servants to study. Even people who are adults from twenty to fifty-five, when they are government servants, will have to study. Under the system of free private enterprise, forcing adults to study will be difficult.

[Conclusion]

When government runs the economy like this, it will successfully achieve the objectives of the People's Party's six principles, as announced to the people. The contentment and progress to the highest level which everyone desires and which can be called *si-ariya*, will arise for everybody with no exception. Why would all of us, who were like-minded about opening the door for the people, hesitate to lead the people further to the *kalapaphruk* tree where they can reap the fruit? This is the fruit of happiness and progress in accordance with the Buddhist prediction about *phra si-ariya*. On this matter, every religious person in making merit wishes to meet *phra si-ariya*. Even in swearing an oath in the court or in any ritual, it is said that a person who is honest and gives truthful testimony will meet *phra si-ariya*. Now that we are following the path to the era of *ariya* [civilization], there are still some people who want to walk backwards into a *khlong*—who if they walk backwards too far will return to the era before Buddha, that is 2475 years ago.

# DRAFT
# ACT ON SOCIAL INSURANCE *(ASSURANCE SOCIALE)*

King Prajadhipok

Clause 1. This Act is called the Act on Social Insurance 1932 [literally: act concerning the guarantee of well-being of the population].
Clause 2. This Act shall be in force from the date of publication in the Royal Gazette.

## PART 1: SALARY AND PENSION OF THE PEOPLE

Clause 3. From the day when the national economic plan is promulgated, all those with Thai nationality living in the country of Siam shall receive payment from the government or a cooperative as established by royal decree according to the minimum scale as follows:[1]

1. those under 1 year          ... baht per month
2. those 1–5 years             ... baht per month
3. those 6–10 years            ... baht per month
4. those 11–15 years           ... baht per month
5. those 16–18 years           ... baht per month
6. those 19–55 years           ... baht per month
7. those over 55 years         ... baht per month

Clause 4. Those who have qualifications or special ability or physical capacity shall receive higher payment according to their qualifications, ability, and physical capacity and according to the kind of work, by the minimum scale as follows:[2]

|  | | |  | | |
|---|---|---|---|---|---|
| Grade | 1 | 80 baht | Grade | 11 | 180 baht |
| Grade | 2 | 90 baht | Grade | 12 | 190 baht |
| Grade | 3 | 100 baht | Grade | 13 | 200 baht |
| Grade | 4 | 110 baht | Grade | 14 | 220 baht |
| Grade | 5 | 120 baht | Grade | 15 | 240 baht |
| Grade | 6 | 130 baht | Grade | 16 | 260 baht |
| Grade | 7 | 140 baht | Grade | 17 | 280 baht |
| Grade | 8 | 150 baht | Grade | 18 | 300 baht |
| Grade | 9 | 160 baht | Grade | 19 | 320 baht |
| Grade | 10 | 170 baht | Grade | 20 | 350 baht |

| | | | |
|---|---|---|---|
| Grade 21 | 400 baht | Grade 26 | 650 baht |
| Grade 22 | 450 baht | Grade 27 | 700 baht |
| Grade 23 | 500 baht | Grade 28 | 800 baht |
| Grade 24 | 550 baht | Grade 29 | 900 baht |
| Grade 25 | 600 baht | Grade 30 | 1,000 baht |

Clause 5. Apart from the salary, those who work or are in government service shall receive bonuses based on their work performance, as determined by government or cooperative.[3]

Clause 6. Those who work or are in government service and receive salary higher than the ordinary grade, on leaving government service shall receive pension higher than the minimum rate laid down in clause 3.[4]

Clause 7. Salaries, bonuses, and pensions shall increase in proportion with increases in the economic output of the government and cooperatives.[5]

## PART 2: CONCERNING EMPLOYMENT

Clause 8. Those aged between eighteen and fifty-five shall enter government service according to the type of work and according to their ability, qualifications, sex, and age as follows:

1. Those with any qualifications shall be enrolled for work which uses their qualification. If for any type of work more people enrol than the number required for that type of work, competitive examinations shall be held and those who pass the requirements shall be enrolled.

2. Those with ability shall be treated the same as those with qualifications.

3. Physical capacity. Those who have no qualifications or special ability or who fail in the competition for work which requires qualifications or special ability, shall be put to work appropriate to their physical capacity and strength.

4. Sex. In general, light work such as maintenance, clerical duties, teaching, child care, and sale of consumer goods, should be allocated to women except in cases where it is necessary to employ men, but with no reduction of rights of women who have qualifications or special abilities to enter the competition for work of types which use qualifications and special abilities.

5. Age. Those of higher age must be given lighter work than those in their prime.

Clause 9. Those aged from eleven to eighteen years and those over fifty-five years ordinarily need not do any work, except in emergency when there is a shortage of labour. To protect the economy from risk these groups may be mobilized to work according to their physical ability but without excess stress or strain, for example, to harvest rice when there is a labour shortage, or to eradicate pests which threaten crops.[6]

Clause 10. The following people, even though they are of the age which must work or enter government service, are exempt from having to work while both they and their children under eighteen shall continue to receive a monthly salary:
1. pregnant women[7]
2. invalids[7]
3. disabled[7]
4. university students and secondary school students who have passed the entrance examinations[8]
5. those who have been in government service long enough to receive a pension

Clause 11. The following people are exempt from government service but they and their children have no right to receive a salary as long as they have not entered government service:[9]
1. those who can demonstrate that they have adequate assets or income for their upkeep
2. those who are in independent occupations such as doctors, lawyers, skilled craftsmen, authors, or those authorized by government to engage in other business such as commerce, industry, and some forms of agriculture, as long as such people can demonstrate that they have income from their independent occupation to maintain themselves and their children throughout their lives.

## PART 3: THE METHOD OF PAYING SALARIES

Clause 12. Government or cooperative shall pay monthly salaries by one of the following methods:
1. In cash in accordance with the rate which that person has the right to receive.
2. By cheque drawn on the national bank in accordance with the rate which that person has the right to receive, after deduction *(compensation)* of money which that person owes to the government or

cooperative from purchase of food, clothing, shelter, and other means of existence. After deduction, if the person is still a creditor of government or cooperative, that person has the right to deposit that money in the national bank, or purchase bonds of the government or cooperative, or withdraw for spending according to preference.

## PART 4: FOREIGNERS IN GOVERNMENT SERVICE

Clause 13. Government may engage foreign nationals with special expertise, who shall have rights as detailed in their contracts.

## PART 5: DISCIPLINE OF GOVERNMENT SERVANTS

Clause 14. All government servants whether administrative officers or workers in government enterprises must have the discipline to work to their full capacity and ability in their role. Those who are found slacking shall be punished, such as by cutting salary or increasing working hours or by other punishment according to regulations.

Promulgated on . . . (date)

# EXPLANATORY NOTES ON THE DRAFT
# ACT ON SOCIAL INSURANCE 1932

1. This minimum rate must be fixed as sufficient for food, clothing, shelter, and so on.

2. These rates are reproduced from the current regular salaries of government servants of *sanyabat* level [i.e. commissioned officers of grade 3 and above] as newly agreed.

3. It is the intention with these bonuses to give workers a part of profits, known as *participation benefice*.

4. The salaries of government servants and workers shall vary according to qualifications and ability. Those who receive high salary should also receive high pension.

5. This is possible. When it is announced that government enterprises have a higher output, increase may be made, such as a 25 percent increase, which would increase salaries from 80 to 100, from 400 to 500, for instance.

6. In some countries, there are laws to mobilize people to help with pest eradication. In our country it may be possible. Or during the time when machinery cannot yet be used for harvesting, when the rice is ready to harvest, people may be mobilized according to their capacity to help on work that is not too heavy.

7. Under social insurance by the method of *assurance sociale*, this group of people has pensions.

8. This is to cultivate experts in arts and sciences.

9. This exception gives wealthy people or those who object to becoming government servants the opportunity to conduct their own independent business when they are able to do so.

# DRAFT
# ACT ON THE ECONOMY

King Prajadhipok

Clause 1. This Act shall be called the Act on the Economy . . . [date].

Clause 2. This Act shall be in force from the date of publication in the Royal Gazette.

Clause 3. From the day when the national economic plan is promulgated, government shall have the power to engage in economic activities, that is, all forms of production both agriculture and industry, inclusive of transport and distribution, except that in those economic activities where government has granted private concessions, the private interests shall have the power to continue according to the following examples:

1. Mining, forestry, and public utilities for which government has already granted concessions or licenses.[1]

2. Private factories already established which government may allow to continue by issuing concessions.

3. Sales outlets of nationals of foreign countries which have special treaties of friendship with Siam.[2]

4. Other economic activities such as commerce, industry, and agriculture for which private interests apply for licences[3] or concessions case by case, as long as that independent business can demonstrate satisfactorily to government that the business has output sufficient for the owner to make a living continuously, and is in accordance with other conditions set out in regulations relating to the national economy.

## PART 1: ON THE PURCHASE OF LAND

Clause 4. Government shall have the power to purchase all land apart from land for private dwellings and apart from land on which private interests have been granted licences or concessions to conduct business.[4]

Waste land which is not controlled or owned by anyone, cannot be controlled or owned except under a concession received from government.

Clause 5. To determine the price of land, the landowner and government shall each appoint one person as arbitrator, and shall jointly appoint one other as adjudicator. The price of land may not be fixed higher than it stood on 24 June 1932.

Clause 6. To pay the purchase price, government may pay by cash or by a bond for the landowner according to the price of the land which government buys. The interest on this bond shall be fixed at the bank interest rate at the time of the transaction, but not higher than 15 percent per annum which is the maximum rate at present.

Those who hold these bonds may still have the right to receive further money as dividend from the returns made by the cooperative to which the land is transferred according to a ratio which the government shall determine.

## PART 2: ON PROVISION OF CAPITAL AND CREDIT

Clause 7. The government shall provide capital and credit for engaging in economic activities as follows:

    1. by collecting inheritance tax[5]

    2. by collecting income tax

    3. by collecting indirect tax on tobacco,[6] matches,[6] salt,[7] etc.

    4. by forcing those who desire to gamble[8] to register for a personal licence and to pay a registration fee in instalments according to the type of gambling they wish to play, while banning registration by those who at the time this Act comes into force do not know how to play. Apart from paying the personal registration fee, gamblers must receive permission and pay an additional fee each time they play.

    5. issuing bonds[9] for the wealthy in the kingdom to buy, with the government providing factories or other assets as collateral

    6. issuing a lottery[10]

    7. borrowing from the national bank[11]

    8. borrowing overseas

    9. negotiating credit and repayment by instalment with overseas companies which sell machinery

## PART 3: ON THE NATIONAL BANK

Clause 8. The government shall establish a national bank using the government reserves and borrowing from the private sector as the capital. The national bank shall conduct business like other banks and have the power to issue banknotes. The mint shall be transferred from the Finance Ministry to the national bank, and the present provincial treasuries shall be transferred to become provincial branches of the national bank.

Clause 9. The central bank shall loan money to the government as the government requires in accordance with the capacity of the national bank.

## PART 4: ON THE NATIONAL ECONOMIC PLAN[12]

Clause 10. A council shall be created with the duty to draw up a national economic plan which shall determine the production, including agriculture, industry, distribution (transport and communications), and the construction of dwellings for all the people, and shall divide the work among various cooperatives.

Clause 11. The national economic plan shall determine the year's activities of the government, and the results shall be announced to the people each week.

Clause 12. During the time this national economic plan is in use, if there is need to adjust the plan, either because the government is unable to provide the capital and labour as required, or because the government has more capital and labour, the members of the council of the national economic plan shall meet to amend the plan and announce the result to the people.

Clause 13. The initial implementation of the national economic plan in any area shall be announced case by case with explanation about the adequacy of land, capital, and labour of government servants, workers, and specialist experts.

## PART 5: PRIVATE OWNERSHIP

Clause 14. Private interests are granted the right in any moveable assets which they have acquired.

Clause 15. Those who invent any article which has the potential for commercial use may acquire the property right as *Brevet d'Invention*. Such people may request a concession to found an enterprise, or sell it to government, or undertake production jointly with government, according to preference.

Promulgated on . . . [date].

## EXPLANATORY NOTES ON THE DRAFT ACT ON THE ECONOMY

1. So as not to affect harshly the private interests which can make an economic living themselves.

2. To prevent any impact on foreigners.

3. To open an opportunity for private interests who object to becoming government servants to do their own business.

4. Forced purchase of land already exists at present, for instance, for roads, railways, etc. This is because at present only roads, railways, etc. are considered public utilities. But this draft plan considers that economic enterprises are public utilities because if the government does not run them, it will be hazardous for the people.

5. This inheritance tax is not motivated by envy of the rich. According to principle, the rich have amassed money, that money has come from using the people, and the rich have saved it by either direct or indirect means. In determining the inheritance tax, those who are very rich to the point of excess should pay a lot *(super tax)*, while the middle class should be allowed to pay a little, so as not to affect the rich too much.

6. The tobacco and match taxes enabled France to have revenue to pay off the German loans in 1870 quickly, and the French currency strengthened because of these taxes. In our country, suppose that there are one million tobacco smokers and we collect indirect tax on sales at one *satang* a day, which will not feel heavy; this should yield an extra 3 million baht or more. But a *monopoly* on tobacco tax would involve the foreign treaties. Hence we should have a policy of collecting tax from shops selling tobacco and from tobacco factories, taking care not to lose advantage against overseas tobacco which is imported.

7. For salt, a way should be found to collect tax indirectly, by government buying the salt from those with salt fields at a specified rate, and selling it either by itself or via a monopoly. Suppose that government collects tax at the rate of 1/10th *satang* per head per day, the annual revenue will be over 3 million baht.

8. It will be impossible to stop those who are already gamblers from playing at all. They will play secretly. Therefore, a way should be found to prevent people of later generations, who do not yet know how to play, from playing. Those who can already play may play, but must register like those addicted to opium. The fee should be collected in instalments, such as one baht five times a year. Suppose that there are a million gamblers, then 5 million baht a year can be collected in personal licence fees. As for collections from each playing occasion, for example, in one tambon there are not fewer than two

poker circles per day, and in the kingdom there are 5,000 tambon. This gives 10,000 circles applying for licences. If the licence fee is 5 baht per circle, the return will be 50,000 baht a day and 18 million baht a year. New restrictions should be placed on time for gambling so as not to waste working time. The previous restriction from noon to 2 A.M. has no principle. Truly the time should be restricted to 4 to 10 P.M. At other times gamblers must work and not impair the economy.

Gambling should also be progressively reduced. Later generations must be prevented from learning how to play. This measure is not for supporting gambling.

9. On this matter we must coordinate with the wealthy, not kill them.

10. Although a lottery is a form of gambling and risk taking, the gain or loss for the risk taker is only a small amount. For instance, in one year there may be a lottery thirty times at one million baht a time, with several million deducted as the government's share, and one person risking about twenty to fifty *satang* each time.

Concerning the organization of a lottery in this way, some Thai people are sensitive to criticism for promoting gambling. But please see the example in France where the *Credit National* bonds to raise money for rebuilding the country which had been destroyed in the war, were bonds of a type which also provided a lottery for the bondholders. In Britain itself there are horse racing courses and there are many British people who like horse racing. But we have no wish to go that far. We wish only for a lottery which people can play in small amounts but have an opportunity to make a lot of money.

11. The national bank can help the government considerably, because the tax returns which are retained in the provincial treasuries could be brought into circulation. Besides that, the surplus salary which government servants deposit in the bank will come into circulation in the same way. Even beyond that, there are many methods for the government to borrow money from the national bank.

12. Besides this, the administrative plan must also be adapted to the national economic plan.

# 11. SOME ASPECTS OF THE ESTABLISHMENT OF THE PEOPLE'S PARTY AND THE DEMOCRACY (1972)

I

The first official meeting of the People's Party was held in February 1927 at a boarding house on the *Rue du Sommerard* where we hired a large room especially for the meeting. The seven people at the meeting were: 1. Lieutenant Prayun Phamonmontri, a reserve military officer who had previously been a commander of the royal bodyguard in the Sixth Reign; 2. Lieutenant Plaek Kittasangkha [Phibun], a graduate of the Siam army general staff school who had come to study at the French artillery school; 3. Second Lieutenant Thasanai Mitphakdi, a reserve officer who had formerly been commander of the fifth cavalry regiment at Nakhon Ratchasima and who had come to study at the French cavalry school; 4. Nai Tua Laphanukrom, a science student in Switzerland who had been a sergeant in the volunteer regiment during the First World War; 5. Luang Siriratchamaitri, previously named Charun Singhaseni, assistant Siamese ambassador in Paris, who had formerly been a law student in the Justice Ministry, and who had been a lance corporal in the volunteer regiment during the First World War; 6. Nai Naep Phahonyothin, a barrister in England; 7. myself.

The meeting passed a unanimous resolution that I should be chairman and head of the People's Party until there was a person appropriate to be leader of the party in the future.

The meeting continued for around five days, and took the following important decisions:

I. The first purpose of the People's Party was to change the system of absolute monarchy into a constitutional monarchy. In those days there were no words *patiwat* or *aphiwat* to translate the French or English word, *revolution*. Hence we used the ordinary words "change the system of government in which the king is above the law to the system of government in which the king is under the law". The second purpose of the party was to enable Siam to achieve six principles: 1. to maintain securely the independence of the country in all forms including political, judicial, and economic, etc.; 2. to maintain public safety within the country and greatly reduce crime; 3. to improve the economic well-being of the people by the new government finding employment for all, and drawing up a national economic plan, not leaving the people to go hungry; 4. to provide the people with equal rights; 5. to provide the people with liberty as far as this does not conflict with the above four principles; 6. to provide the people with full education.

II. Siam was surrounded by the colonial powers of England and France, both of which had agreed to treat Siam as a buffer state, but either of which might be ready to invade, seize, and divide Siam as a dependency or client state of these two countries. Given this situation, we saw that the method of changing the system of government must be through *coup d'état*, for which we used the ordinary Thai words "rapid seizure of power" because at that time nobody had coined the Thai word *ratthaprahan* to translate the French phrase. A coup was necessary to prevent an intervention by the great powers. Once the People's Party had seized power, the great powers would face the situation called in French a *fait accompli*.

III. Those who attended the first meeting would form the central committee of the People's Party for the time being. Each would head up a branch to select trusted people by a process of personal scrutiny, and propose them to the central committee of the People's Party for membership. The committee could accept them as members only by unanimous resolution. At the first stage, each committee member was to find only two additional members, then divide up into separate branches.

IV. The selection of additional members of the People's Party would have to take account of their readiness to make a sacrifice for the country, their courage, and their ability to maintain confidence. Those who wanted to change the system of government were classified into three types, namely:

1. Those who should be invited to join the People's Party before the start of the seizure of power. These were further subdivided into those who should be invited early on, and those invited close to the time of the start of the seizure of power. Any friend with whom a member dined and socialized should not simply be invited to be a member of the People's Party immediately. Such a friend might like joking too much and saying things true or untrue just to amuse his listeners. He

might disclose the secrets of the party just for a joke. Some friends might have many good qualities, but when they drank they might be unable to control themselves and might speak nonsense. They might make the mistake of speaking about the party when drunk. Such people would not be invited to join the People's Party before the attempted seizure of power. But once we had seized power on the 24th June, there was no secret to keep hidden so they could be invited to join.

2. Those who would be invited once the process of seizing power had begun. They would agree to have a role as the force of the People's Party.

3. Those who would be invited on the day of seizing power itself, but after the seizure promised to be successful rather than unsuccessful.

V. As to the policies to be pursued after the People's Party had the power of government, the meeting entrusted me to make proposals in line with the six principles. I proposed general principles for an economic plan, and was later entrusted to draft an economic plan.

VI. The meeting also considered that if the activity of the People's Party was suppressed or failed, there should be one leader whose membership of the party we should keep unexposed to outside view, by allowing him not to attend the general committee meetings often, whether in France or after return to Siam. He would conduct himself like someone who stays quietly at home. This person would have the duty to carry out the work of the People's Party through to completion in case the party was suppressed or failed. This duty would include helping out the families of friends who were jailed or dead. The meeting agreed to entrust this duty to Nai Naep Phahonyothin, who was a man with considerable property inherited from his father.

When the meeting to form the People's Party was over, I returned to Siam in March of the same year. For another two or three months, the friends still in Paris selected people suitable to invite into the People's Party. They invited Nai Thawi Bunyaket, an agriculture student; Nai Banchong Sicharun, a Thai-Muslim from Egypt who came to visit Paris and took on the task of organizing other Thai-Muslims such as Nai Chaem Musthapha (son of the Islamic leader in Siam who is known by the name Khru Fa; later Nai Chaem changed his last name to Phromyong, similar to mine). Later they invited Midshipman Sin Kamonnawin, a naval student in Denmark who came to visit Paris. Later Phraya Songsuradet came for a study tour on the military in France. Friends still in Paris tried sounding out how he felt about the absolute monarchy, and found that he was dissatisfied. However he was not yet invited to join the People's Party. After that, friends who formed the People's Party in Paris came back to Siam one by one, and gradually invited student friends who they had earlier observed in casual conversation. It was not limited only to students from Paris. Hence later in Siam those invited included M.L. Udom Sanitwong, a student from Switzerland; M.L. Kri Dechatiwong, Nai Saphrang Thep-hatsadin na Ayutthaya, and Leng Sisomwong, students from England; and others including friends in the army, navy, and other civilians in Siam. At the end of 1931, Phraya Phahon Phonphayuhasena, Phraya Songsuradet, Phraya Ritthiakhane were invited, and Phraya Phahon was made head of the People's Party.

## II

The People's Party called type-1 members "promoters of change in the system of government" or for short "promoters". This indicated that people of this type were just the vanguard of the mass of the people who wanted more freedom and equality than under the absolute monarchy. Members of types 2 and 3 were the next levels of support. However, the major power which helped the People's Party to succeed was the mass of the people who gave support both directly and implicitly.

Some people with the vision *(thatsana)* of the old order have stated that the People's Party claimed the people without the people's consent. This accusation follows the vision and standpoint of their own class-caste status *(chon chan wanna)* from which they receive benefits or of which they admiringly approve.

Progressive social science divides people into two main types: 1. Reactionaries are those who want the old social system to remain or even regress backwards further; 2. Others who are not reactionaries are the *people* which we translate as *ratsadon*. Most of the citizens of Siam who were subordinate to the power of the government of that era called themselves *ratsadon*. For example, when district officers recruited civilians for public works, they called them *ratsadon* recruits. Individuals pondering their own troubles would say: "*ratsadon* everywhere are beset by difficulties", which indicates the condition of people governed by the absolute monarchy.

The Thai people's wish to change the absolute monarchy did not begin with the People's Party. Those really interested in social science have already studied the theory on how people's social vision is formed, and have applied this to the reality evident in Siam ever since the time when Siam had to make treaties with various capitalist countries from the middle of the nineteenth century onwards.

I have already dealt with this topic somewhat in the book *The Impermanence of Society* and here I will just summarize it. When the tools for producing a society's necessities of life have developed, the men who make and use those tools must develop too. Productive power leads to greater abundance in the production of the necessities of life. As a result, the economic relations of man in society must change to avoid an economic crisis. When the economic system which is the basis of society has changed, the political system must change too. Otherwise conflict between the political system and the economic system at the base will create an economic crisis. The thing which guides the movement to bring about the changes demanded by the new economic system is man's social vision. In the book just mentioned, I dealt with the development of the social vision to change from primitive society to slave society, then from slave society to *sakdina* or *feudal* society, and from this system finally to capitalism. The social vision of capitalism is now ascendant. In the time ahead, other progressive visions will arise.

Here let me talk briefly about the birth of the social vision to abolish the absolute monarchy which is a feudal system. In Europe, this vision did not arise among the feudal lords. Rather, it arose because in western Europe at the end of the eighteenth century, the invention of steam power created a major revolution in production machinery and gave rise to what is known as the industrial revolution. The need arose to develop man to be capable of making and using this modern machinery. The serfs and slaves were expert only at using animals for ploughing or at making handicrafts. They were incapable of making and using the modern production machinery with any efficiency. The modern capitalists who owned businesses using the modern production machinery needed modern workers who had more knowledge and ability than the workers in the old feudal system. They also had to change the relations between business owners and workers into a new form—that is the modern capitalist system where the modern wage workers have more freedom than the feudal serfs and slaves who were forced to work. The serfs and slaves had no incentive to pay attention to the modern and more complex machinery. So the modern capitalists wanted to change the feudal political system to accord with the developing system of modern capitalism. The capitalist vision of society arose because of the need to change the feudal political system so that people would have more freedom and democratic rights. The thinking and vision which demanded the change of absolutism in Europe spread widely at the end of the eighteenth century. The feudal lords tried to retain the system from which they received the most benefit. They tried to use the old vision from the feudal system to oppose the new, progressive vision. Violent conflict arose between the old system and vision on one side and the new system and thinking on the other.

After modern capitalism had arisen in western Europe, it developed further into large-scale financial capitalism and imperialism which spread their power into Siam and other underdeveloped countries. Siam was forced to make treaties with various capitalist powers. Thereby Siam was forced to accommodate the capitalist economic system alongside the old Siamese feudal economy. Thus the vision arising from the modern capitalist system in Europe also came into Siam. Meanwhile, inside Siam itself, there was also a demand for change. People who had studied in Europe and America and who were not too stubbornly tied to the backward feudal system wanted to change the absolute monarchy towards a system of constitutional monarchy. But this demand had several levels. Some groups wanted only a little change, while others wanted to be completely under a constitution with full democratic principles. These different levels of demand arose from the varying boundaries on each individual's vision.

According to the scientific principle of the origin of human consciousness, "material existence determines human consciousness". Hence those who exist as feudal lords or tribute-lords have the consciousness to preserve that system. But there are exceptions, as I have recounted in the above-mentioned book [*The Impermanence of Society*, 18–19] as follows:

When talking of the "residual power" of the old order, we must understand that this residual power is not identical with the people of the old class. Some members of this old class are progressive and they understand the law of impermanence. They value the general benefit of society above the benefit of their class alone. They are people with ethics and they are worthy of admiration. The founding father of modern social science stated objectively as follows: "Finally, in times when the class struggle nears the decisive hour, the process of dissolution going on within the ruling class, in fact within the whole range of old society, assumes such a violent, glaring character that a small section of the ruling class cuts itself adrift and joins the revolutionary class, the class that holds the future in its hands. Just as, therefore, at an earlier period, a section of the nobility went over to the bourgeoisie, so now a portion of the bourgeoisie goes over to the proletariat, and in particular a portion of the bourgeois ideologists, who have raised themselves to the level of comprehending theoretically the historical movement as a whole." [from Marx and Engels, *Manifesto of the Communist Party*, 1888]

At the other extreme to the people described in the last paragraph, there arise people who seem like a new class, but who do not understand the law of impermanence. They believe the old state of affairs is permanent. They are not happy with the new state of affairs which is developing by natural law. These people may not be the offspring of the old class. But they act as servants of the old order even more than those who come from the high ranks of the old class. This situation arises because the old order which is crumbling away loses control only of the outer casing of the political system. These people are still embedded in the power mechanisms of the state and economy. They still have the social vision of the backward old system. Unlike the progressive segment of the old class, this residual element of the old order has a vision which conflicts with natural law. They oppose natural law and the law of impermanence. They drag the society backwards even more than the old ruling class itself would do. However, "society can be dragged backwards only temporarily, because in the end the law of impermanence must prevail" [*The Impermanence of Society*, 20].

From the law above, we can conclude that those belonging to the new order are not simply the same as those born and living in the new era. We must look whether the vision guiding their lives is the new vision arising from the new changes in the economy at the base of society. Or whether they hold the vision from the old order, as described by the proverb: "old wine in new bottles".

Let us apply these principles to examine which people initiated the vision to change the absolute monarchy in Siam. Those who represent the residual part of the old order believe the change came from people in the old order. But those who belong to the new order, especially those at the forefront, believe it came only from people in the new order. However, those who are philosophers and as described above, "have raised themselves to the level of comprehending theoretically the historical movement as a whole" do not limit themselves to either the new order or the old. They look at both sides and discover the truth.

Within the old order of Siam, there were people more progressive than those who clung to the old thinking. Around a hundred years ago there were three younger brothers of the king, Krommun Naretworarit, Phraongchao Sonabandit (later, Kromkhun Phitayalap), Phraongchao Sawatdisophon (later Somdet Kromphra Sawat) and Phraongchao Prisadang. They joined with some officials from the Siamese embassy in London, including Luang Wisetsali (Nak na Pombejra, later Phraya Chaiwichit Sitthisattra, governor of Ayutthaya), and Sub-Lieutenant Sa-at Singhaseni (later General Phraya Prasitsalayakan, Siamese ambassador in London, and then Phraya Singhaseni, commissioner of monthon Nakhon Ratchasima). They sent a petition to King Rama V to modernize the government. They were progressive, but not to the extent of petitioning for Siam to have a parliamentary system under which people would participate in elections and ministers would have to command the confidence of parliament. Yet they were very brave to have made a petition. Current intellectuals who truly belong to the new order should not be surprised to find that there were once relatives of the king who had such progressive thinking. Please follow up for yourselves how this matter concluded, how the king responded to this petition, what the king said on the occasion of his birthday about government by the parliamentary system, and what the king wrote to his daughter from Norway (in the book *Klai Ban* [Far from home, vol. 2, p. 36])—I quoted this letter in my lectures on administrative law at the Justice Ministry law school in 1931. [The quote in these lectures runs: "Today at dinner there were not many important people. We waited for the prime minister for a while and then were told he could not come as he was engaged at the Storting [the Norwegian parliament]. That is, the parliament was making trouble. This prime minister is the one who thought of separating Norway from Sweden. Very clever. Speaks good English. He urged me strongly not to have a Storting in Thailand at all. The king also said the same thing."].

Those interested in the history of democratic thinking among the Siamese should research what happened to those who sent this petition to the king when they returned to Siam and whether they expressed any opinion about democracy anywhere. I was once a law student in the Justice Ministry at the time when Somdet Kromphra Sawat was chief judge of the high court. I had the opportunity to study whether judgements written by him revealed any democratic vision. For example judgement no. 326/1912 has this passage:

> in a case so severe as to warrant capital punishment, if the hearing has not come to a clear enough result, to find that Nai Thomya is guilty and should receive the death penalty would be risky and improper. According to a Buddhist saying, when cases are in doubt, to let even ten wrongdoers go free is better than punishing one person who is innocent.

The democratic principle of judicial practice laid down here was followed by judges then and later for many years, until the time when the old carcass of the ancient feudal system was revived. Then some judges with the old vision threw away this Buddhist saying which had been the basis for a democratic vision of judicial practice.

At that time, law students at the Justice Ministry had to study various laws, so people from that group should still remember the law about private schools of 1917. The history of this affair is that the Education Ministry of the time submitted to King Rama VI a draft law to regulate the schools which previously had been founded by private interests with no need to ask government permission. The Education Ministry wanted to require private schools to have permission as well as other strict controls. King Rama VI sent the ministry's draft bill to the law-drafting council, of which Somdet Kromphra Sawat (then Kromluang) was the head. He inspected the draft, and then redrafted it according to his own democratic vision. He wanted freedom in the provision of education and he wanted education to spread widely among the people. Hence he drafted a provision whose essence was that if someone wanting to found a public school applied to the Education Ministry and the ministry did not reply within a specified time, it would be as if the application was approved. King Rama VI agreed and promulgated this Private Schools Act. This made the Education Ministry very unhappy. The ministry tried many times to amend the law, but without success. This illustrates that Somdet Kromphra Sawat, even while in the bureaucracy, still had some democratic vision.

Those who really belong to the new order must not look down on ordinary commoners as if they had no thought to demand change in the absolute monarchy.

When I was studying in upper secondary over sixty years ago, I heard about, read about, and met two elderly commoners. The first was K. S. R. Kulap, who issued the magazine *Sayam Praphet* [Siam type, a pun on *Sayam prathet*, the country of Siam] which picked at the absolute monarchy until some people charged that he had a screw loose. But when I met him, I did not think he had a screw loose. The second was Thianwan who had the alias, Wannapho. He had very democratic principles. At that time, he had a grey beard and was almost seventy. I met him in a rowhouse near Wat Bowonniwet. He was once imprisoned for writing and speaking in opposition to the absolute monarchy. He did not think he had broken the law. His case is of the type described by the old saying "the rule of law cannot compete with the rule of the mob", which is a reference to the cliquiness of judges in old times. But Thianwan, who was imprisoned, extended the saying as: "the rule of law cannot compete with the rule of the mob; the rule of the mob cannot compete with a boot on the neck; and a boot on the neck cannot compete with a king breaking the neck." This indicates the vision Thianwan had towards the absolute monarchy. Many of the new generation in Siam at that time who read and talked with Thianwan may still remember this saying of his. But he was an ordinary commoner who attracted no interest from those who held the vision of the old order. It is as if people of the old order do not like to mention K. S. R. Kulap or Thianwan, who in their youth over a hundred years ago openly called for change in the absolute monarchy.

Students who studied Thai from the book *Basic Elementary (Munlabot bapphakit)* before the time of *Speed Reader (Baep rian reo)* may remember that they were taught about the decline of the absolute monarchy from the start of reading ABC. Those who studied after *Speed Reader* had come into being may have heard earlier students mention this. Phraya Sisunthonwohan (Noi Acharayangkun) composed a text about the decline of the imaginary kingdom of Sawatthi. I can remember a bit:

Praise be to the Buddhist trinity, fathers, mothers, teachers, angels in the zodiac . . . as time went by, the servants sought young girls with beautiful faces to make music and provide entertainment night and morning at the residence . . . whatever was obtained, the wife became mad with greed . . . some warnings were issued, but the king did not pay attention, so whoever could make some gain for himself, did so, and the people were all sick in their hearts.

In this text there was a saying which people revived and discussed a lot during the Sixth Reign. Some senior royal family members in Paris warned me to keep in mind this saying which ran:

The king who ruled Sawatthi was fooled by his army commander who was very cunning. Hence the kingdom was destroyed.

Hence it can be seen that among students who studied *Basic Elementary* or among later students who heard their predecessors relate it for them, there arose some general appreciation of the decline of the absolutist or backward feudal system. I would like to honour King Rama V who had a more progressive heart than some very backward people. Even though this book appeared in his reign, he approved its use as a textbook to create a sentiment to help the king get rid of bureaucrats who were corrupt, who cunningly told him lies, and who acted more royalist than the king.

During the Sixth Reign there was a call for change in the absolute monarchy in many newspapers and magazines. Several English-language newspapers in Siam displayed a daring vision. These papers are probably difficult to find now. But anyone really interested should be able to find some. This vision helped some Siamese become a little more aroused to the point where some people thought of seizing power by force—the so-called Ro. So. 130 group.

Later there were many newspapers which, although under the absolute monarchy, dared to risk jail by writing articles calling for change in the absolute monarchy. Some papers were closed down, and several editors jailed. But still people put out many little papers and magazines.

When I came back to Thailand in 1927 after being in France almost seven years, the youth of that time who had never been to see democracy overseas were nevertheless aroused to change the absolute monarchy. This shows that those who did not live in the feudal style had developed a consciousness that this system was not suitable as a result of their own experience and the influence of the progressive journalists of that time who called for change from the feudal system to constitutional monarchy. Hence my little group returning from Europe did not have much difficulty in inviting those aroused in Siam to be members of the People's Party because they had the basic want already. The fact we invited only just over a hundred people as type-1 members was because that was enough to create the vanguard of the people and because of the need to maintain confidence within a limited circle. But when we had seized power on 24 June, we received support from huge numbers of people. Some came in person to offer congratulations at the Ananta Samakhom throne hall where the command headquarters of the People's Party was established. Others sent letters and telegrams. As further evidence, when the party deputed Thawi Bunyaket to accept applications from people wanting to join the People's Party at Suan Saranrom, there were so many applicants that the membership cards we had prepared ran out and people fought over them.

Hence we maintain we were the "People's Party" because we acted according to the needs of the people, not the wishes of the reactionaries.

Many decades passed from the time the demand to change the absolute monarchy into a constitutional monarchy appeared in the various documents mentioned above, until 1932. It is normal that the law of social science, which I described in *The Impermanence of Society*, must apply. Let me insert an extract here [p. 75]:

> By natural law, the form (the political system) must be in line with the substance (the economic system). If the form of society changes slower than the material basis of society for too long a time, nature will force the form to fall into line with the substance. Hence, when this does not happen by evolution, it must happen by revolution. For instance, the change in the system of government on 24 June 1932 had to be this way because the form of society changed slower than the material basis of society. The change in the absolute monarchy in France at the end of the eighteenth century had to take place through revolution because the feudal form refused to change by evolution to fall into line with the material basis which had progressed much farther.

## III

Some people understand wrongly that the founders of the People's Party in Paris were dissatisfied with the Siamese ambassador of the time over the inadequate payment of monthly allowances, and hence thought of changing the absolute monarchy. This misunderstanding has spread more widely since Nai Khuang Aphaiwong, who became a member of the People's Party only three months before the day of the revolution and who hence does not know what truly motivated the founders and who has had a social vision from

134

before that time, spoke at the teacher's council *(khurusapha)* on 23 November 1963 to distance himself from any responsibility for the People's Party. He made many incorrect statements to show that he had a large personal income and belonged to the class of the feudal nobility and bourgeoisie, and hence was different from other students who joined together to fight for justice at that time, especially myself and Lieutenant Plaek whose monthly salaries were not enough. The file of information which shows who received what salary—whether son of a millionaire or not—and how the Siamese ambassador was equally strict with everyone, is probably still there at the Thai embassy in Paris, as I will explain at a more suitable opportunity in the future.

Here let me state that I and the six friends who founded the People's Party in February 1927 already had the idea that the absolute monarchy must be changed. The social vision to change the absolute monarchy had arisen because of the laws and facts I have noted above. But at another level, each of us had different ideas about the need to develop society, and about the principles and methods of social development. After we had the power of the state, these differences led to conflict among us.

In particular, in Siam there were some young people who had already decided together to be serious about changing the absolute monarchy. They joined the People's Party after I and friends who founded the party in Paris returned to Siam. As for me and the friends who had been in Paris, we had been talking together for many years earlier. People of that time who are still alive today, including some royal family members who uphold the Buddhist saying "truth never dies", could probably relate how great was the demand for a change in the absolute monarchy around 1925 at the end of the Sixth Reign. When Lieutenant Prayun Phamonmontri, who had been the commander of the royal bodyguard and a royal page close to King Rama VI, came to Paris and met me in 1925, he talked about the decline of the absolute monarchy and the demand of the people in Siam for a change in the system. Hence in 1925 itself, after I had talked with Lieutenant Prayun several times, I invited him to take a walk on *Henri Martin* street, and remarked that I had heard that the people who wanted to change the absolute monarchy were already many in number, but there was nobody who had decided to do anything committed. Thus we had to go beyond mere talk. We had to start small and grow big by gradually inviting friends who we could rely on to join in the first unit. Hence subsequently we invited other friends including Lieutenant Plaek and Second Lieutenant Thasanai, who moved from their old lodging to the same as mine in the *Quartier-Latin*, and we talked together almost every day.

We laid plans to stimulate the idea among friends and students in general that the absolute monarchy must be changed. The best opportunity was

135

during the 1925 annual meeting of the S.I.A.M. [Association Siamoise d' Intellectualité et d'Assistance Mutuelle] of which I was then the head. The society had organized for Thai friends to assemble at a big mansion which the society hired for fifteen days in the district of Chatrettes. We organized almost every kind of sport including target shooting so that we had grounds for practising using weapons. In the evenings we had lectures about international and domestic affairs, debates on educational topics, meaningful drama performances such as "Lo-le-buri" [Wobble-ville] by King Rama VI about the disintegration of the courts and judges in the imaginary city of "Lo-le", and some music and singing but no dancing to arouse sensual desires. This gathering in the summer of 1925 resulted in the creation of close friendships among the Thai student friends who attended, to the point that at the end of the fifteen days several people regretted that the group had to split up. So I and the founding friends named earlier consulted together and agreed that at the next annual meeting in July 1926 we should develop the consciousness of our student friends to a higher level to challenge the ambassador who was the overseas representative of the absolute monarchy. But we would challenge in a way which custom and tradition allowed, that is by petitioning King Prajadhipok who had just ascended the throne in succession to King Rama VI. And we would take as our basis the dissatisfaction shared by most of the students because the ambassador paid too little allowance money, even though each person had an adequate budget which either the government or their family had entrusted to the ambassador. In line with the law of social science on the development of consciousness, we used economics as the basis to develop a consciousness of politics.

The king rightly judged that I must accept responsibility for subverting the student association to become like a labour union, a *syndicate*. In France at that time the workers' movement was active but the ideology of *syndicalism* came later. May I print here the king's ruling as it appeared in a telegram from Phraongchao Traithot (Krommun Thewawongwarothai), the foreign minister, to the Siamese ambassador in Paris, together with the permission for me to study further up to doctorate.

[In English] Copy No 14080 (Received 22nd October 1926)
His Majesty, having examined all the documents submitted concerning Prince Charoon's dispute with the S.I.A.M. and students' petition, has come to the conclusion that the Students' Society has deviated from the purposes for which it was formed. The object of the Society should be entirely social among students under the care of the Paris Legation. It seems that the Society has now become a sort of Syndicate of students, in

which the students meet to discuss the actions of the Minister and to form resolutions and take actions contrary to the wishes of the Minister. The students have discussed and condemned the manner in which the Minister has been paying out their allowances, they have sent representatives to England well knowing that it was against the wishes of the Minister. They have shown themselves to be thoroughly hostile to the Minister and the actions of the President of the society has been on the verge of insolence. Such a state of affair cannot be tolerated for if students are allowed to form themselves into a syndicate hostile to the Minister in this way, no Minister can possibly accept the responsibility of looking after the students' welfare in the future. His Majesty, therefore, orders that the S.I.A.M. in its present form should be dissolved. If it is still desired to form some Society that will afford the Students some social intercourse among themselves, new statutes must be framed in which the Students will be allowed to have free hand as to social arrangements but otherwise must be under the strict control of the Legation. Moreover junior students of the Preparatory and Public School class should not be full members and have votes. They can join the holiday camp under the special person or persons chosen by the Minister. They should live as much as possible apart from the elder students while joining in some of the sports and entertainments. His Majesty considers that Nai Pridi Panomyong must be held chiefly responsible for the Society's deviation from its original purpose and for inciting a feeling of indiscipline and mistrust of the Minister among the students, His Majesty, therefore, commands that Nai Pridi Panomyong be immediately recalled.

As to the second part of the students petition asking for their allowance to be paid in pounds instead of francs, His Majesty is willing to consider the matter after having received explanations from the Minister. If it has not already been done so, a copy of the petition should be supplied to Prince Charoon and Prince Charoon is requested to submit explanations with reference to the said petition concerning allowances.

His Majesty deeply regrets to learn of indisciplinary feelings among students and wishes to call them to their sense of duty.

Sd/TRAIDOS

Div.A / Copy of telegram from H.H. the Minister for Foreign Affairs in Sect. 1 / Bangkok to H.H. the Siamese Minister in Paris. Despatched from No 3007/ Bangkok on the 25th November 1926. Received in Paris on the next day.

SIAMADUTO

BANGKOK

With regard to the question of recalling Pridi Panomyong as contained in my letter of 178, 27th October, I am now commanded by H.M. the King to communicate to Pridi the following message. BEGINS. With reference to your recall, your father has now petitioned His Majesty that it may be postponed until you have passed examination the degree of Doctor of Law which will take place shortly. His Majesty has been most graciously pleased to grant that petition on condition that, however, you tender to the Siamese Minister in Paris (a) written apologies and the expression of regrets for your attitude in connection with the recent unfortunate incidents. END.

Please take note of the content of the above communication and act accordingly.

Sd/ TRAIDOS

IV

Those who have studied the natural law of conflict, under which positive and negative, new and old fight one another, and who apply this natural law to human society, will understand that within human society new and positive forces clash with old and negative forces. Hence the People's Party which made the revolution on 24 June to change the absolute monarchy into constitutional monarchy had to face a negative side, or various reactionary elements, which opposed the people making the revolution. These can be classified into several types, for example:

1. Some of those who lost benefit from the change in the system were not resigned to the law of impermanence, and tried to revive the old system in some form. This is common and in conformity with the law of conflict. The exceptions were those who were resigned to the law of impermanence, among whom may I honour King Prajadhipok, who ceded more royal power than others, and also many princes and nobles of the Chakri dynasty who followed the example of the king in pardoning the People's Party.

2. Others who did not lose any benefit from the change of system yet embraced the old order with both body and soul as I described above. Even though these people were born and lived in the new era, they were not of the new generation. That is, they belonged to the new generation, but in soul and vision which were the leading principles in how they conducted their

lives, they belonged to the old order. This group used their external physical power, which was more robust than that of the past generation who were then old, to oppose the revolution more violently than did the old generation of the old order who lost benefit from the change in system. This group's opposition to the revolution had many aspects including being more royalist than the king *(ultra-royalist)*.

3. *Social scum (sawa sangkhom)* are the *rotten mass (set somom)* which the old society discarded but which left remnants in the new society. Social theorists of the right wing and the left have the same view that social scum are a dangerous class which neither wing wants to associate with its movement because social scum are egoist and show the *self-conceit* that they are more important than others. At the end of the great French Revolution there were people who, it was said, were such social scum that they could even sell their own fathers to further their own interests. Napoleon I took what was being said at the time about social scum and applied it to Talleyrand, a vacillator who changed his view back and forth according to his own benefit, as follows: "Monsieur could even sell his own father".

## V

Some people tell falsehoods to many of the present generation to make them lose their beliefs and fall into doubt. For instance, consider the false charge that the People's Party knew that King Prajadhipok would grant a constitution but forestalled him by making the revolution of 24 June.

Before the Second World War, Nai Chai Ruangsin, *po mo* [*pathamaphon mongkutthai,* royal decoration] and Thai barrister who was an official in the Education Ministry came to ask me whether it was true, as he had heard from someone who had been a minister before 24 June, that King Prajadhipok had already drafted a constitution, and that the People's Party knew about it but forestalled him by acting first. I explained to him as I had stated in parliament on 9 May 1946 as follows:

The People's Party came to know six days after the change in government, that is on 30 June. Phraya Phahon Phonphayuhasena, Phraya Pricha Chonlayut, Phraya Manopakon Nitithada, Phraya Siwisanwacha, and myself were summoned to attend in audience on the king. Chaophraya Mahithon, who was the royal secretary, took down the record. The king said that he had wished to grant a constitution, but when he consulted high-ranking officials of the time, they disagreed. Finally when he returned from a visit to America he asked someone who attended in audience on that day to consider the issue. That person offered his opinion that it was not yet time, and the advisors agreed. The People's Party had no foreknowledge of the royal wish and performed the change honestly, not to forestall, as some people have pretended, twisting the truth. The complete truth appears in the record of the meeting on that day. The fact is that King Prajadhipok had a prior wish but there were people who advised against it. Hence when the People's Party asked the king to grant a constitution, the king was pleased to make this gracious gift to the Thai people. I would like all present and the Thai people as a whole to remember the king's graciousness and to have high esteem for His Majesty at all times.

I can remember the impressive scene of that audience. The king had tears in his eyes when he pointed his finger at Phraya Siwisan, who joined the audience on that day, and said: "Siwisan, I sent a matter for you to consider, and you wrote a memo that it was not yet time. You also sent the memo of Stevens (an American adviser on foreign affairs) which agreed with you."

After I came to Paris in 1970 some people of the new generation came to ask me the truth about what they had heard. People who lost benefit because of the People's Party informed some of the new generation that the People's Party changed the system of government because they knew that King Prajadhipok would grant a constitution and wanted to forestall him. Some people of the new generation with the vision of the old order believed this and spread the information more widely during the time I had to escape from Siam. Some still believe this to the present day.

I thus explained the truth as above. For the sake of historical accuracy, please take the opportunity to consult a copy of the memos of Phraya Sriwisan and Mr Stevens, the American adviser, and the statement of King Prajadhipok. The Ministry of Foreign Affairs or the government organization which took over the affairs of the royal secretary and the Ministry of the Privy Seal ought to have kept these documents. But if these memos and the royal statement have disappeared, then please use the Buddhist wisdom that used to be inscribed on the certificates for primary and elementary school: *su ci pu li*, which is a guide to becoming a scholar or intellectual. Once you have heard *(su)* anything, use your brain to consider *(ci)* carefully whether it can be so according to reason, then ask *(pu)* to make certain, and finally write *(li)*. Many of the young generation of earlier times can probably remember the verse that secondary teachers in many schools taught them to memorize:

*su*  hear whatever in the world
*ci*  consider intently and searchingly

*pu*  ask questions to find hidden truth
*li*  write down to prevent forgetfulness

I'm happy for people to come and ask me rather than listening to or enquiring from the opponents of the People's Party. I have advised that if it is impossible to get copies of those memos and royal statement from the aforementioned places, please think how those in the People's Party could have known the royal intention—beginning with Phraya Phahon who was the party head.

Before 24 June, Phraya Phahon was an assistant inspector of the army, and assistant aide-de-camp who had the duty to guard the king at certain times according to a rota. He was not a permanent royal aide-de-camp. Please consider whether a temporary royal aide-de-camp has the duty to attend the king and hear high-level political matters. You will find there was no way Phraya Phahon could have known the royal wish to grant a constitution. As for other members of the People's Party in the army and navy, their positions gave them even less chance to know the royal wish. As for those who were civilians, several were farmers and workers. Among those who were bureaucrats and who had posts higher than ordinary civilians, I was one who had the regular post of assistant secretary in the law-drafting department, and who taught at the law school of the Justice Ministry for two or four hours a week. How could I and other civilian members of the People's Party know the royal wish? If you claim that the post of assistant secretary of the law-drafting department provided a way, I must ask whether King Prajadhipok sent his draft constitution for the law-drafting department to scrutinize. I and all my friends in the law-drafting department can confirm that the law-drafting department never received a draft constitution to scrutinize. Nevertheless, according to bureaucratic practice there is a ledger to register the receipt and despatch of all documents. Please let those interested look at this ledger belonging to the royal secretary and the Royal Secretariat. You will not find a draft constitution by the king sent to the law-drafting department to scrutinize. With all these facts, those interested should write *(li)* the truth, instead of just listening *(su)* and writing the distorted truth which someone tells them. The king's wish to grant a constitution was known only to those people whom the king entrusted to know, including Phraya Phahon and myself six days after 24 June, and the king's ministers who would not talk to outsiders about a secret government matter. Any minister who agreed with King Prajadhipok should have supported his wish in the ministers' meeting. To sit quiet would make it seem as if the king stood alone on this measure and was opposed by his ministers.

I would like to thank the students who came to ask me, and who told me they thought those in the People's Party were not so confused that they knew in advance that the king would grant a constitution but still risked their lives on 24 June.

I advised those who came to ask me, to think according to the method of the Buddha. To know something clearly you must use "critical method", which is the same method that Greek philosophers taught. That is, intellectuals should not just accept anything passed on from a teacher or other person. They must be able to categorize and analyse down to the details. For instance, when you want to be knowledgeable about fish, it is not enough to know that all aquatic animals which have gills and can swim belong to the one category of fish. You must know that this aquatic animal is a snake-head fish *(pla chon)* or an anabas *(pla mo)* or whatever. By the same token, when you hear that King Prajadhipok would grant a constitution, you should enquire from the informant what type of constitution the king would grant.

On 30 June 1932, the day Phraya Phahon and I had an audience with the king along with Phraya Mano, Phraya Siwisan, and Phraya Pricha-chonlayut, the king informed us of his desire to grant a constitution in stages. At the first stage, ministers would hold meetings without the king as chairman, but with the minister of the privy seal instead. This was Chaophraya Mahithon who had changed from royal secretary to this position. As for parliament, the king would adapt the Privy Council, which he had set up on a trial basis earlier, to have the position of a parliament. I think that the new generation who have an interest in the history of the Thai parliamentary system should research the truth about both the law and practice of the Privy Council. They should explain to students the full truth about what issues this Council met over, and what result came from the meetings. Documents on this would be better sources than listening to an informant whose knowledge is incomplete. As far as I can recall, document sources reporting the meetings of this Council should exist at some organization under the Prime Minister's Office which took over the affairs of His Majesty's principal private secretary and the Ministry of the Privy Seal.

On that day King Prajadhipok announced only the general principle about the essence of his constitution as far as I can remember. If any minister attests he knows more detail than this, let those interested ask him whether in King Prajadhipok's draft constitution the members of parliament would be appointed, elected, or both types; and whether the cabinet must have the confidence of the parliament or not. If anyone knows these details from a minister and approves of King Prajadhipok's draft constitution, then he should propose to the "Revolutionary Party" [i.e. Thanom and Praphat], which is now studying the announcement of a constitution, to take it as a model for drawing up the new constitution.

# VI

Some people who used to be King Prajadhipok's junior pages, and some who received information which junior pages relayed incorrectly without completely knowing the real views of the king, tried to revive and expand the issue of conflict between King Prajadhipok and the People's Party, to show themselves as more royalist than the king. The new generation who want the real truth, instead of just listening to some junior pages, should ask for an opportunity to consult Queen Rambhai Barni [wife of Prajadhipok], and some royal family members who were close to the king after he abdicated, to find out what was the king's outlook towards the People's Party and those in the People's Party.

I and many friends in the People's Party have followed the advice which King Prajadhipok delivered in the ceremony to ask for royal amnesty, as follows:

> I am very happy that you thought to come yourselves and make an apology today, which I did not request at all. That you have done so gives you great honour, as you have all shown you have truth in your hearts, and are people who are honest and courageous. That is, when you felt you had done something which was somewhat excessive and mistaken, you accepted the fault fully and openly. This is a difficult thing to do, and truly requires courage. That you have made this ceremony today shows clearly that whatever you did, you did for the true benefit of the country. You have shown that you are people with sympathy and bravery. You dared to accept responsibility when you felt you had made mistakes. This will make the people have even more trust in you. This makes me feel very pleased.

I and many friends in the People's Party were conscious of the mistakes which caused King Prajadhipok to abdicate the throne. We accepted the situation and tried to correct the mistakes. For instance, after the Second World War had begun in Europe and before the death of King Prajadhipok, the king sent a letter to the government with the wish to return and live in Trang with the rank and status of a prince which the king had reserved at abdication. The government was considering this wish but before a reply could be made, the king passed away. It was a disappointment to me and many friends in the People's Party. Junior pages who did not accompany the king to England had no knowledge of this. I remember that the letter was in the king's own hand to Field Marshal Phibun who read it in the cabinet meeting.

When the war was over, I re-established the status of king of Thailand in full, as appears in the note from M.C. Suphasawat Sawatdiwat and the communication from Queen Rambhai Barni as follows [facsimile of handwritten letter]:

Bridge House
Trumps Green Road
Virginia Water
Wentworth 2185
20 March 1946

Dear Khun Luang [Pridi],

All of us have arrived safely in England. The English arranged a grand welcome, including the British Foreign Ministry and Defence Ministry organising a reception in our honour. They *make speech* explaining how clever we were . . . thanking us enormously. I made a *speech* in reply telling them that we thanked them for helping us to have the chance to save our face, and I stated that especially our group would probably not have done as we did. What we achieved was largely because the resistance group in Thailand set a standard of acting bravely without any fear of danger at all. All of the English thanked the resistance group in Thailand with great sympathy and sincerity. The welcome on this occasion was not done just because they had to. Everyone who spoke really *appreciate* us. I explained to everyone about the decisive actions of our resistance group including Khun Luang . . .

All of us from the queen [Rambhai Barni] down are well. The queen thanks you and Khun Phoonsuk very much for sending the offerings (*khruang sakkara*) for the royal ashes. And she was very pleased that you have helped to re-establish the honour of King Prajadhipok as king of our country in full, including your resolve to try to *justify* action of him also. This means all of us have *appreciation* for you as I *appreciate* everyone. The queen was greatly amused to know that now she herself has the surname of Banomyong. Another thing which you said, that really you yourself are Sawatdiwat too, pleased her a lot, and she said she agreed to accept you as Sawatdiwat! I hope you will come over here soon so we will meet again. I don't need to say how much I miss you because the love and respect which I have for you *has no bound.* As to how much I miss you it is very low language to explain the real feeling I have.

With much respect and regards,
Chin

So fair-minded people should see that anyone who claims to honour King Prajadhipok but who makes the mistake of believing the publicity by some junior pages, does not study the matter in full, and does not have enough sympathy and courage to be sensible—such people appear to be using King Prajadhipok as a tool to criticize the People's Party for reactionary purposes, in the manner of those who act as more royalist than the king.

About King Prajadhipok's abdication, the king explained in the documents of abdication how he had some disagreements with the government of the time. The government tried to explain matters to the king and thus appointed Chaophraya Sithammathibet, who was a minister in that government and who had previously been a minister of the king, to be the government's representative at an audience with the king. But the king decided to abdicate.

People have analysed that King Prajadhipok should not have abdicated because he did not have to accept the responsibility for putting his signature to matters which the government proposed. I reply to these critics that the government of the time was very disappointed that King Prajadhipok abdicated. But if we look at it from his side, we should respect his wish to preserve the dignity of the monarchy. When he saw that the government of the time was acting against his wish, he decided to give up his personal comfort by abdicating rather than having to sign approving matters against his integrity. For this the Thai people should respect, honour, and uphold the utmost dignity of King Prajadhipok for ever.

## VII

Many people still misunderstand the democratic system in Thailand established by the revolution of 24 June 1932 and maintained until today. Let me explain that the word *"prachathipatai"* means "government by the people" which is the same as the English word *democracy*. President Lincoln analysed the word thoroughly as: *"The government of the people, by the people, for the people"*.

The intentions and actions of the People's Party followed this ideal, as is shown by the provisional constitution of Siam of 27 June 1932 and the constitution of 10 December 1932. But at a turning point when an old system which had existed since ancient times was being changed towards a system of full democracy, there was initially a need for some temporary provision of semi-democracy.

After the Second World War, the People's Party delivered on its promise to the people to provide full democratic rights. The MPs of type 2, who were mostly members of the People's Party, joined with the elected MPs of type 1 to draft a constitution with full democracy, which King Ananda Mahidol signed and promulgated as the constitution of the kingdom of Thailand on 9 May 1946 in place of the charter of 10 December 1932.

The constitution of 9 May 1946 gave the Thai people the most complete democratic rights. Clause 13 gave complete freedom of religion or faith. Clause 14 gave complete freedom of person, dwelling, property, speech, writing, printing, publicity, education, public assembly, association, political parties, occupation—with the qualification that these freedoms were circumscribed by law. But law did not infringe democratic right as it was designed to create peace, order, and morality for the people. Hence newspapers became widely distributed, and parties could be widely founded with no limitation on a party's political ideology.

The parliament consisted of the Senate and Assembly, both of whose members were elected, not appointed. For members of the Assembly, election was direct and secret. Election for members of the Senate was indirect and secret—by the principle popular everywhere known as two-stage election. At the first stage, the people elect representatives (who may be members of the Assembly), and these representatives of the people pass motions to elect senators at the next stage.

Later, on 8 November 1947, a coup abrogated the full democracy established by the constitution of 9 May 1946. The coup group established a new political system by the constitution of 9 November 1947 known as the under-the-water-jar constitution because those who made the coup announced that they kept the draft constitution hidden under a water jar. According to the system of this coup group, the parliament consisted of a Senate and Assembly. Members of the Senate were selected by the king. The number was the same as the Assembly. But in practice it was laid down that any royal command concerned with administration of the kingdom must be countersigned by a minister. Hence the government of the coup group itself appointed the senators. The king merely applied his signature to the government's proposal. As for members of the Assembly, although they were elected by the people, the new system laid down that the minimum age for electoral candidates was thirty-five years. This differed from the constitution of 9 May 1946 which specified twenty-three years in the electoral law in order to give opportunity for many of the younger generation to stand and be elected. As for freedom in founding political parties, the under-the-water-jar constitution cut this out. There were many other provisions including revival of the system of the Supreme Council of State from the absolutist period [abolished in 1932]. Hence it can be seen that the system which arose from the coup of 8 November 1947 was different from the democratic system of the People's Party, even though in the coup group there were people who had previously belonged to the People's Party, but who had disassociated themselves from the People's Party and joined with people who had the political vision of this coup group. Hence the duty of the People's Party, laid down in the party's objectives, to be responsible to the people was rejected by the coup group both in law and practice. From that time on, nothing could be achieved according to the objectives of the People's Party. From then on, the responsibility for the conduct of public affairs fell to the coup group and subsequent governments which succeeded to the coup group.

Some people have asked me why the Thai democratic system has had such ups-and-downs in the latter period. In particular, they relate this back to the People's Party. I explained that although there were conflicts inside the People's Party at times, ultimately the People's Party as a whole cooperated with the MPs elected by the people to establish a full democratic system by the constitution of 9 May 1946. The fact that after 8 November 1947 there was a system of constitutional government under which the constitution was amended ten times, was not the work of the People's Party. So please let those who are fair-minded distinguish the outcome of the People's Party from that of the coup group and its successors, and from that of the "Revolutionary Party" which openly referred to the system through which it governed Thailand as dictatorship. People should not misunderstand this as democracy.

Some people have broadcast that the constitution of 23 March 1949 was the most democratic of all constitutions. Maybe they are comparing this constitution with the various constitutions written after the coup of 8 November 1947.

The new generation interested in Thailand's constitutional system should compare all the constitutions in full detail to see which is the most democratic according to the meaning of the word "democracy".

The constitution of 9 May 1946 laid down the minimum age for candidates for election to the Senate as thirty-five years and for the Assembly as twenty-three years. But the constitution of 23 March 1949 laid down the minimum age for senators as forty years and for MPs as thirty years. No constitution in the world sets the minimum age for MPs so high. This amounted to reducing the rights of the new generation, as many people aged under thirty had been elected MPs under the constitution of 9 May 1946. The new generation of that time saw that the constitution of 23 March 1949 was not democratic because it gave rights to those older than themselves. Many of the new generation knew that constitutional monarchy holds that "the king can do no wrong", because the king does nothing of his own accord but merely affixes his signature to approve whatever the government proposes. The real perpetrators were those who countersigned the royal command and their group. If any king actually did anything of his own accord, he would have to be responsible. The current British constitution and the Thai constitutions which the People's Party requested from the king, did not intend that the king be responsible for his official actions. But the constitution of 23 March 1949 was written in such a way that readers misunderstand that the king chose and appointed the senators by himself. But there was a rider that the chairman of the Privy Council must countersign the royal command. It sounded as if the king selected and appointed senators of his own accord, but the chairman of the Privy Council agreed to be responsible for the king's action. The new generation of the time could interpret this as a political ploy, because they could see that in practice when the constitution was announced, King Bhumibol Adulyadej was still a minor and the Privy Council performed the king's regnal duties on his behalf. Thus in practice, the Privy Council itself selected and appointed the senators. Granting this power to the Privy Council may be connected to the idea, put around by certain people, that King Prajadhipok had allowed members of the Privy Council to debate issues along the lines of parliamentary debate as the first stage in granting a constitution. Giving the chairman of the Privy Council the right to countersign the royal signature for selecting and appointing senators was an innovation in the world of constitutional monarchy. But whether it is a form which is more democratic than any which exist in that world, those who study constitutional systems comprehensively will have to decide.

24 June 1972

# 12. THE PEOPLE'S PARTY AND THE DEMOCRATIC REVOLUTION OF 24 JUNE (1982)

Respectful greetings to the Thai people who love nation and democracy and who are fair-minded.

Khun Sawet Piamphongsan, chairman of the organizing committee of the celebration of Half a Century of Democracy, has notified me that since 24 June 1982 is the fiftieth anniversary of democracy in Thailand, various private organizations and groups in the country have joined together to organize a celebration of Half a Century of Democracy at Chulalongkorn University on 24–27 June 1982 with the objectives:

1. to commemorate the great work of those who dedicated themselves to establish the democratic system in Thailand;
2. to reflect on the problems of developing the democratic system in Thailand;
3. to disseminate democratic principles and promote political participation among the people;
4. to propose ideas for developing the democratic system of the government and relevant people;
5. to create harmony among democracy groups.

Let me express my gratitude to the chairman and members of the organizing committee, private organizations, and various people for recalling those who dedicated themselves to promote democracy, and for having the desire to help the Thai nation achieve full democracy following these aims.

Moreover, the chairman informed me that the committee, seeing I had a part in establishing the democratic system of government in Thailand, would like a speech from me to present to the Thai people on the occasion of the opening ceremony. I am happy to accord with the wish of you all.

Now to the subject of my speech. I think all of you, and the Thai people who love the nation and democracy and are fair-minded, see that the People's Party dedicated itself to serve the nation by founding democracy. Yet there are still a number of people who set themselves up as enemies, and who through their own actions and through their underlings, vilify the People's Party in various ways which are opposite to your aims. When the news that you had initiated the celebration of Half a Century of Democracy had spread widely, these opponents increased their vilification of the People's Party. This reached a peak recently when someone wrote and distributed an article with the title "The first age of dictatorship" *(phadetkan yuk raek),* which began as follows:

> The first age of dictatorship was born in the democratic system which the People's Party established on 24 June 1932. The first dictator was none other than an important person in the People's Party. After the victory over the Boworadej revolt in October 1933, he gradually extended his "shadow" until within less than seven years he totally commanded the power of dictatorship, and the whole country was in fear.
>
> To the question why the People's Party should have destroyed democratic ideology so quickly, contemporaries of the People's Party might not give a clear answer, especially the members of the People's Party themselves, because the situation outside and inside the People's Party encouraged everyone to believe it necessary to entrust the central power to Luang Phibunsongkhram alone . . .

This article vilifies all members of the People's Party to damage their reputation and make them appear loathsome. Yet in truth many members of the People's Party dedicated themselves to opposing Field Marshal Phibunsongkhram when he acted against democratic principles, causing him to resign from the post of prime minister. On many other occasions, those who opposed him were imprisoned or had to flee overseas. The members whose reputations are damaged, or their heirs, have the right to ask the courts to investigate these slanderers. The above article goes against the aims of your committee.

However, so that my speech complies with the objectives of your committee, let me present on "The People's Party and the Democratic Revolution of 24 June".

In order to relieve me from having to speak in my old age, I have asked the chairman of the Thai Students Association in France to read my text. As for the summary at the end, I will deliver that myself.

# THE NAME OF THE PEOPLE'S PARTY

*The situation for founding political parties in the absolutist period*
Certain academics who set themselves up as opponents of the People's Party have scoured up many reasons to attack the People's Party. One such reason which they and their group have taught their disciples is that those who promoted the change of government of 24 June called themselves the "People's Party" without the people's consent. This is to persuade their disciples not to recognize the existence of the People's Party from its foundation. Thus let me ask those still living who can remember the absolutist period to please think back, and those born after that time to please study the situation for founding political groups in the absolutist period, and the proper analysis as follows.

In the absolutist period, people did not have the right to join together to form a political party. Hence founding a political party had to be done secretly, and in the case of a political party with the aim of overthrowing the absolute monarchy, very secretly indeed. It was not possible to call many people openly to join with a political party. Hence it is not possible to take the Kuomintang under the leadership of Sun Yat Sen as a model for Thai politics under the absolute monarchy because the Kuomintang used the concession zones which the Chinese government granted to foreign countries to call on large numbers of Chinese to join.

The seven people who initiated the foundation of the People's Party in Paris were full Thai citizens. Later they acted in secret, as was appropriate to that time, along with more than a hundred other Thai people who joined the People's Party as type-1 members who were the vanguard. Later there were many people of type 2 and type 3 who supported and joined with this vanguard. This all shows clearly that a considerable number of Thai people were of similar mind about changing the system of government on 24 June. However, they were not like those who want to act according to the Chinese strategy of countryside surrounding city, which requires millions of people to be of similar mind and to fight against the government, with many casualties.

Let me ask academics who are fair-minded to check whether there are political science texts of any country which teach that if you are going to found a political party whose name translates as "people", you must first present your case to a certain number of people of similar mind beforehand.

Suppose an academic states there is such a text. In the time since Thai governments have allowed the establishment of political parties, people have established parties called People's Party, Citizens Party, and Thai People's Party (led by Field Marshal Thanom) [*phak ratsadon/prachachon/sahaprachathai*]. Please judge whether any doctor or academic protested that these parties used these names without the people or the citizens or the Thai people giving their consent.

*The regent in charge of the capital and King Prajadhipok, the head of state of the Thai people, recognized the name of the People's Party from 24 June 1932*

Genuine government documents show clearly that when the People's Party revealed itself to the people on the morning of 24 June 1932, the regent in charge of the capital and King Prajadhipok, who was the head of state of the Thai people, recognized the name of the People's Party from then onwards.

Before 24 June 1932 King Prajadhipok had travelled to Hua Hin and appointed Somdet Chaofa Boriphat, Kromphra Nakhonsawan to the post of regent in charge of the capital, with power in lieu of the king. On the morning of 24 June 1932, the People's Party invited him to the Ananta Samakhom throne hall. He made an announcement which indicates recognition of the People's Party, as follows:

Announcement
of the regent in charge of the capital

As the People's Party has seized the power of government of the country with the major intention that Siam should have a constitution, I ask soldiers, officials, and all people to help maintain peace and prevent Thais spilling one another's blood needlessly.

(signed) Boriphat

At 16.00 hours on 24 June 1932 Phraya Phahon Phonphayuhasena, military governor of the capital, invited the ministers and under-secretaries of various ministries to a meeting with the People's Party in the Ananta Samakhom throne hall to come to an agreement with the People's Party on the procedures ministries should follow, which was agreed as follows:

Agreement on the procedures for ministries to follow
Ananta Samakhom throne hall
24 June 1932

Today at 16.00 hours, the ministers and under-secretaries of the various ministries have agreed with the People's Party on the conduct of official business that:

1. For any ordinary matter for which there is a procedure already in use, continue as before.
2. For any matter previously forwarded to the king, bring the matter to the military commander of the capital.

3. In the case of conflict or doubt, bring the matter to the military commander of the capital.
4. Each ministry must inform its departments that now the military commander of the capital holds the provisional power of government. As for their responsibilities, the conduct of official business will proceed as before. Do not be excited.

> Supphayok (Phraongchao)
> Thani (Phraongchao)
> Phichaiyat (Chaophraya)
> Sithammathibet (Chaophraya)
> Rachanikun (Phraya)
> Phiphitasombat (Phraya)
> Wimwathit (Momchao)
> Mahosotsiphiphat (Phraya)
> Withayaprichamat (Phraya)
> Prasoetsongkhram (Phraya)

King Prajadhipok returned to Bangkok by special train leaving Hua Hin at 19.45 hours on 25 June, disembarking at Chitlada station at 0.33 hours on 26 June, and proceeding to Sukhothai Palace. He granted an audience to the People's Party at Sukhothai Palace at 11.00 hours on that 26 June.

Representatives of the People's Party attended the audience and took along a draft royal decree of amnesty for the change of government of 1932 for the king to sign in approval.

At that time there was no national constitution limiting the royal power. King Prajadhipok still had the absolute royal power to do anything on behalf of the people of Siam without anyone representing the people of Siam having to countersign the royal command.

King Prajadhipok graciously signed the royal decree whose content indicates recognition that the People's Party had a proper legal status, as follows:

**Royal decree of amnesty for the change in government of the country, 1932**

The People's Party is a party which has a strong desire to remove some rotten aspects of the Siamese government and Thai nation, and to develop the Siamese government and Thai nation to prosper, progress, and strengthen to equality with other countries and nations in the future. Hence it has seized the power of governing the country with the major aim of having a constitution, and has called on us to remain as king of Siam under the constitution. Hence even though this action conflicts with the wishes of some members of the royal family and offends some of the members of the previous government, such events are common and unavoidable in all countries, no matter how advanced. Nevertheless, this is the first occurrence in the history of the world that such an event has taken place peacefully and without violence.

Although they invited high-ranking members of the royal family and some officials to come and remain in the Ananta Samakhom throne hall, that was only for the safety of the party and to ensure a smooth operation. No harm or contempt was inflicted on them, nor was there any such intention. All were treated considerately and according to due dignity.

In fact, we have already contemplated government by constitution. What the People's Party has done is correct, is in line with our views, and truly demonstrates good intentions towards the nation and people. They did nothing wrong nor did they have bad intentions.

For this reason a royal decree is issued as follows.

Clause 1.　This decree is entitled "Royal Decree of Amnesty for the Change of Government, 1932".

Clause 2.　This decree is in force from the time when the royal signature is affixed.

Clause 3.　If any action committed in this affair by anyone in the People's Party was against the law, let it not be held as against the law.

Promulgated on 26 June 1932
(signed) Prajadhipok

Besides the fact that Somdet Chaofa Boriphat, regent of the capital, and King Prajadhipok recognized the People's Party and held that it acted on behalf of the people, a large number of Thai people recognized the People's Party directly as well.

When the People's Party revealed itself to the people from 24 June onwards, a large number of those who knew about the matter accepted and approved the People's Party's action. The exceptions were only the minority who approved of absolutism even more than the king—the *ultra-royalists*.

The People's Party and the People's Party government invited the Sangha, which most of the people respect, to request every *wat* in the kingdom to explain to their adherents that King Prajadhipok, who is the supreme head of the Buddhist order, had graciously conferred the system of democratic government under the provisional constitution of 27 June 1932, which the People's Party requested in the name of the people. Later when the permanent constitution of 10 December 1932 replaced the provisional constitution of 27 June, the People's Party and the People's Party government invited the Sangha to request every *wat* to explain to their worshippers in the same way. In addition, the Ministry of Education asked the Islamic head to explain to the Thai Muslims, and the head of the Christian church to explain to Thai Christians all over the kingdom in the same way. The Ministry of Education reported that the Buddhist, Thai Muslim, and Thai Christian adherents approved of the action of the People's Party, and also supported the People's Party and its government to implement the party's six principles. The ministry also confirmed that schools throughout the kingdom at that time taught students to understand the democratic system of government and the six principles of the People's Party. The Ministry of the Interior also confirmed that its officials arranged for staff at provincial, amphoe, and village levels to call meetings to let the people know and understand the administration which the king had granted at the request of the People's Party, and the six principles of the People's Party. The outcome was that the vast majority of people (with the exception of the minority mentioned above) approved what the People's Party had done for the people.

In addition, in over thirteen years that the People's Party was responsible for administering the country and overseeing the work of the bureaucracy, the People's Party and its governments arranged for regular annual celebration of the constitution (except in some years when there was war or emergency) both in Bangkok and every province. This demonstrated to the people that the People's Party governments acted according to the democratic system and the six principles. Nobody appeared to protest that the People's Party established the People's Party without the people's consent.

*Why the promoter group was called the "People's Party"*

Before people thought of promoting a change in government, and before many people and groups united together, each group had its own reputation and some had no name. But when those who wanted to change the government joined together, they used the name "People's Party", as I proposed in the meeting to establish the People's Party in Paris in February 1927. Subsequently, those who joined in the promotion of a change in government, both overseas and in Siam, used the name "People's Party" as it appeared in the announcement of the People's Party on 24 June 1932, when the regent of the capital and King Prajadhipok, the head of state of the Thai people, and the Thai people recognized the name of the People's Party as noted above. The promoters of a change in the system of government who became members of the Assembly took an oath in the meeting of the Assembly on 28 June to be loyal to the People's Party and securely uphold the party's six principles. In addition, the first cabinet and many subsequent cabinets announced to the Assembly that they took the six principles of the People's Party as the policy of their governments (those interested can research this in official documents).

*The reasons I used the name "People's Party"* (khana ratsadon)
*The origins of the Thai words* "khana" *and* "phak"
The people who thought of joining together to change the system of government from absolutism to constitutional democracy—which at that time was called the system of government in which the king is under the constitution—had to establish an organization or political association, as called in English a *"political party"* or in short, a *"party"*.

Before 1932, the word *phak* was not used to describe a political grouping or party either in the dictionary of the Education Ministry or in official usage. The navy used the word *phak* to mean various units of the navy, which was divided into three major units namely: 1. *phak klin* meaning the unit of regular ship's engineers; 2. *phak nawikayothin* (marine corps) meaning the regular land-based fighting unit; and 3. *phak nawin* (sailors) meaning the regular fighting unit.

At that time, academics used the work *khana* to translate the English word *"party"* which is reduced from the old phrase *"political party"*. For instance, the phrase *"Conservative Party"* was translated as *"khana khonsoerwetif"*, *"Socialist Party"* as *"khana sochialit"* and *"Chinese Nationalist Party"* or the Chinese Kuomintang as *"khana chat chin"* or *"chin khana chat"*. The Kuomintang is still popularly called *chin khana chat* to this day rather than *"phak chat chin"* or *"chin phak chat"*.

The organization or political association which was formed in Ro. So. 130 [1912] to overthrow absolutism in Thailand used the word *"khana"* as *"khana ro. so. 130"*.

Let me ask those of you who are interested in the history of the Thai language to look at the true documentary sources. You will easily find that after King Prajadhipok granted the provisional constitution of 27 June 1932, a group of people set up an organization or political association with conservative aims under the name *"khana chat"* (national party), with Luang Wichitwathakan as general secretary. He had studied for a *parian* [the exam certificate given to a graduate of Buddhist theology], and knew Pali and Thai as well as English and French. But as the Thai dictionaries did not yet use the word *"phak"* for a political grouping or association, Luang Wichit used the word *"khana"* for his political organization or association.

Around 1937, H.R.H. Krommun Narathip, at the time he held the title Momchao Wanwaithayakon, proposed using the Thai term *"khana phak"* to translate the English *"political party"* or in short *"party"*.

Officially the term *"khana phak"* was recognized to describe political organizations and associations from the time that the constitution of 9 May 1946, clause 14 included the passage: "people have the freedom . . . to establish political parties *(khana phak kan muang)"*.

Later the constitution of 24 March 1949, clause 39 changed the term *"khana phak kan muang"* of the 1946 constitution into *"phak kan muang"*, that is, the word *"khana"* which came ahead of *"phak"* was dropped. The phrase *"phak kan muang"* began to be used officially only from 1949.

*Remarks*

According to this history of the Thai words *"khana"* and *"phak"*, the name of the People's Party was established at a time when the dictionary of the Education Ministry and the Thai constitution had not yet used the word *"phak"*. English-language documents from that period called it the "People's Party".

The Chinese encyclopaedia called *su chia chu su nian chian* which translates as "world knowledge annual", and the Chinese encyclopaedia called *su chia chu su* which translates as "world knowledge", printed in Beijing for many years running, called political groupings or parties in Chinese as *"tang"* as in *"sian lo kong chan tang"* and *"tai kua kong chan tang"*. Later after the Second World War, *"sian lo kong chan tang"* was translated as *"phak kommiunit haeng sayam"* [Communist Party of Siam]. It was claimed to have been founded in Siam from 1930. And *"tai kua kong chan tang"*, which was claimed to have been founded in Siam from 1942, was translated as *"phak kommiunit haeng prathet Thai"* [Communist Party of Thailand]. Hence there is a problem because, as I noted above, leaders only used the Thai word *"phak"* to describe political parties several years after these two organizations were claimed to have been established in Siam or Thailand. Hence did these two organizations translate their names into Thai using transliteration of the Chinese *"tang"* or did they use some Thai word?

*Why the word "people" was used as the name of the party*

I proposed the party should name the party as "People's Party" because all the promoters were true Thai people, and the members of the People's Party dedicated themselves and their efforts to the people to achieve democracy. As all democrats know, President Lincoln summed up the word democracy appropriately as "government of the people, by the people, for the people".

*The word "promoter"*

I proposed to the founding meeting that in founding a party or political association there must be *phu ko kan* which in English are called *"promoters"* who form the vanguard of the people. We thus agreed to divide the members of the People's Party into three types:

type 1: people who should be invited to join as members of the People's Party before the day of the attempted seizure of power;

type 2: those who should be invited after the attempted seizure of power had been launched;

type 3: those who should be invited on the day of seizure of power after there was a prospect of success rather than failure.

I explained in the book *Some Aspects of the Establishment of the People's Party and Democracy,* printed for the first time in 1972, as follows:

The People's Party called type-1 members "promoters of change in the system of government" or for short, "promoters". This indicated that people of this type were just the vanguard of the mass of the people who wanted more freedom and equality than under the absolute monarchy.

The monopolization of a political party's name appeared at a meeting of the Communist International after the death of Stalin. The Soviet Communist Party had re-established friendship with the Communist League of Yugoslavia which had also been invited to the meeting. Wu Siew Chuan, central committee member of the Chinese Communist Party, objected that the Communist League of Yugoslavia was not communist but had stolen the word "communist" to use in its party name. This shows that these central committee members of the Chinese Communist Party monopolized the use of the word "communist" only for their coterie.

## AIMS OF THE PEOPLE'S PARTY

The aims of the People's Party were: 1. to change the government from the absolute monarchy to monarchy under a democratic constitution; 2. to develop the Thai nation according to the six principles.

*To change the government from the absolute monarchy to monarchy under a democratic constitution*

First, remember that the absolutist government had no law to limit the power of government. The king was above the law, and had absolute power to govern the country according to the royal will.

Hence on 24 June 1932 the People's Party seized the power of the state to change the government from the absolute monarchy to a monarchy under a democratic constitution by stages, as follows.

On 26 June the People's Party sent representatives to present the "constitution for governing the country drafted by the People's Party" for the king to consider.

On the 27th, while King Prajadhipok still had the absolute power to act on behalf of the people of Siam, he graciously agreed to affix his signature and confer the above-mentioned constitution. He added the word "provisional" to the title "constitution for governing the country". He told the People's Party to use this constitution temporarily and proposed that the Assembly set up a sub-committee to draft a permanent constitution for subsequent use.

*Remarks*

The provisional constitution of 27 June 1932 was drawn up totally in conformity with law and practice according to legal principle. This differs from many constitutions which are invalid.

The constitution of 27 June established the system of monarchy under a democratic constitution as the transition between the absolute monarchy which had governed Siam for several thousand years and the democratic system which had just begun (see the details in that constitution).

On the morning of the 28th, the Assembly established under the provisional constitution of 27 June held its first meeting. Among the many agenda items in the report of this meeting 1/1932 of the Assembly, there was one important item, namely to establish a sub-committee to complete a draft of the new constitution. The report of the meeting runs:

9. Chaophraya Thammasakmontri (speaker of the Assembly) stated that the next item was the establishment of a sub-committee to complete a draft of the new constitution.

Luang Pradimanutham announced that this constitution is provisional because we created it in a time of emergency, and hence there may be some errors. So a sub-committee of people with knowledge and expertise in this matter should thoroughly check, amend, and expand to a complete new draft.

Chaophraya Thammasakmontri stated that, if this is the case, let a sub-committee be chosen and entrusted with drafting an amended constitution.

The meeting selected:
Phraya Manopakon Nitithada
Phraya Thepwithunphahun Sarutabodi
Phraya Manwaratchasewi
Phraya Nitisatphaisan
Phraya Pridanarubet

Luang Praditmanutham
Luang Sinatyotharak
as the seven members of the sub-committee.

Later the Assembly resolved to add two members, namely Vice-Admiral Phraya Ratchawangsan and Phraya Sriwisanwacha.

Those who teach and study the history of the Thai constitution using authentic documents rather than gossip (or what the British law of evidence calls hearsay) should give justice to the People's Party that among the nine names on the constitution sub-committee, only one was a member of the People's Party, namely "Luang Praditmanutham". The other eight were highly qualified persons who were not members of the People's Party. Some teachers have taught their students to misunderstand that the constitution later known as the "constitution of the kingdom of Thailand" (1932) was drafted according to the wish of Luang Praditmanutham (Pridi Banomyong). This is teaching falsehoods. The first point is that, in practice, Luang Praditmanutham alone could not force or influence the eight other highly qualified persons to agree to his views alone. The second point is that, Phraya Manopakon, the chairman of the drafting committee, announced to the Assembly on Friday 25 November 1932 that the constitution, hereafter called the 1932 constitution, was communicated to King Rama VII, as appeared in the report of the meeting of the Assembly on 25 November 1932, as follows:

> In addition let me (Phraya Mano) advise that in drafting this constitution, the sub-committee communicated with the king throughout, to the point where it could be said that it was a joint process throughout. The draft proposed here has been submitted for royal approval on every point, and been approved. And to say the king approved does not mean merely that he approved the content presented to him. It was more than that. The king was very pleased with the draft. On this point, let me take this occasion to speak to certain points of the constitution as points to lead your thinking when considering and debating in the days ahead.

Those who teach about and study the constitution of 10 December 1932 will find that clause 16, which has been an enduring article of that constitution, provides that: "the Assembly is composed of members elected by the people". This shows that this enduring clause of the constitution follows the democratic system, in that the members of the Assembly were elected by the people, not appointed.

The parliament under this constitution consisted of the Assembly as a single chamber with no Senate.

The chairman of the drafting committee of the constitution of 10 December 1932, as recorded in the minutes of the meeting of the Assembly on 25 November 1932, explained as follows.

Section 7 is temporary. The provisional constitution laid down three time periods. These temporary sections will be in force only before the third and final period. The importance of this section lies in clause 65, which establishes that the Assembly has type-1 members elected by the people and type-2 members appointed by the king. The reason for having two types of member is that we have only just had a constitution, and familiarity of working with a constitution is not yet widespread. That is the reason for including as members people who are familiar with the work and who can help the process, along with type-1 members elected by the people.

If we read other new constitutions, such practice is always found. When in future the members elected by the people can work on their own, we will proceed like that from that time on.

In addition, before speaking in the Assembly, Phraya Mano informed the cabinet that the king approved the inclusion of this temporary item, saying that changing the government from absolutism to constitutional monarchy was "an important change of basic principle" in the system of government, and hence required sufficient time for the new system to supercede it smoothly.

Clause 65 of the provisional section of the constitution of 10 December 1932 runs as follows.

Clause 65. As long as the people who have the right to elect members of the Assembly according to the provisions of this constitution still include more who have not completed primary education than those who have, but not exceeding ten years counted from the inauguration of the provisional constitution of Siam, 1932, the Assembly shall consist of members of two types in equal numbers:

1. type-1 members elected by the people according to conditions laid down in clauses 16 and 17;

2. type-2 members appointed by the king according to the Act on the Election of Members of the Assembly for the Duration of the Provisional Section of the Constitution of the Kingdom of Siam, 1932.

On 15 August 1940, Khun Buratsakankitti Khadi, MP (type-1) for Ubon Ratchathani, with the support of not less than one-in-four of all type-1 MPs, proposed to amend the [term of the] provisional clauses of the constitution from ten years to twenty years, citing many reasons concerning national security.

The government of the time (Field Marshal Phibun was premier) saw that a major war had begun in Europe since 1939, and the Japanese war on China had penetrated to Indochina and was expanding towards Thailand. Hence the government agreed with the amendment proposed by this type-1 MP.

The meeting of the Assembly passed a resolution on the principle of amending the constitution by a majority of at least three-quarters of all members. Then according to the procedure for amending the constitution as provided in clause 63, it debated and passed the new law on 19 September 1940.

After the temporary section had been in force for fourteen years, it was abolished, as noted in the preface of the constitution of the kingdom of Thailand of 1946 as follows:

Then Nai Pridi Banomyong, currently holding the post of regent, advised Nai Khuang Aphaiwong, the prime minister, that the king had granted the constitution to the Thai people now for fourteen years. Although the democratic constitutional government had brought progress to the country in many different ways, and the people were truly grateful for the benefits of this system of government, public affairs had changed considerably. Hence it was time to abolish the temporary section of the constitution, and to amend the constitution. The prime minister took this matter for consultation with type-2 MPs and the promoters of the constitution. When agreement was reached, on 29 July 1945 the government of Nai Khuang Aphaiwong proposed to the Assembly a motion to establish a special commission to examine whether and in what ways the constitution should be amended to be appropriate to the situation of the country and to make the democratic system of government more complete.

The Assembly established a special commission to examine the constitution according to this proposal. This commission worked all through the governments of Nai Khuang Aphaiwong, Nai Thawi Bunyaket, and M.R. Seni Pramoj.

Subsequently M.R. Seni Pramoj's government established a committee to collect opinions and draw up the provisions of a draft constitution. When this committee had finished, the cabinet deliberated and amended the draft further, and then proposed it to the regent. The regent met and consulted with type-2 MPs and the promoters of the constitution. The meeting set up a committee which studied and made amendments. Then a type-2 MP proposed the motion to the Assembly to amend the constitution. The Assembly deliberated, accepted the principle, and appointed a special commission.

The Assembly's special commission deliberated, made amendments to the constitution, and introduced the matter to the Assembly. The Assembly deliberated and then submitted the matter for royal assent. The king studied the matter and considered that his people had achieved the qualifications for looking after state policy and were capable of developing the country to progress towards international civilization *(sakon arayatham haeng lok)*.

Hence there is a royal command, according to the advice and approval of the Assembly, to promulgate this constitution from 10 May 1946 onwards for use in place of the constitution of 1932, the constitution amended with the name of the country of 1939 [i.e. from Siam to Thailand], the constitution amended with provisional clauses of 1940, and the constitution amended on elections of 1943.

The constitution of 9 May 1946 provided for a parliament consisting of a Senate and Assembly.

Members of both Assembly and Senate were elected by the people, not appointed, and hence were the full representatives of the mass of the people in considering resolutions in the Assembly and upper house. Hence the constitution of 1946 was a democratic constitution which fits the definition of "full democracy" according to the Royal Institute dictionary's definition of "democracy" as "the system of government which holds that the will of the people is paramount".

Clause 24 of the 1946 constitution laid down that from then on:

The Senate is composed of members elected by the people, with eighty members in total.

Members of the Senate must not be serving officials.

Election of members of the Senate shall be indirect and secret.

*Notes*

Apart from stipulating that senators be representatives elected by the people, the constitution of 1946 also laid down that "members of the Senate must not be serving officials" to prevent the government ordering officials under its own authority to stand for the Senate. This would have given the government, which is the executive, power over senators, who are the legislature, which would violate the principle of democracy.

The number of senators was limited to eighty persons, which was less than half the number of 178 MPs elected under the rules of clause 91 of the 1946 constitution.

The 1949 constitution, which was the model for the 1974 constitution, which people have proclaimed was the most democratic of any Thai constitution, provided that senators would be appointed, not elected by the people.

Even so, it still stipulated that the number of senators would be a hundred. This meant that, at the onset of the 1949 constitution, senators outnumbered MPs by one as the provisional section of the 1949 charter had ninety-nine MPs (elected by the rules of the provisional constitution of 9 November 1947 which the "8 November Coup Group" established and which is known as the under-the-water-jar constitution) and they remained as MPs under the constitution of 1949 as well. Subsequently additional MPs were elected under the rules of that constitution, but the number was only twenty-one, which when added together with the ninety-nine transferred from the under-the-water-jar charter, brought the total number of MPs under the 1949 charter to 120, only twenty more than the number of senators.

After the promulgation of the full democracy constitution of 9 May 1946, which the People's Party held fulfilled the duty announced to the people on 24 June 1932, the People's Party dissolved itself. The promoters and People's Party members parted company to undertake their own activities. One group went into personal businesses not connected with politics. Another group, who preferred to serve the nation through politics, entered various political parties in accordance with each person's vision. For instance, Nai Khuang Aphaiwong and friends entered the Democrat Party; Rear-Admiral Thawan Thamrongnawasawat and friends entered the Constitutionalist Party; Nai Sanguan Tularak and friends entered the Sahachip (unionist) Party; and so on. I entered no party.

*Remarks*

The democratic system of the 1946 constitution was in force for only one year, five months, and thirty days. Then a group of people called the "Coup Party" *(khana ratthaprahan)* seized the power of the state and demolished the democratic system set up by the 1946 constitution.

Subsequently many other people and groups, who were not the People's Party, governed the country by systems different to that of the People's Party. These parties and people went by many different names, for instance

1. The Coup Party (8 November 1947)
2. The Provisional National Executive Party (29 November 1951)
3. The Military Party (16 September 1957)
4. The Revolutionary Party (20 October 1958)
5. The Revolutionary Party (17 November 1971)
6. The National Forum (10 December 1973)
7. The National Reform Party (6 October 1976)
8. The Revolutionary Party (20 October 1977)

9. Governments established under various systems other than a democratic constitution.

The six principles of the People's Party, which were announced to the people on 24 June 1932 and which the People's Party fulfilled before dissolving itself on 9 November 1946, were as follows

*Principle 1. To maintain the independence of the country in all forms including political, judicial, economic, etc.*

Let those interested please recall the status of Siam or Thailand before 24 June 1932. At that time Thailand had no independence or full sovereignty because it had had to make unequal treaties with several modern capitalist countries under what is known as "imperialism". These countries had special rights over Thailand. For instance, the Thai courts had no power to try and convict people under the jurisdiction of foreign countries who committed crimes on Thai soil. The government had to send these criminals to the foreign consular court. Later, however, some countries such as Britain and France allowed the formation of foreign courts where cases concerning those under the jurisdiction of these two countries were heard and decided jointly by Thai judges and European legal advisers. Yet the treaties laid down that if the views of the Thai judges and the European legal advisers conflicted, those of the European legal advisers would prevail over those of the Thai judges with no accounting whether the Thai judges outnumbered the European advisers. Even further, the treaties laid down that the British consul had the power to withdraw cases from the foreign court and transfer them to the consular court. Several countries' consulates had courts and jails specially for people under their jurisdiction. There were other special rights which in the language of international law are called "extraterritoriality".

On the economic side, those imperialist countries had special rights under the unequal treaties. Originally Thailand was forced under the treaties to collect import duty at only 3 percent ad valorem. Although the absolutist government amended the treaties to increase its rights, the customs duty was still limited in many ways. Further, several imperialist countries had special rights of forest, mining, and shipping concessions, and had power and political influence over the country.

In 1937 the government in which Phraya Phahon, head of the People's Party, was prime minister abrogated the unequal treaties with several imperialist countries, and negotiated new treaties which gave Thailand independence and full sovereignty.

Later during the Second World War when Thailand was invaded by the Japanese army, many members of the People's Party participated in the Seri Thai movement which joined with the Allies to fight the Japanese invaders.

This caused the Allies to recognize the independence of the Thai nation, as is shown by several documents which I printed in the book *Letters from Pridi Banomyong to Phra Phisan Sukhumwit about the records of the Seri Thai concerning actions in Kandy, New Delhi, and USA.*

*Principle 2. To maintain public safety within the country and greatly reduce crime.*

I hope that those of you who are fair-minded can compare the statistics of crime before 24 June 1932 and after, and see how much the numbers were reduced after 24 June. And compare the statistics of crime from 8 November 1947, the day of the demolition of the democratic system of the constitution of 9 May 1946, to the present, and see how much they have increased.

*Principle 3. To improve the economic well-being of the people by the new government finding employment for all, and drawing up a national economic plan, not leaving the people to go hungry.*

I hope many people already know that I, on behalf of the majority of members of the People's Party, proposed an outline national economic plan according to the third principle. But obstacles arose which prevented implementation of the plan I proposed. Even so, the People's Party attempted to improve the economic well-being of the Thai people by finding employment for large numbers of people, thus not leaving the people to go hungry. Let those of you who have good will please study the statistics of theft resulting from hunger from before 24 June 1932, after 24 June 1932, and since 8 November 1947.

*Principle 4. To provide the people with equal rights.*

Please study the history of inequality among Thai people. You will find that before 24 June 1932, royal family members from Momchao upwards had many rights superior to those of commoners. For instance, if these people were accused in a criminal case, they did not have to appear before the criminal court but before the specially established court of the Ministry of the Palace. And so on.

Later, the provisional constitution of Siam of 27 June 1932 established the equal rights of all Thai people. This was the model for the constitutions of 10 December 1932 and 9 May 1946.

*Principle 5. To provide the people with liberty and freedom as long as this freedom does not conflict with the above four points.*

I hope those of you who are fair-minded can compare the extent of the freedom enjoyed by people before 24 June 1932, after 24 June 1932, and after the coup of 8 November 1947, the day of the demolition of the democratic system under the 1946 constitution. Even though the rights and free-doms of the people have been written down, in practice they have been evaded by declaring emergencies and declaring martial law beyond the call of necessity.

*Principle 6. To provide the people with full education.*
I hope those of you who are fair-minded can compare how education was limited before 24 June 1932, how people had full rights to education after 24 June 1932, and how people were limited in education from 8 November 1947 to the present.

# THE CAUSES OF THE ERRORS OF THE DEMOCRATIC REVOLUTION OF 24 JUNE

The causes of the errors of the democratic revolution of 24 June fall into two types: 1. causes of errors similar to those of all political movements; 2. causes of errors specific to the People's Party.

*Causes of errors similar to those of all political movements, namely conflict within the movement*
Every political party which competes in a parliamentary system has conflict within the party. Even though a party may have the power of government, conflict inside the party may still persist. Hence many parties break into parts or dissolve completely.

As for parties or movements in armed struggle, conflict and division is evident in the same way.

The history of the feudal age displays examples of groups of people successfully using armed struggle against those in command of the state. Inside such groups there were people with greed and jealousy founded on massive egoism, who destroyed people in the same party to ensure they alone became the centre of the affair *(egocentrism)*.

History displays an example in which a party or movement changed an absolute monarchy into a bourgeois democracy—namely the great revolution in France in 1789. After the movement was victorious over the old system, conflict arose inside the movement between progressives and reactionaries.

In China in 1850, the Taiping movement was able to triumph over the Manchu court in the southern region of China. It established its capital at Nanking and soon Hong Siw Chuan [Hong Xiuquan], the leader of the Taiping movement, established himself as the new emperor of China and appointed his deputies as lords of descending rank. As a result, mutual conflict arose within the movement. In the end, the Manchu court returned to triumph over the Taipings. Later in 1911, the revolution under the leadership of Sun Yat Sen triumphed over and successfully demolished Chinese absolutism. Inside the movement, conflict arose and the movement broke into many parts.

Subsequently the Chinese people's liberation movement under the leadership of the Communist Party triumphed over the Kuomintang on the Chinese mainland and established the People's Republic of China in 1949. Conflict arose inside the Chinese people's movement and the Chinese Communist Party. The party was purged of those who followed the capitalist line and the groups which strayed outside the communist line.

In the Soviet Union and the socialist states of Eastern Europe, there has been evidence of violent conflict inside parties to the extent that people were purged for following far right or far left lines.

Conflict also arose within counter-revolutionary parties which triumphed over revolutions. For example, the French royalist faction made a successful counter-revolution but then conflict arose over the royal succession.

The Italian fascist and German nazi movements made victorious counter-revolutions over democracy, but internal conflict arose resulting in purges of people whose vision differed from that of the leaders.

Every party, every movement, calls on its members to be united and harmonious, but there is no evidence of any movement whose members have been united and harmonious throughout. This follows the natural law of conflict within human groups and societies, which is a long-standing and profound issue which deserves study.

Within parties or organizations which aim to change an old system of society into a new progressive system, conflicts have the following major causes.

1. These parties or movements are born in the old society before the new social system has come into being. The newborn party or revolutionary movement represents a new society which does not yet exist. A philosopher expressed the gist of this as: "The birth of a revolution is like a human before life who must first be born in the mother's womb". The old society is the birthplace of the revolution for a new society.

2. The party or revolutionary movement to establish a new society is thus comprised of people who were born in the old society. They form a progressive element, who forsake their standing in the old system and devote their lives to establish a progressive new society.

But as this progressive element is born and lives in the old society, they carry the residual vision and habits of the old society embedded within themselves. There are differences in the degree to which different people can abandon these old traces. These differences can be categorized as follows.

Those of the first type forsake the vision and habits of the old society significantly and permanently, and help the newly established society to develop and progress to achieve fuller democracy. Those of the second type forsake just enough to establish the new social system and no more. Those of the third type likewise forsake just enough until the new society is established. Then they revive the vision of dictatorship, slavery, and feudalism until it becomes a counter-revolution against the revolution to which they themselves had once devoted their lives by joining the party or movement. These are the people who come into conflict with the revolutionary element inside the party or movement.

*Causes of errors specific to the People's Party*

Point 1. Lack of study of the law of conflict inside political movements and of the historical examples mentioned above made the majority of members unheedful that some would revive the vision of dictatorship, slavery, and feudalism as a counter-revolution against the revolution to which they themselves had devoted their lives.

Point 2. Members focused on achieving victory through the tactics of seizing the power of the state without thinking carefully about how to sustain victory and avoid a counter-revolution which would cause the nation to walk backwards into a *khlong* [i.e. to regress].

Point 3. Because three of the People's Party leaders, namely Phraya Phahon Phonphayuhasena, Phraya Songsuradet, and Phraya Ritthiakhane, had military knowledge and expertise, they were able to lead the party to success in seizing the power of the state. Many members had theoretical knowledge about establishing a country, but lacked practical expertise and lacked expertise in communicating with the people on a broad basis.

Point 4. Old bureaucrats were invited to join the government. I had hoped they would be more progressive than they acted. This created violent conflict within the revolutionary movement to the point where the parliament was closed and the permanent constitution of 10 December 1932 was abrogated.

# SUMMARY

Let me present "The People's Party and the Democratic Revolution of 24 June" as I have outlined above, and let me confirm that the People's Party as a whole had the ideal and pure desire for full democracy, but its actions in pursuit of this ideal and desire had errors which delayed the establishment of the democratic constitution until 9 May 1946.

Although during the process the People's Party as a whole had to face counter-revolution both inside and outside the party, the People's Party as a whole successfully developed the Thai nation according to the six principles, as I outlined above.

Please observe that in over thirty-five years—from the coup of 8 November 1947, which demolished government by the fully democratic constitution of 9 May 1946, up to 24 June 1982—democracy is still facing many setbacks.

Some learned academics who claim to be progressive have not helped the new generation to understand the true causes of the obstacles to the development of democracy. Rather they have been intent upon digging up the dissolved People's Party so they can fight against it. They have hunted down hearsay and used that hearsay as an academic basis to malign the People's Party, as I explained already. They accused the People's Party of failing to make the people understand the democratic constitution, such that some understood that "'constitution' is Phraya Phahon's son". Those who have intellectual capacity must have noticed the symbol of the constitution with a pedestal as the base. That symbol was created since the time when the People's Party had the duty of governing or overseeing the government of the country. Thus the Thai people should not misunderstand that the "'constitution' is Phraya Phahon's son". Some groups of academics should not show contempt for the Sangha for having been invited by the People's Party government to order every *wat* to explain to the people the essence of the constitution. They should not show contempt for the Islamic head, Christian head, officials of province, amphoe, and village who had enough intellectual capacity to explain to the people the essence of the democratic constitution.

I thus request the Thai people who love the nation, love democracy, and have a fair mind, to study the aims and correct methods to bring forth full democracy in Thailand within a time span no longer than the time the People's Party served the nation and the people.

Before ending this speech, let me thank the chairman and all the committee members of the celebration of Half a Century of Democracy again for the good intentions of your five objectives. And let me wish that all of you, including the Thai people who love nation and democracy and are fair-minded, be blessed with long life, good status, good health, and physical strength to achieve success in serving the nation and people to achieve full democracy in every detail.

Paris suburbs
24 June 1982

# PART III: AFTER THE REVOLUTION

*Senior statesman Pridi on his return from a tour of China, USA, and Europe,
20 February 1947*

# INTRODUCTION

## LIFE

After the 1932 promoters had made a second coup in June 1933, Pridi returned to Siam in September and was cleared of the charge of being a communist. Between 1934 and 1941, as minister of interior, then foreign affairs, and then finance, he tried to implement some of his vision of a country free of colonial pressure, being led by enlightened and efficient bureaucracy towards a more prosperous and equitable future. But from 1935–36 onwards, the People's Party became more seriously divided—partly over domestic strategy, but more drastically over how to manage the split in the developed world between liberal and fascist camps. On 8 December 1941, Japanese troops occupied Thailand. Eight days later Pridi was pushed out of the Cabinet and appointed one of the regents for the young (and absent) king. He became the local leader of the Seri Thai resistance movement against the Japanese. In 1946, Pridi and his allies were briefly in the ascendant. Pridi became prime minister. Parliament accepted the constitution which Pridi claimed finally fulfilled the promise of the 1932 revolution. The People's Party was dissolved. But after June 1946, royalists began to blame Pridi for the mysterious death of King Rama VIII. In 1947, the army seized power, and scrapped Pridi's constitution. For the next four years, Pridi tried to organize his Seri Thai remnants in armed resistance to military dictatorship. In 1949, he escaped to China.

## WRITINGS

The first piece, from the *Concise Autobiography*, is Pridi's own brief record of his achievements as a minister in the mid and late 1930s. As in the earlier extract from this book, the note style of the original is preserved in the translation. The following three speeches were broadcast by radio on the anniversary of the first constitution (27 June 1932) in 1934, 1935, and 1936. The *Establishment of the Anti-Japan Resistance Movement and Seri Thai* was printed in the 1981 memorial volume of Pramot Phungsunthon, a 1932 promoter, MP, and aide to Pridi in the 1930s, member of Seri Thai, publisher of many of Pridi's writings, and the first manager of the Ratcha-damnoen boxing stadium. "What Happened inside the Regency Council" was the first of Pridi's retrospective pieces on Thai politics to appear, published by the Nittivet press of Pramot Phungsunthon and Proeng Siriphat in 1972. The 1946 speech was delivered in the Assembly after the passage of the 1946 constitution, just a month before the death of King Rama VIII. "Uphold the Aim for full Democracy of the Heroes of 14 October" was written in the two months following the student revolution of 1973, and sent to be included in a Thammasat student publication in December of that year. The final excerpt is taken from *Ma vie mouvementée et mes 21 ans d'exil en Chine populaire,* which was published privately in Paris in 1972, subsequently distributed in Thailand by UNESCO and the *Bangkok Post,* and translated into Thai as *Chiwit phan phuan khong khaphachao lae 21 pi thi liphai nai satharanarat Chin.*

# PREFACE

Again this section contains a mix of contemporary documents on the one hand, and later attempts to reflect and intepret on the other. As brief records of a political career spanning seventeen critical years for both Siam and the world, they offer a very fragmentary view. But a handful of themes stand out.

Siam at the time of the 1932 revolution was still a very undeveloped country, even within the Asian context. Its economy was based on agriculture (in the outline economic plan, Pridi devoted only a handful of paragraphs to the modern urban economy). The monarchic state was oriented to defence, control, extraction. Against such a background, the ideals which Pridi had summarized into the six principles translated into an intensely practical challenge for the post-1932 government. The three speeches from the mid-1930s trace a nice progression. The first is largely a lecture on the importance of the constitution and the rule of law, with some comments on economics and education. The emphasis is on principles and ideals. The second is a laundry list of projects and practical achievements—statistics of crime reduced, mental hospitals built, electricity plants funded, law codes completed, numbers of medical staff trained, length of water pipes laid. The climax of the speech is a list of road construction projects and an announcement on the reduction of electricity tariffs. The speech presents constitutional democracy as a more efficient and effective form of social management. The third speech switches to Siam's position in the world, and the interaction between domestic progress and international pressures. This speech presents constitutional democracy as Siam's calling card in the modern "civilized" world. It anticipates how much Siam's fate over the next decade will be decided by international rather than local forces. Over the course of these three speeches, Pridi has progressed from philosophy, to administrative practicality, to global realism.

Pridi saw that the enemy of progress was not monarchy or any particular king, but the corrupting reign of privilege which sheltered under the umbrella of monarchy and blocked any programme of progress for the mass of the population. Pridi was consistent on this. In the announcement of 24 June 1932, he denied any aspiration to "snatch" the throne, but inveighed against the *chao nai* who "farm on the backs" of the population. From the reflective standpoint of his later years, this point took on even greater importance. He painted the ideal framework for Thailand as a constitution-based democracy with the king at its head. After Thailand's post-war experience of military dictatorship, he became more aware than ever of the important role the monarchy could play in blocking the aspirations of dictators. But the danger was that monarchy and monarchism could also be manipulated to serve dictatorship. In later life he stressed that the 1932 objective of a constitutional monarchy had not been enough; the proper aim was "constitutional democratic monarchy". The most vituperative passages in his later writings were reserved for those who perverted constitutions and sought personal advantage by manipulating the power and prestige of monarchy.

This conviction has to be seen in the context of the three-way battle which developed through the 1930s and 1940s. The People's Party (at least in Pridi's imagining) had conducted a revolution against privilege and inefficiency in the name of law, constitutionalism, equity, rights, and progress—the outline programme of new nationalists the world over in this era. But in the 1930s, this nationalism underwent a split—again on a world rather than a local scale. Some were attracted to the "strong state" version of emergent fascism. Others clung to a "liberal" model based on the supremacy of elected parliaments as the best possible expression of a popular will. Within Thailand, this led to increasing estrangement between Pridi and Phibun, between (roughly) the civilian and military elements of the People's Party. This estrangement was exacerbated by the difficulties of managing Thailand's position in a global war between the two nationalist tendencies.

Even so, this estrangement was manageable in the local arena. Despite these strains, the People's Party stuck together and managed its own internal conflicts reasonably well through to 1946. But the situation changed in the immediate post-war period. Many of the royalists who had fled or lain low since 1932–33, now returned or re-emerged. The political struggle now became a more complex three-cornered fight. The focus became the full restoration of monarchy following King Rama VII's abdication, the long minority of his successor, and the resulting fifteen years without a resident, reigning king. The issue was not so much the restoration itself, but rather in the service of what political cause the restoration would be carried out— Pridi-style democratic constitutionalism, military-led dictatorship, or the revival of aristocratic norms and privileges. Pridi tried to build an alliance with the royalists in opposition to militarism. He invited Seni Pramoj to return and become prime minister; released many royalists held as political prisoners; restored ranks and titles; and lifted political restrictions on royal family members. But these overtures were rejected. "What Happened inside the Regency Council" may be read as a rueful and angry account of his attempt to work with the royalists. The 1946 speech in the Assembly shows Pridi at the point of realizing that the royalists will not help him defend democracy against dictatorship.

Ultimately, Pridi's vision was defeated by an alliance of the other two. This royalist-military alliance took a decade or so to work out its terms and conditions, and required an American helping hand. But the decisive point was the political turmoil of 1946–47 marked by a revolving door of premierships, the mysterious death of King Rama VIII, and the first in a long series of classic military coups.

This is why Pridi returned again and again in his later writings to this period, and particularly to the contrast between the 1946 and 1947 constitutions. The 1946 constitution made both chambers elective. The 1947 constitution substituted an appointed senate. The military dictators were able to appoint a tame senate, while claiming that the appointments were officially made by the king. This tame senate allowed the dictators to control and manipulate parliament. Only in 2000 has the senate again been made elective. At times, Pridi's reiterations about the age limit of electoral candidates, the appointment of senators, the drafting of clauses on the royal signature, and the ranks of appointees, can seem obsessive. But for him these were the means by which his constitutionalist ideal was not just hijacked, but turned into the basis of a pact between dictatorial nationalism and aristocratic privilege which shaped Thailand's political course for a generation.

This conviction in turn framed Pridi's reaction to the 1973 student uprising. For a quarter-century, the political tide had been running against him. In 1973, he seized immediately on the hope that the student uprising signalled that the tide had turned. "Uphold the Aim for Full Democracy of the Heroes of 14 October" appeared within two months of the event. It was followed by a stream of pieces through which Pridi hoped to pass on the lessons of his experience to the student leaders, politicians, and makers of the new constitution. These messages ranged from discourses on general constitutional principles down to detailed plans on how to divide the country up into electoral constituencies. Like the two essays on 1932 in part 2 above, "Uphold the Aim" dwells on the question of why the ideals of the People's Party were blocked and reversed by military dictatorship. But the hope engendered in Pridi by the 1973 uprising makes the tone different and the analysis deeper in this piece. Perhaps emboldened by the king's alignment on the student side in October 1973, he is more detailed in his account of King Prajadhipok's role in 1932–33, and more explicit about his own ideal of a constitutional democratic monarchy as a bulwark against dictatorship. And finally, he is also more explicit and more acid about the corrupting influence of lingering aristocratic privilege.

# 13. EXCERPT FROM:
## *CONCISE AUTOBIOGRAPHY OF NAI PRIDI BANOMYONG*

## 16. AS MINISTER OF THE INTERIOR

Received royal appointment as minister of the interior on 21 March 1934.

Pridi acted to give the people participation in local government.

Established municipalities throughout the kingdom of Siam through the Municipality Act which Pridi drafted for the government of Phraya Phahon to submit to the Assembly so that local government would follow the democratic system.

Ensured election of village heads *(phuyaiban)* and sub-district heads *(kamnan)* by the Local Government Act.

Established the department of municipal public works to accord with municipal administration and built local roads in many provinces.

Reduced crime by prevention and suppression.

Built hospitals in several places, including hospital boats on the Mekong, by using proceeeds of the local lottery.

Built weirs and dams in many places to help paddy farmers and other agriculturists.

Built penal projects so convicts could have land.

Etc. Etc. Etc.

## 17. ESTABLISHED THE UNIVERSITY
### of Moral and Political Sciences [Thammasat]

Proposed to the government to set up the University of Moral and Political Sciences as an academic centre for study in law, economics, and other disciplines connected with moral and political sciences, to promote officials and other people to have the opportunity to study widely, to extend and root the democratic system, to know the duties of governmental administration in this system. The government approved and entrusted Pridi to draft the Act of the University of Moral and Political Sciences 1934 to submit to the Assembly. The Assembly approved the bill into law on 14 March 1934 (according to the old calendar).

Then the government submitted to the king the Assembly's proposal to appoint Pridi as rector of the University of Moral and Political Sciences on 11 April 1934. Pridi held this post for eighteen years and quit the post because the government that descended from the coup group of 1947 submitted a new Thammasat University bill on 18 March 1952 rescinding the post of rector.

While Pridi was rector, he worked to have students favour the democratic system, as the majority of Thammasat students already know.

## 18. TRAVEL OVERSEAS
### to Negotiate Reduction in Interest on the Loans made by the Government of the Sixth Reign, and to Sound out Foreign Governments about Amending the Unequal Treaties

During the Sixth Reign the government borrowed money from British banks for building public utilities at an interest rate of 6 percent. Hence in 1935 Phraya Phahon's government assigned Pridi to travel to London to negotiate reduction in interest. Pridi negotiated with the British banks to reduce the interest rate from 6 to 4 percent which greatly reduced the Thai nation's interest liability.

At the same time, Pridi travelled to the great powers to sound out the Siamese government's opening new negotiations to cancel the unequal treaties.

## 19. NEGOTIATION
### for Siam's Full Independence and Sovereignty and Some Territorial Gains while Minister for Foreign Affairs

Appointed minister for foreign affairs on 9 August 1937 and held the post until 15 December 1938. Important matters were as follows.

In the absolutist period, Siam was forced by several imperialist countries to make unequal treaties, allowing imperialist countries several special rights. For instance, if people under the jurisdiction of those countries committed a crime on Thai territory, the Thai court had no power of judgement. The Thai government had to send the foreign national who committed a crime for the foreign consular court to hear the case. Later some countries such as Britain and France allowed Siam to establish a foreign court consisting of

Thai judges and European legal advisers jointly hearing and passing judgement on cases involving people under the jurisdiction of Britain and France. Yet in the treaties it was further specified that if the opinion of the Thai judges and the European legal advisers conflicted, the opinion of the European advisers would have greater weight than that of the Thai judges, with no account taken whether the Thai judges outnumbered the European advisers. Even so, the treaty laid down further that the British consul still had the power to withdraw a case from the foreign court to be heard in the British consular court. The consular offices of many countries had a court and jail especially for people under their jurisdiction. There were other special rights which are known according to the language of international law as extraterritoriality.

In economic affairs, the imperialist countries had special rights under the treaties. For example, import tax could be collected only at 3 percent *ad valorem*. Although the absolutist government had made some treaty amendments to improve Siam's rights, there were still several provisions determining the rate of customs duties. Furthermore, several imperialist countries had other special privileges, for instance forest, mining, and shipping concessions, and political power and influence over the country.

When Pridi was appointed minister for foreign affairs in Phraya Phahon's government, the prime minister allocated him the duty to negotiate new treaties with various countries so that Siam would have full independence and sovereignty. Pridi used the tactic of announcing cancellation of the unequal treaties with various imperialist countries, and submitting for the imperialist countries' consideration a new draft treaty in which Siam had full independence and sovereignty. Pridi tried strongly to negotiate by the principle of "balance of power" to make each imperialist country agree to a new treaty granting Siam full independence and sovereignty. In the end, every imperialist country agreed to make a new treaty allowing Siam full independence and sovereignty—political, judicial, and economic independence, etc.

Negotiated with the British government to transfer that part of Siam's territory which Britain acquired from Siam by the treaty defining the border with Britain in 1868 (during the Fourth Reign) at the mouth of the Chan river between Ranong province and British Victoria Point, and along the edge of the Sai river in Chiang Rai province. In both places land jutted out on the Thai side. The British government agreed that the territory which jutted out on the Thai side was Thai territory.

Etc. Etc. Etc.

## 20. FAIR TAX REFORM;
### Cancellation of the Poll Tax and Land Tax; Establishment of a Revenue Code for the First Time in Thailand

Received royal appointment as minister of finance from 20 December 1938, and held the post until 16 December 1941.

While holding the post of minister of finance, undertook several measures concerning fairness in society, for instance:

Repealed the poll tax which was a corpse left over from the dues *(ngoen suai)* which people who were *phrai* had to pay to their feudal lord.

Cancelled the land tax which was a corpse of the tribute *(bannakan)* which people who cultivated paddy land had to pay to the highest feudal lord who held that all the land throughout the kingdom belonged to the head of state.

Reformed taxes for fairness in society, that is, anyone with income paid more tax, anyone who enjoyed luxury consumption paid high indirect tax, and anyone who bought consumer goods that were not necessities paid higher levels of tax.

Established a revenue code, the first ever in Thailand, including provisions on direct taxes which were fair to society.

When major war began in Europe before spreading all over the world, Pridi arranged to protect the Thai nation's overseas assets in good time, as follows.

During the absolutist time, the currency reserves were kept in sterling bonds in British banks in Britain. Pridi foresaw that sterling bonds would gradually fall in value, so he arranged to use one part of the bond money held as currency reserves to buy gold of around one million ounces (35 million grams) at a price of around 35 US dollars an ounce, and kept this gold in the strong-room of the Finance Ministry. This is probably still being kept as reserves for the baht today. At present gold in the world market has a price of about 350 US dollars an ounce. Hence the investment which Pridi as minister of finance made to buy the gold to keep in the strong-room of the Finance Ministry was 35 million US dollars, and currently that gold belonging to the Thai nation has a value of 350 million US dollars.

Apart from this, there is other gold which Pridi asked the Japanese to bring to exchange for Thai currency before the outbreak of the great East Asian war. Also there is another amount of gold which Pridi as head of Seri Thai asked the Khuang government, when lending to Japan during the Second World War, to have Japan bring from the Japanese central bank as collateral for the Thai government. The Allies handed this over to the Thai government after the Second World War.

# 21. TRANSFERRED THE ANGLO-AMERICAN TOBACCO COMPANY
## to the Thai Government before the Japanese Could Seize It

According to the unequal treaties with Britain and the US, British and American companies had special rights to run a monopoly on the sale of cigarettes in Thailand.

After Pridi had made new treaties with various countries cancelling various special rights, had moved to the post of finance minister, had reformed taxes for social equity, and had announced the revenue code, he proposed to the government to submit a tobacco bill to the Assembly. When the law was enacted, Pridi arranged to transfer the business of the Anglo-American company to the Thai government. This was completed about six months before Japan invaded Thailand. If the Anglo-American company had still owned the business, the Japanese invaders would probably have seized it as property of Japan's enemies, and manufactured and sold tobacco in Thailand throughout the Second World War, with Japan getting profit of many billion baht.

# 14. SPEECHES 1934–36

## "THE TWO YEARS THAT HAVE PASSED"
## BY LUANG PRADITMANUTHAM
## (NAI PRIDI BANOMYONG)

Broadcast on radio on 27 June 1934

Dear listeners,

Today is an auspicious day, an occasion to recall 27 June of two years ago, the important day for the nation when the king graciously affixed his signature to the provisional constitution. The Thai people advanced onto a new path. Siam entered into the constitutional system. Even though the constitution adopted on that 27 June was only a provisional constitution, it was the first step on a ladder to the permanent constitution, promulgated on 10 December 1932.

In the time that has passed from the day the provisional constitution was announced until now, the government taking care of the constitution has devoted itself single-mindedly to improving the state of the country. The constitutional system has benefited the country. On the evening of the 24th, General Phibunsongkhram gave you the views of the military. Then on the 25th, Momchao Wanwaithayakon relayed to the nation the observations of the king. This evening, the board of directors of the radio has given me the honour of passing on some of my feelings.

The change in the system of government, as Momchao Wanwaithayakon has already recounted, was an all-round change—not just a minor change, or a change in some areas, some departments. It was a change in the method of running the country. Hence the change must deliver results both in theory and practice. But the results of this change will not be achieved quickly. In the West there is a saying: Rome was not built in a day. Siam is the same. To judge the effects of the change in government, you must view things fairly and in all aspects. Some people have found fault with the government for doing nothing but putting out laws. Those who find fault in this way are looking only at the material side. They do not realize that passing laws is very necessary. Under a constitutional system such as this, government can only do something when there is a law which gives it the power. Neither the government nor any individual can act according to will without a law which grants the power to do so. Acting on the basis of law is acting according to the consent of the people who have their representatives in parliament, in keeping with the rights and freedoms granted by the constitution. Besides, law is the working framework of the government. It is the blueprint for letting the people know what the government will do.

It is vital to think before you act. In Buddhism, there is a teaching always to put thought before action. This teaching tells us not to do anything without thinking thoroughly first, not to do anything without principle or direction, not to set out before knowing for sure where we are going. We Siamese are in a situation like people in a boat together in the middle of the ocean. The boat is trying to find its way through the wind and waves to reach landfall. If there is no compass on the boat, the boatmen do not know which direction to steer. It will be impossible for the boat to reach safety. Our country is in the same situation. If we do not make a definite plan of work, it will be difficult for us to make things better for our country.

During the two years that have passed, what has the government done? Or to put it another way, what have been the beneficial effects produced by the change in government? I will divide my opinions on this issue under the six principles and explain each to you in turn.

Principle 1. The issue of independence. In the area of law in particular, we have speedily completed many new law codes in a very short time. Before the announcement of the permanent constitution, that is, before 10 December 1932, the law-drafting department which at present is the Juridical Council, proposed the draft of section 5 to parliament. Then by 31 March of this year, it proposed to the cabinet section 6 and the codes of civil and criminal procedure. But the very next day, the Assembly was closed. Hence the work is delayed. But consider the time taken on this work before the change of government and after the change. The drafting of the civil code began from 1909. By 1932, only sections 1, 2, 3, and 4 were done, and a start had been made on laying down the principles for section 5, at a cost of around 2 million baht. Then after the change in government, sections 5 and 6 and the codes of civil and criminal procedure, which are important laws, were all four completed in just eight months at a cost of 115,000 baht. Now these completed drafts are under consideration by a commission established by the government, which will hasten to complete the task within December of this year according to the cabinet resolution.

As for economic and political independence, the government has speedily arranged other matters which I will consider under the points below.

Principle 2. The issue of internal peace-keeping. Government has utilized the power of the military, police, and civilians to ensure lasting peace within the country. This was not done only by strengthening the suppressive authorities, but also by strengthening in other ways within the six principles as a whole, such as through the economy and education. The six principles are all interconnected like a chain. As time has past over the two years, change has begun in the central bureaucracy. The aspiration to maintain the peace internally will be realized when various local governments have been organized in the form of municipalities *(thesaban)* under which the local people have the right to manage the administration of their own locality.

The government has prepared the way to draft a law about maintaining peace and order in the locality to replace the old law on local government. It has prepared ways to prevent wrongdoing occurring through administrative practice. It is also considering organizing a general registration of the people as a regulatory measure once the municipal administration has begun. And it is also considering a system of identity cards for convenience in maintaining the peace and monitoring public order in general. Hence it will be imperative to prepare the funds and the personnel for administering this.

But keeping the peace internally is a very heavy task. When the change was achieved, there were dissatisfied people who generated jealousy, and who tried by various ways to generate disorder to the point there arose a rebellion which caused the destruction of lives and property of the country. Attempts to stir up disorder like this still remain. This creates delay in arranging other matters. Work that is going well and smoothly gets disrupted. Nevertheless, the government will boldly persevere to overcome all obstacles. I myself believe strongly in my heart in the fairness of the majority of the people to help maintain peace and order within this nation of ours.

Principle 3. The economy is an important problem talked about constantly. It is often asked when the government will make the economy improve. It is fitting to pay such attention to the economy. If we change only the way of governing without changing the economy, the change in government will have no effect. Some people believe that up to the present point the government has done nothing to strengthen the economy. This statement is slander and without truth, because the government has already done many things to help the economy. For example, it has established an office to find employment to help farmers; passed a law to prevent seizure of certain property; reduced various taxes; placed a legal ceiling on the charging of interest rates; reduced the poll tax; expanded cooperatives; and passed a law stipulating that a certain proportion of workers must be Thai. In addition, as General Phibunsongkhram has said already on the 24th, the government has also expanded communications by making roads and has been building irrigation works ceaselessly. But the economic problem is more difficult than any other problem. The various obstacles and obstructions which arise over the economic problem are no fewer than over other problems. There are many reasons for this. For instance, some understand that the government must ensure that money pours in so that lazy people can have money without working. This is beyond the bounds of possibility. There is no government that can do that. There is no honest person that can get money without working. A second obstacle arises from not knowing how the economy must be strengthened. For instance, when the government invests in building a long road, there is talk about why ever is the government building a road? How come it's not strengthening the economy? People who speak like this don't know that the economy will not improve unless we have roads. They say the government is always looking into things, not doing things. This is because they do not ponder that looking into something amounts to doing something. If you do not look into something first, what can you do? But no obstacle is as great as seeking personal benefit above the benefit of the majority. Anything that government does is for the common benefit, not to grab money for individuals. So every time the government tries to help the poor, such as the farmers, the government will face difficulty, criticism, and dissent. All these laws such as the law forbidding the seizure of certain property from farmers, or the law controlling the charging of interest beyond a certain rate, were passed with difficulty. The difficulty in the economic problem lies here. I hope the people will sympathize. We cannot accomplish matters faster than this because the government faces many obstacles as I have stated. But the government is ever more committed to the effort. The country's finances are one issue on which the enemies of the constitution have tried to stir up concern that since the change in government the country's finances have declined, to the point of having almost no budget reserves left in the treasury. Fomenting lies such as this is shameful. In truth, the financial situation is something which you cannot be deceitful about. Whatever the truth is, the government has to make that public, because our finances are connected with those of other countries.

Before the change, the budget prepared for 1932 was almost out of balance, causing difficulty in financial matters. After the overthrow, the People's Party government studied the budget again and at the end of the year produced more revenue than expenditure.

About the financial reserves, you should know that:

on 1 April 1932, the treasury reserve was over 34 million baht
on 1 April 1933, the treasury reserve was over 47 million baht
on 1 April 1934, the treasury reserve was over 54 million baht
on 1 May 1934, the treasury reserve was over 58 million baht.

This means that in two years since the change of government, the treasury reserve has increased by over 23 million baht. Besides this, on March 1932, Siam repaid a loan of over 20 million baht borrowed at 7 percent. The money came from funds accumulated for repaying debt. This lifted the burden of the country by no small amount.

Principle 4. The issue of equal rights. The people have acquired these rights already under the constitution. In addition, the government has done many things to foster the equal rights of the people. The government has arranged to pass the civilian bureaucracy law so that all people will be treated equally in entering government service. Government has established the University of Moral and Political Sciences [Thammasat]. Previously, education on politics was a matter of heavy concern. Ordinary people had no opportunity to study. But now everyone has equality in learning about politics and has a part in their country's affairs.

Principle 5. The freedom of the people. This is an outcome of the constitution. Over the issue of freedom, there are many people who misunderstand or pretend to misunderstand. Freedom does not mean that human beings can do anything they like. That would become anarchy, the lack of any government. Freedom must have rules. Freedom must exist within the scope of law and morality. We humans have freedom to do anything but we must not cause harm to others, and must not cause turmoil in the country. The government which looks after our constitution has granted more freedom than in other countries which changed to a new government. The government has patiently allowed the expression of many hostile opinions. There is no country which has changed to a new government which is as tolerant as the constitutional government of ours. Hence I dare say that the government has granted freedom correctly according to the constitutional system.

Principle 6. How far has education advanced after the change of government? You may know that education in public elementary schools has progressed a lot. Apart from the help from government, the monkhood has generously helped national education. At present there are more than five hundred monks in various provinces who are happy to be trained to help as teachers in public elementary schools, and another almost eight hundred monks who have pledged to help by teaching for nothing. And apart from this, the Sangha is thinking of setting up *wat* schools to help public elementary education even further. This all shows clearly that the constitutional system has coordinated work between the government and the Sangha very well.

On education in general, compare the number of schools before and after the change of government. There are thirty-six more elementary schools, twenty-two more lower secondary, and forty-three more middle secondary. In 1934, higher secondary has expanded to the provinces.

Vocational education, which means schools teaching occupations, has expanded greatly through various technical and agricultural schools. After the change in government, seven new technical schools have been opened, five new agricultural schools, and ten new commercial schools both in Bangkok and the provinces. Apart from these, there is a vocational school for housekeeping, one for secretarial, and one for languages which have been newly established in Bangkok and Phuket.

These advances in education are clearly a result of the change of government. The important item is the University of Moral and Political Sciences which was opened today, and which has enrolled 7,094 students. The subject of politics, which previously was only for a limited circle, is now the opposite. The government is glad to extend its teaching as widely as possible.

In addition, with respect to the arts of the nation, the government has promoted schools for various crafts, and a newly established school of music and dance which has been operating very smoothly.

In conclusion, from everything I have said, you listeners who truly have fair minds, will see that within two years, the work has progressed considerably. The people who made the change of government aspire only for progress in these matters. If any matter has not been able to progress easily, it is because enemies of the constitution oppose and create trouble. But if the people in general have love, and if the constitution is everywhere appreciated, the constitution itself will be what fuses all of us together as one unity. When each person does his own duty, and helps others to think and create without envy and without being destructive, the path of the constitution will be smooth, and we will move together towards contentment and prosperity, which is the goal at the end of our road. I do not appeal to you to favour the government or anyone personally, but I appeal to you to have concern for the nation, have concern for the people in general, and help to raise up the constitution of ours to endure permanently. The permanence of the constitution is the foundation for securing the contentment and prosperity of the people, while the extinction of the constitution would be the end of the country and the nation. May all of us Thais help to maintain the constitution of the kingdom of Siam to endure forever.

May I wish happiness to all you listeners.

# SPEECH BY LUANG PRADITMANUTHAM
## (NAI PRIDI BANOMYONG),
## MINISTER OF THE INTERIOR

Broadcast on radio on 27 June 1935

Dear listeners,

Today marks the third anniversary of 27 June, the auspicious day on which the Thai nation entered the constitutional system. In the one year that has passed since I had the occasion to talk about the two previous years, the government has striven constantly to raise the country to further progress.

The life of the country will prosper when the various organs of the nation are sound. Unity is something which will make the nation have the strength to attain prosperity. The prime minister has already spoken on the 24th and our nation must face any obstacle that there is. On the evening of the 26th, Luang Thamrongnawasawat, secretary-general of the cabinet, informed you that our country is deficient in financial resources and in people—that is, deficient in people with scientific knowledge and expertise. On entering the constitutional system, Siam has to start anew not only in the matter of government. Siam has to cultivate people, cultivate more people with knowledge and expertise, to strengthen the organs of the nation even further. A saying of Western people, which I referred to a year ago, is that Rome was not built in a day. I must refer to it again today in respect of Siam, our beloved nation.

Let me explain to you briefly what have been the results from the change of government over this past year under the headings of the six principles, with special emphasis on the duty of the Interior Ministry.

Principle 1. On independence. I shall talk especially about the various law codes of ours which were still pending. They have all been speedily revised, proposed to the Assembly, and enacted. This includes section 65 of the civil and commercial code concerning the family; section 6 concerning inheritance; the code of criminal procedure code; the code of civil procedure; and the constitution of the courts of justice, which will come into

189

force from 1 October 1935. Next we shall start to negotiate the foreign treaties.

Concerning economic and political independence, the government has speedily arranged other measures to promote greater independence and security.

Principle 2. On internal peace-keeping. I shall talk especially about the robbers who were widespread in 1933 and the beginning of 1934. Now they have decreased. You can see that in March 1934 there were seventy-five fewer cases of serious crime than in March 1933; in April 1935 there were forty fewer cases than in April 1934; and in May 1935 there were seventy-three fewer cases than in May 1934. In the first three weeks of this June compared to last June, the number of cases of serious crime has reduced a lot.

Regarding imprisonment, we have tried to train criminals to earn a living and change their character for the better. We have tried to find occupations for those who have completed their sentence; have begun to establish a prison with a new design as a reform colony in Nakhon Ratchasima province; and have prepared to extend this project to Yala province. The revenue from the penitentiary department in 1934 was 289,702 baht, more than planned by 189,702 baht. The difference has partly been subtracted from the investment for 1934, partly from 1935, and the remainder remitted to the treasury as revenue. In addition, more new reform schools will be established.

Administration, health, and public works, which are important supports for maintaining internal peace, have advanced from the previous year.

The regulations for municipal administration will come into force shortly with the inauguration of provincial councils in various provinces, and with the conversion of thirty-four existing sanitary districts *(sukhaphiban)* into municipalities. The Chiang Mai sanitary district which has a dense population will be raised to the status of a city *(nakhon)*. Similarly, cities will be established in Phranakhon and Thonburi provinces. Apart from this, there will be a budget for setting up urban *(muang)* and rural (tambon) municipalities in many other important locations. The people will thus have even more of a role and a voice in the management of their local government.

As for health measures and medicine for the good health of the people, health institutions have been built in many places using some money from the government, some from the lottery, some from those of you with the goodwill to make donations, and some labour power from those ready to make a sacrifice. For instance, in Thonburi the Chaokhun Phra Prayu-rawong health centre received donations from those with the surname after which the centre is named. Singburi province has built a health centre with money from the sanitation district and from donations. Udon Thani province has built additional accommodation for patients in the grounds of the health centre. In addition, new hospitals are being built in many places such as the Phranakhon central hospital, Nong Khai hospital, and Ubon Ratchathani hospital. Nakhon Phanom province will begin shortly. Phrae province will arrange to have a health centre, and the Phrapadaeng charitable hospital will build additional accommodation for women with tuberculosis. People on the banks of the Mekong river will have better access to medical care as the government has created a regular motorized floating hospital. The boat will sail up and down the Mekong in Loei, Nong Khai, and Nakhon Phanom provinces and the Kam river in Sakon Nakhon. Apart from this, any place which has not yet been able to build a hospital or health centre, will have to open a treatment centre at a doctor's residence, for instance at amphoe Ban Sao in Lopburi province and amphoe Tha Bo in Nong Khai.

People who have mental disease were previously kept in the jails in the provinces. From now on they will be sent to the mental hospitals which will be built, one in the southern region and one in the north.

As for the important problem of medical staff, we have trained thirty people as doctor's assistants for Isan already, and this year will begin training another twenty at Chiang Mai. Two laws concerning medicine have already been promulgated—the Health and Sanitation Act, and the Infectious Diseases Act. Apart from this, the health and medical committee established by the government has helped to draw up a plan for the improvement of health and medicine.

Municipal public works, which are one of the important supports of administration, have progressed in many ways, especially roads. Let me say that the Phrae–Nan route has the budget for earthworks which are hoped to be finished this year. On the Sawankhalok–Tak route, the gravel foundation will be finished. The rural Roi-et–Ubon route, Ubon–Mukdahan–Nakhon Phanom, Taphan Hin–Phetchabun, Paetriu–Sattahip, Prachin–Aranyaprathet, Chumphon–Kraburi, Huai Yot–Krabi, Yala–Betong, Tha Nun–Takua Pa—these main roads have a total length of 1,301 kilometres. The forest has been cleared on 655 kilometres, the earthworks finished on 477 kilometres, the gravel foundation completed on 99 kilometres, concrete bridges built at 46 places, and water drainage pipes laid in 262 places.

In addition, the Paetriu–Chonburi–Sattahip route will be expedited because the earthworks are finished, the gravel foundation finished in places, and the navy has helped on the section from Sattahip back to Chonburi.

On both the Bangkok–Don Muang and Bangkok–Samut Prakan roads, the earthworks are complete, currently the bridges and water drainage pipes are being built, and preparations are being made for the gravel work.

The important highways on which construction will proceed as soon as survey work is complete are Sattahip–Rayong, Ratchaburi–Ban Pong,

Phetchabun–Lomsak, Bua Yai–Chaiyaphum, Chakkarat–Phimai, Khon Kaen–Loei, and Udon–Loei–Chiang Khan.

Phranakhon–Thonburi has received budget to build improved roads. On the Phranakhon side, the roads which will have asphalt surface are Songwat, Songsawat, Dinso, Ban Tanao, Chakphet, Phrasumen, Ti-thong, and Triphet. Also, the area in front of the main railway station has already been concreted. On the Thonburi side, Lat Ya road will have gravel work and bridges built from Wongwian Yai to the Bangkok Yai canal; and some gravel work, earthwork, and bridging will be done from Lat Ya road to Talat Phlu, where the road around the market will also have gravel fill.

Electricity and piped water supply in the main urban centres will be expedited for the convenience of the population. A law has been passed to enable the government to lend 500,000 baht to sanitary districts or municipalities to set up electricity plants at Chachoengsao, Uttaradit, Uthai Thani, and in the localities of Chumsaeng and Bangmunnak. Water supply pipes will be built in Ayutthaya, Lopburi, Nakhon Sawan, and Phitsanulok.

As for Phranakhon and Thonburi, there is some important news which I am very pleased to let you all know today. The electricity rate and equipment rental charges which are expensive will be reduced in future. The Ministry of the Interior has agreed with Siam Electricity Corporation, Limited to reduce the electricity supply rate from the current level. Beginning from 1 July 1935, the upper rate for the supply of electricity for lighting, power appliances, and heating will come down by two *satang* per unit, and on 1 July 1936 it will come down by three *satang*. This means that within this year we have reduced the rate by two *satang* and by next year by a total of five *satang*. The rental charge for electricity metering equipment of ten amperes and below will come down as follows:

from 1 July 1935, charged at 80 *satang*, a reduction of 20 *satang*
from 1 July 1936, charged at 50 *satang*, a reduction of 50 *satang*.

As noted, these are matters which are related specifically to the Ministry of the Interior.

In addition, internal peace-keeping has depended on the army, police, and civilians to help the country to survive.

Principle 3. The economy. This is an important problem. I have already talked about this in detail a year ago and I will leave it for those responsible to inform you.

Principle 4, the right to equality, and principle 5, the liberty of the people. I spoke on these a year ago. Matters have taken place in accordance with the permanent constitution. The government has established a committee to revise laws which conflict with the constitution. This indicates the good intention of the government to ensure greater equality and freedom.

Principle 6. Education. This has progressed further. Public elementary schools will be established in every tambon. An indication of the honesty of the government is that it has set a policy to return back to the provinces that portion of education funds which the previous government borrowed from the provinces. It is hoped that when each province has prepared a plan under this policy and has received back this money, it will help the public school education for our youth even further, and will successfully strengthen municipal administration.

The results of the constitution over the past one year are as I have outlined. Those of you who have a fair state of mind will probably wish to see these results progress further. I must appeal to you listeners in the same way I appealed last year. May I beg all of us Thais to have love in our hearts, to appreciate the constitution with honesty, to help one another to solve things, to think, to create, without being destructive. If things can be thus, our constitution will endure permanently. I do not ask you to favour the government or anyone personally, but I appeal to you to have concern for the nation, for the people in general. Let us Thai people help one another to maintain the constitution of the kingdom of Siam to endure forever.

May I wish happiness to all you listeners.

# SPEECH BY LUANG PRADITMANUTHAM
## (NAI PRIDI BANOMYONG)

Broadcast on radio on 27 June 1936, the fourth anniversary of the
constitutional system

Dear listeners,

Before I say anything, let me invite all of you to think back to 27 June 1932.
On that day, the hearts of us Siamese, the whole country, were nervous and
unsure. We did not know what the future of the nation would be. Those
who could listen to the radio were determined to wait to hear whether Siam
would have a constitution or not. When the radio announced that the king
had fixed his signature to the provisional constitution, the anxiety was
reduced.

The constitutional system has been established as a democratic system
which respects a human being as a human being, which respects the Thai-
ness *(khwam pen Thai)* of the Siamese people as free *(thai)* people and not as
slaves, which accepts that sovereignty comes from the Siamese people, and
which has the king as the head of state whom we respect and revere. Siam
with the king as head of state in accordance with the constitution has progressed and prospered further day by day to the point that today is the
fourth anniversary of the constitutional system.

I spoke on the radio on 27 June in 1934 and in 1935. In the speeches on
those occasions, I explained the progress which the constitutional
government had made over the three years. Let me say that whatever
progress was made in those three years has been extended even further over
the following year up to today. On the 25th, Luang Thamrongnawasawat
informed you about matters connected with the Ministry of the Interior,
and I hope that you will learn about matters concerning other ministries
from those ministries at an appropriate time.

The constitutional government has worked with effort and care to
progress gradually and steadfastly on all fronts. The constitutional system is
not a system which leaps ahead, but is a system which needs security and
permanence, and which proceeds by calm and meticulous detail. Some
things have to be done slowly. But anything we have done, you can be sure

we have thought it through thoroughly. Each step ahead we must proceed steadfastly. We must choose the footholds which are not muddy lest we slip carelessly. Any path we walk along, we have first cleared and made into a permanent path so that the whole nation can walk along after without hindrance. The nation belongs to the whole Siamese people, not just to the people in the government. When the provisional clauses specified in the constitution expire, those of you who will be entrusted with the task, will be able to use this permanent path conveniently.

The characteristics of the constitutional system have found favour inside the country. In addition, Siam as a constitutional state has gained high favour and credibility from foreign countries. This credibility has conspicuous value which cannot be gained by exchange for assets. We have not exchanged anything with foreign countries to gain this credibility. They find us credible because the constitutional system is a system which brings peace and contentment to humanity. We listen to the voice of the people rather than acting arbitrarily, and we can see that humanity desires peace and comfort. This is the height of happiness, namely peace and contentment. Hence the credibility of foreign countries has conspicuous value as one of the important instruments to protect the kingdom and sustain the independence of the nation. If this credibility should somehow be lost, the future of the nation may be destroyed.

Please study a map of the world. You will see clearly that Siam is one of the small countries among the many, many countries in the world. We cannot exist on our own. We must have trade and friendly relations with other countries. We can plant rice, mine tin, plant rubber, raise animals. We must ask foreign countries to help us by buying the surplus beyond what is used inside the country, in return for money or exchange of goods which we still cannot make, to build our nation to greater prosperity. At the present time, we are always saying that Siam has a very extensive territory. We have land which could be used to expand rice cultivation or animal raising. We have valuable forests. We have mines. And so on. To put it briefly, there are assets in the fields, wealth in the water. But we have not yet made full use of our assets. We live in Siam, but the territory of Siam is left to the ownership of nature. We the people of the Siam cannot yet become owners of these assets in total.

This is because we know we lack people with expertise, and we lack one other important thing—capital for investment. If we are to save up the capital ourselves, it will take a long time. If we wanted to move more quickly, we would have to raise taxes very high, beyond the capacity of the people. But with the credibility of foreign countries, we can solve this problem by hoping for help over capital. We have this credibility already. We have evidence of this. For instance last year, instead of repaying 3 million pounds of loans borrowed overseas and paying interest at 6 percent interest, because of our credibility we could keep that money to invest inside the country and managed to reduce the rate of interest from 6 to 4 percent a year. This gave us benefits both through investment to strengthen the country, and through reduction of the amount of interest due.

We still need to make use of capital, markets, and assistance from abroad to strengthen our country. Shortly we will begin to negotiate new treaties so that our country has equality with others. This matter requires the credibility which we already have because of the constitutional system. The more secure the constitutional system, the more prosperous the people. Siam will have rights on a par with foreign countries. The benefits which we get from the constitutional system are real benefits in reality, not imaginary benefits, benefits in dreams. We can see benefits that are very close at hand. Please help us to clear our path ahead to other destinations and new directions. We may not be sure where we are going. If we suffer a setback, the nation will be lost.

The constitution is the highest dhamma to enable the Siamese people to survive as an independent nation. For those of you who abide by the constitution, who abide by the dhamma, good things will result.

*Dhammo ha veragati dhammacāriṃ*
Dhamma always protects those who practise dhamma.

May you all be resolute to sustain the constitutional system for ever. May I request the power of the three jewels—that is, the Buddha, the Dhamma, and the Sangha—and all the sacred things in the world to protect you all to have happiness and prosperity under the constitutional system at all times. Any wish that you have which is legitimate within the scope of the constitution, may that wish be fulfilled in all respects.

[Translators' Note: The original text of this speech had almost no paragraphing. We have inserted paragraph breaks to improve readability.]

# 15. ESTABLISHMENT OF THE ANTI-JAPAN RESISTANCE MOVEMENT AND SERI THAI (1981)

## THE FEELINGS OF THE THAI PEOPLE
### from Their Own Experience and from Knowing that the Nation Was Invaded by Japan

The majority of Thai people are patriots. Whether they were in Thailand and experienced for themselves that the nation was invaded, or were overseas and heard about it, the feeling arose that they must fight the invaders to recover the independence of the nation.

While I was at a cabinet meeting on the afternoon of 8 December [1941], the Japanese army moved from Battambang to Bangkok, as was reported in the cabinet minutes, which I print here as part 2 [not included in this translation]. When the cabinet meeting ended at 17.55, I returned home by car and noticed many groups of Thai people gathered on both sides of the road and crying. This exact situation appeared in the American newspaper, *Washington Times Herald,* of 18 December from a story which the paper's reporter slipped out of the country, as follows: "The Thailanders, shocked by the news of the surrender, wept as they stood dazed in the streets."

When I reached home, I found several friends waiting for me, such as Luang Bannakonkowit (Pao Chakkaphak), Nai Sanguan Tularak, Nai Chamkat Phalangkun, Nai Wichit Lulitanon, Nai Tiang Sirikhan, Nai Thawin Udon, M.L. Kri Detchatiwong (Luang Detchatiwongwarawat) and so on. The friends who had come to see me explained the feelings of themselves and the majority of the people who had experienced the sight of the Japanese army, a foreign army, invading Thailand. The Thai people had cried, not out of cowardice and fear for their lives, but because of anguish and resentment. Anguish because foreigners had invaded. Resentment because the government had not, as it had announced both in the news-papers and on the radio, made them sacrifice themselves to fight the invaders. Even though they could not fight with weapons, they could burn houses and granaries before the enemy invaded, leaving just the earth for the invaders to seize. As the government slogan ran: "Let the enemy seize only the surface of the earth." The government spokesman had also announced that the citizens should use every weapon available such as guns, swords, pikes, spears, and so on, even poisonous animals and plants such as snakes, centipedes, scorpions, horse-eye beans [*fak mamui*, an irritant plant], and so on (those still alive today who heard the government radio broadcast of that time can probably remember). When the Japanese actually invaded, the army, police, and people at the border were ready to sacrifice their lives to fight them. But the government allowed the Japanese in by not calling on the people to fight.

The group of friends who came to discuss together saw that the people should not rely on the government to preserve the independence of the Thai nation. That is, the government would increasingly have to follow the demands of the Japanese to the point where the country would be totally bound to Japan.

When we had talked together for some time, those at the meeting agreed to dedicate their lives to recover the full independence of the Thai nation. To that end, they agreed to establish an "anti-Japan resistance organization" consisting of patriotic Thai people of all classes and social levels both inside and outside the country. The meeting entrusted me with the duty of being the head and deciding on the future plan of action.


# THE TWO TASKS
## of the Anti-Japan Resistance Organization

The organization had two tasks to perform: first, to fight the Japanese invaders with the Thai patriotic forces, in cooperation with the Allies; second, to make sure the Allies recognized the true intention of the Thai people not to be their enemies.

After the government of Prime Minister Field Marshal Phibun-songkhram declared war and created a state of war with the Allies, this second task was extended as: "to make sure the Allies recognize that Thailand is not on the losing side in the war, and to do anything to lessen the severity of the situation".

If we merely took up armed resistance against the Japanese without making the Allies understand, Thailand would be considered an enemy by the Allies, and Thailand would be on the losing side in the war. But if we used only words to talk with the Allies with no armed action against the Japanese inside Thailand, the Allies would not think this was enough to overcome the problem that Thailand had been involved in the war.

# DISCIPLINE AND CAUTION
## of the Members inside Thailand

I appealed to the founders and later members of the anti-Japan movement in Thailand to bear in mind at all times that for the activities to succeed without loss to the organization, all founders and members must maintain secrecy and act with tight discipline, to prevent the enemy destroying the movement. They must always bear in mind that the activity zone of the movement of resistance against Japan inside the country was territory which had fallen under the occupation of Japan and of a Thai government which was under the power and influence of Japan. The Japanese army which had invaded Thailand had only fighting units and supply units. Suppose Japan brought in units of the special military police which the Japanese call Kempeitai. They had the same nature as the special military police of Italy and Germany known as Gestapo. They had the power to arrest people suspected of being enemies of Japan, and might imprison, torture, or kill them, as Japan had done in the Chinese territory under Japanese occupation.

Besides, the Thai police and military police who had not joined our resistance movement were intent upon suppressing anyone who resisted the Japanese, or who was suspected of preparing to resist the Japanese, against the wishes of the Thai government. Such people could be arrested and jailed by the Thai police or military police. Hence as the members of the resistance movement were still surrounded by the Japanese and by a government under the power and influence of Japan, it was necessary to use caution and work in an "underground" way, or as is known in English as *"cover story"*.

But if the organization were able to seize some territory outside Bangkok and form a resistance government, those who joined the resistance government would not need to work underground but could fight Japan openly and let the Allies know and openly support the resistance government.

Any member of the organization who was ordered by the organization command to work openly in the Allied countries would be free from the threat of the Kempeitai or Japanese Gestapo and of the Thai police and military police under Japanese influence.

# THE PLAN TO SEIZE THE NORTHERN REGION
## to Set Up a Government of Resistance against Japan

When those who came to the meeting to found the anti-Japan resistance movement had talked together and come to this understanding, I asked them all to return home and help one another to study the situation, to

199

consider the thoughts and feelings of the people in general, and to discuss together again after thinking the matter over.

The meeting ended at 11 P.M. on that 8 December.

I asked M.L. Kri Detchatiwong, who was chief engineer in the highway department and a well-known figure in the north (his wife's mother was from the family of Chiang Rai rulers), to talk with me further whether it was appropriate for the resistance movement to seize the northern region, because this region had a back door to Burma which was then under the British. M.L. Kri agreed and advised we should hurry to seize the rail route at Paknampho (Nakhon Sawan) before Japan did. The northern road route at that time reached only to Saraburi and Lopburi.

While I was talking with M.L. Kri around midnight of 8 December, Group Captain Kat Kengradomying (Luang Katsongkhram) arrived at my house and asked to meet me urgently. I had M.L. Kri hide in one room while I met with Gp. Cpt. Kat who was one of the promoters of 24 June. Gp. Cpt. Kat greeted me and stated that he could see nobody who could help the nation. He swore that he was loyal to me and would act on my command to recover the independence of the Thai nation. Then he announced that he was ready to use one army company to take me, him, and trusted friends to travel to Kanchanaburi, and to enter British Burma to organize a government in exile to resist Japan. He hoped that the British government would lend support. I expressed my thanks to Gp. Cpt. Kat, and explained to him that it was not yet time to form a government in exile in Burma because we should establish a government to resist Japan inside our own country, in particular in the northern or northeastern region. The north was more appropriate because it had a back door to British Burma. Besides, Gp. Cpt. Kat was from Chiang Mai and could probably assist with this plan. Gp. Cpt. Kat said he agreed with my plan. I thus asked him whether he had trusted friends in the military stationed at Nakhon Sawan. He replied that he had friends who were sufficiently close and reliable. I thus asked him whether he was willing to travel by motorboat as quickly as possible to Paknampho (Nakhon Sawan) and contact his military friends to help the nation by seizing the railway line at and around Paknampho, and blocking the Japanese from moving troops to the north where our group would secretly go to establish the government to resist Japan. Gp. Cpt. Kat travelled by motorboat in the early morning of 9 December. On the 11th, he returned and reported to me that when he reached Nakhon Sawan, the Japanese had already seized the railway. Hence we had to find another way.

I saw that even though the plan to seize the railway at Nakhon Sawan could not be carried through, that had not wrecked the plan to organize forces in the provinces by the method of setting up several units secretly in various localities. This plan is covered in the report of 7 May 1946 of the special committee of the Assembly to investigate the national property which the Seri Thai had expended both inside and outside the country. I also had it published in the book *Letters of Nai Pridi Banomyong to Phra Phisan Sukhumwit about the Records of Seri Thai Concerning Actions in Kandy, New Delhi, and the USA, with appendices on several matters concerning Seri Thai,* in both Thai and English [the English version: *Political and Military Task of the Free-Thai Movement to Regain National Sovereignty and Independence,* Bangkok: American, 1979].

## JAPAN DEMANDS THE THAI GOVERNMENT
### to Remove Me and Nai Wilat Osathanon from the Cabinet by Making Me a Regent

On 16 December 1941 the Assembly passed a resolution approving the proposal of the cabinet to appoint me to one of the vacant posts of regent (as Chaophraya Yommarat had passed away).

The background of this event appears in the primary documents as follows.

Testimony of Police Major General Adun Adundetcharat, deputy prime minister, given under oath before the war crimes tribunal on 17 December 1945.

"I went to the Suan Kulap palace, the residence of the prime minister. I met the prime minister and Nai Wanit Pananon. Nai Wanit said that the Japanese disliked Luang Praditmanutham and Nai Wilat Osathanon because these two leant towards the British. Any matter that the cabinet agreed with Japan could not be pursued smoothly because these two did not see eye to eye with Japan. He wanted these two out of the cabinet. As for Luang Pradit in particular, the Japanese proposed he should be appointed to the Regency Council. As to why Japan wanted Luang Pradit as regent, I think they understood that Luang Pradit was someone who had influence, and who commanded the respect of officials and people. If he became a regent, he would be removed from political duty but it would not appear, the Japanese thought, that the Japanese were mistreating him. After Nai Wanit had spoken with me, the prime minister spoke with me in the same vein. He asked me to inform Luang Pradit, Nai Wilat Osathanon, and Nai Thawi Bunyaket and then proceed with the matter further. Thus I asked the three individuals to Suan Kulap palace and explained to them what was desired and why. Luang Pradit responded that he would consult with his group first. Nai Wilat had no objection. That evening Luang Pradit came to meet me at my residence at Parusakawan palace, and explained that he had consulted with his group but still felt uneasy that joining the Regency Council might appear inappropriate or unseemly. I tried several ways to explain the long-term necessity. Finally Luang Pradit agreed. Nai Thawi Bunyaket arranged matters for Luang Pradit and Nai Wilat to leave the cabinet and for Luang Pradit to join the Regency Council."

A note by Nai Thawi Bunyaket under the title "Additional facts about events in Thailand during the Second World War by Nai Thawi Bunyaket" was printed in the book by Nai Direk Jayanama entitled *Siam and World War II,* published in 1957, pages 357–59, as follows [N.B. this passage was not included in the English version of Direk's book]:

Later, on what date I cannot recall, but I think between 10 and 12 December or thereabouts, and certainly not many days after the government signed the agreement allowing the Japanese army to pass through Thailand, the Japanese government began negotiations to borrow a first instalment of money from Thailand to pay Japanese military expenses. Nai Pridi Banomyong, minister of finance, proposed to the cabinet meeting that we should realize that giving the Japanese government money for their military expenses would not end here. Probably they would ask for loans again and again without end according to their military needs. If we gave the loans, we would have to print more banknotes, which would rapidly increase the number of banknotes in circulation in the market. This would have a bad effect on the economy. It would create inflation. Hence it would be better to make the Japanese military print their own notes to use inside their own army, and call them invasion notes. Thus when the war was over, we could cancel these notes. In that way, when the war was over the finance and economy of the country would not be affected, and there would be no inflation. The prime minister countered that although acting on the opinion and proposal of the minister of finance would prevent inflation, it would be equivalent to showing that we had lost independence and sovereignty, and hence he did not agree. The minister of finance replied that the fact we had allowed the Japanese army to enter all over the place and do whatever they liked, surely implied that we had already lost independence and sovereignty. On this point there was violent argument between the prime minister and the finance minister, but in the end the prime minister remained steadfast in his opinion in favour of lending baht to the Japanese army by printing additional notes according to necessity. A few days later, the cabinet was reshuffled. Nai Pridi Banomyong was removed from the post of minister of finance and became a regent, for which one position was vacant. About the same time another two or three ministers were removed from their posts. As far as I can remember, Nai Direk Jayanama was removed as minister of foreign affairs (later sent as ambassador to Tokyo), and Nai Wilat Osathanon. As it happened, we had to go on continuously printing notes for the Japanese army to borrow and use with a certain amount of gold stored in Japan as guarantee and later with a large amount of yen as guarantee also. Besides, the Japanese government adjusted the exchange rate between baht and yen, increasing the value of the yen up to one yen to one baht, which before had been 1.50 yen to one baht. This arose from the loan because Japan wanted to repay us with a smaller amount of yen.

# THAMMASAT UNIVERSITY AS THE SECRET LOCATION
of the Command Headquarters for the Resistance Organization Which Later used the Name "Seri Thai Movement", and as Detention Camp for British and Americans during the War

I was still rector of the University of Moral and Political Sciences.

I established an understanding with the prime minister (Phibun) and deputy prime minister (Adun) that while the Japanese were not happy for me to be in the cabinet which was a political post, the rectorship was not a political post. Besides I had accepted this post with the approval of the Assembly according to the act establishing Thammasat University. I maintained I should continue in the rectorship. The government had no objection.

I used the university as the command headquarters of the anti-Japan movement which later united with the Seri Thai in the USA and Britain and used the name "Seri Thai movement".

# DETENTION CAMP FOR BRITISH AND AMERICANS
during the War

On 11 December 1941 the Thai government and the Japanese concluded an agreement on military cooperation. The Thai government made preparations to arrest British and American nationals and detain them as enemy nationals. If the Thai government did not make such arrangements, the Japanese army would. The Thai government entrusted Police Major General Adun, deputy prime minister, to carry this out.

The deputy prime minister came to see me and asked to divide off part of

Thammasat University to detain these nationals. He also asked the university to arrange for its staff to take care of this detention camp. As camp commander, the army appointed M.R. Phongphrom Chakraphan, a reserve major serving as an official in the customs department of the Finance Ministry. He had previously been one of my subordinates. The army asked the university staff to arrange the best possible accommodation for the detainees.

As rector I accepted the deputy prime minister's proposals, because I saw that first, these nationals in Thailand would avoid detention by the Japanese who might use the torture methods which the Japanese had already inflicted on British and Americans inside Japan; and second, helping nationals of the Allied countries was one way to make the Allies treat Thailand less harshly in the event that the Allies won the war.

I entrusted Nai Wichit Lulitanon, secretary general of the university, who was also secretary general of the resistance movement henceforth known as the Seri Thai movement, to be head of the university staff in charge of accommodation for the detainees.

The university welcomed and watched over these detainees to the best of its ability to prevent the Japanese grabbing and torturing them.

After the Second World War, Lord Mountbatten divulged to the *Times* newspaper of 18 December 1946 as follows:

> There are, I know, many who were prisoners of war in Siam who have good reason to be grateful for Pradit's good will to us. So let us honour a man who has rendered high service to the allied cause and to his own country, and who from my personal knowledge of him is a firm advocate of Anglo-Siamese friendship. The chain of local resistance to Japanese oppression in the occupied lands of South-East Asia had very few gaps in it, and one of the strongest links was forged by Pradit in Siam. (Loud and prolonged cheers.)

In addition, there are documents of the British Special Forces Club of 17 December 1970 concerning me as follows:

01-589-0490
01-589-4315

SPECIAL FORCES CLUB
8 Herbert Crescent
Knightsbridge
London S.W.1

17th December 1970

H.E. Nai Pridi Banamyong
E.c. 3 – 5
17, rue Emile Dubois,
PARIS XIVe.

Your Excellency,
It was the unanimous decision of the Committee that I should write to express the wish that you would accept our invitation to be an Honorary Member of this Club.

As you know, the Club was formed in 1945 by and for those who served in Special Forces and who were engaged in resistance and underground movements during the 1939/45 war.

It would give us, and all members of the Club, great pleasure to learn that Your Excellency will accept this Honorary Membership. I know that it would give particular pleasure to those members, both Thai and British formerly in the Siam Country Section of Force 136 who in the war years worked so closely with and received at all times such steadfast support and encouragement from you.

This invitation is offered as a mark of our acknowledgement and high appreciation of the outstanding part played by Your Excellency in promoting and sustaining the resistance movement which in days of peril and hazard rendered service to both our countries.

I am, Your Excellency,
Yours sincerely,
[signed] Geoffrey H. Walford
CHAIRMAN

As the university had given a good welcome to the detainees, and protected them safely from the Japanese, one day Professor Hutchenson, a Thammasat professor detained in the camp, told a student who was on the staff looking after the camp that he had observed the university's conduct towards the detainees was better than Japanese conduct towards detainees in

205

China. He wondered whether the students had set up a movement like the Free French. The student replied that he should put the question to someone senior. This surmise among the detainees got through to the staff of the US embassy in Bangkok who were detained inside the embassy itself. The facts appeared in the report of 18 August 1942 by Mr. Chapman, former second secretary in the American embassy in Bangkok. This report was disclosed twenty-five years after the event in the US government volume on "Foreign Relations of the United States" 1942, volume 1, pages 917–920:

> At the time of my departure from Bangkok on June 29, 1942, the Thai Government appeared to be under the control of and subservient to the Japanese military although still nominally independent. The pre-war Council of Ministers remained in office with a few exceptions. As previously noted, Luang Pradist Manudharm, pre-war Minister of Finance, who has so stoutly resisted Japanese attempts at financial penetration and who has staunch pro-Allied sentiments, has been "promoted" to the Council of Regency to eliminate him from political activities inimical to Japan. . . Luang Vichitr had recently become Foreign Minister. Nai Direck, the pre-war Foreign Minister, was safely under observation as Thai Ambassador in Tokyo. As indicated in a previous paragraph the only notable absentee was Nai Vilas Osathananda, formerly Director General of the Publicity Department.
>
> Indications of the development of a "Free Thai" movement organized by university students were reported. Evidently the objectives of such a movement would be to create an underground revolutionary group which at a propitious moment would seize the power and free the country from the Japanese yoke and the control of its present . . . leaders. Whether the small group of liberal and pro-Allied leaders who are still in the Government . . . are connected with this movement is not known.

## THE ESTABLISHMENT OF SERI THAI
### in the USA and Britain

Let me recount the feeling of the majority of patriotic Thais in the USA and Britain, and the attitude of the US and British governments towards the establishment of Seri Thai in the two countries.

I have already related how the Thais in Thailand experienced firsthand the Japanese invasion from 8 December 1941 onwards which created the desire to found the anti-Japan resistance movement to recover the full independence of the Thai nation. Among the Thais in the USA and Britain also, the desire arose to form an organization to resist the Japanese and recover the independence of the Thai nation. Although they received news somewhat late, these overseas Thais did not waste much time in putting out a statement opposing Japan, and considering forming a resistance organization.

On 11 December 1941, three days after Japan invaded Thailand, M.R. Seni Pramoj, Thai ambassador in Washington, made a statement to the press and sent a telegram to the Thai government in Bangkok. The gist was that the Thai embassy in Washington would carry out those orders from the government which the embassy saw were not orders issued on the command of the Japanese. One day later on 12 December, the embassy heard the news that the Thai government had made an agreement of military cooperation with Japan. The embassy informed the American government that the embassy did not recognize this agreement with the Japanese government, and that the ambassador and embassy officials were preparing to form the Seri Thai organization. The American government consulted with the British government. However, the British government replied to the American government in a memo from the British embassy on 24 January 1941 which appeared in the US government volume already mentioned (Foreign Relations of the United States) 1941, volume 5, page 302, as follows:

711.92/33
    The British Embassy to the Department of State
                 AIDE-MEMOIRE

His Majesty's Government in the United Kingdom welcomes the proposal made in the State Department's memorandum of December 18th to continue to recognize the Thai Minister in Washington as the representative in the United States of the free people of Thailand. When the question of setting up a Free Thai movement arises, the personalities of possible leaders will naturally require careful consideration, and His Majesty's Government are now going into this question so far as the United Kingdom is concerned. The Thai Minister in London has shown no wish to come out into open opposition to the regime in Bangkok, and His Majesty's Government consider that it will be best to arrange for his departure.

When the American government received this memo from the British embassy, it replied by a memo on 19 January 1942, which appeared in the same volume for 1942, volume 1, pages 913–914, as follows:

With regard to the Thai Minister in Washington this Government has decided, after careful consideration of all factors involved, not to proceed at present with the proposal to recognize the minister as "the representative in the United States of the free people of Thailand", and intends for the time being to continue to recognize him as "Minister of Thailand".

With regards to the text of the statement which the British Government proposes to issue in London, this Government considers that it would be preferable to defer the issuance of any statements by the British and the United States Governments until such time as word shall have been received that the British and the American Ministers to Thailand have safely departed from the country. This Government agrees that any statements issued in regard to Thailand by the British Government, the Netherlands Government and the United States Government should not conflict.

Washington, January 19, 1942

Although the British government reserved judgement on recognizing the Thai ambassador in Washington as the head of the Seri Thai movement, yet the ambassador and embassy officials in Washington received assistance from the US government to establish Seri Thai forces of Thai patriots and volunteers to go to Thailand to fight the Japanese.

The Seri Thai movement in the USA called the organization in English the *"Free Thai Movement"*.

The great majority of Thais in Great Britain joined the Seri Thai in Britain. Males were trained as British soldiers to go and fight the Japanese in Thailand. Those interested in the details should read the chapter by Nai Puey Ungphakorn, "Temporary soldier", published in the book by Nai Direk Jayanama on Siam in World War II.

As the British government still referred to Thailand as *"Siam"* and the Thais as *"Siamese"*, in Britain the Seri Thai movement was called the *"Free Siamese Movement"*.

Later when the anti-Japanese resistance movement inside the country had united with the Seri Thai in the USA and Britain, we called our movement the "Seri Thai movement".

Yet the British government documents still referred to the *"Resistance Movement"*, hence in announcements and official agreements with the British government, we called it in English the *"Thai Resistance Movement"*.

# SOME DIFFERENCES BETWEEN THE SERI THAI MOVEMENT
and the Claims of the CPT in Resisting Japan

The Chinese annual encyclopedia *"su chia chu su nian tian"* or "encyclopedia of world knowledge" which was published several years running from 1958, claimed that the Communist Party of Thailand was founded on 1 December 1942. That means the CPT was founded eleven months and twenty-three days after the Japanese army invaded Thailand. Documents of the Communist Party of Thailand after 1949 uphold the same claim as this encyclopedia. This day was regularly celebrated as foundation day. This indicates that the party was founded later than the anti-Japan resistance organization and the Seri Thai in the USA and Britain.

Many Chinese journals and documents have pronouncements by the CPT claiming that it led the Thai people to fight the Japanese. But a new announcement was made later maintaining 7 August 1965 as the day known in Isan language as the "day of the gun shot", meaning the day when the CPT shot an enemy. This was twenty-three years after the Chinese encyclopedia and the CPT claim that the party was founded in 1942, and twenty years after the end of the Second World War.

There is no evidence that the CPT communicated to any Allied country that it had joined the armed struggle against the Japanese. Moreover, there is a point for concern. If two parties making war against the common Japanese enemy each fought in its own different way without a common military plan, they would be at a disadvantage. One party might strike before the right time and provoke the Japanese to destroy Thailand before Allied help could arrive. Take the example of the Polish communists who rushed to launch their struggle against Germany before the Allies could send troops to help. Or consider if the Allies had mobilized forces to attack the Japanese when the CPT was not yet ready. That would have resulted in damage to the Allies and the people's forces organized by the CPT.

In the Chinese encyclopedia and documents of the CPT, there is no evidence they made any understanding with the Allies. Communists in the Allied nations have not stated that the CPT made any agreement that if the CPT led forces to fight the Japanese, the Allies would recognize Thailand as not on the losing side of the war. Hence when Japan admitted defeat, what could the CPT have done to make the Allied countries recognize Thailand was not on the losing side of the war—even after the Thai government had declared war and created a state of war with Great Britain, USA, and China? Would the CPT have led the Thai people to fight on alone against Britain, USA, and China until these countries recognized that Thailand was not on the losing side?

# 16. WHAT HAPPENED INSIDE THE REGENCY COUNCIL

[Translators' note: In section II of this piece, we have simplified some of the elaborate royal names and titles. Please see appendix 3 for a description of most of the titles and ranks mentioned. From section VI onwards, Pridi consistently refers to Phibun as *chom phon po*, Field Marshal P., the usual Thai contraction of his name. We have rendered these as "Phibun".]

I

When King Prajadhipok travelled to Europe in January 1934, the Assembly passed a resolution to approve the royal wish to appoint Somdet Chaofa Kromphra Naritsaranuwatiwong as regent from 12 January onwards by royal decree.

II

Later King Prajadhipok abdicated the throne on 2 March 1935 at 13.45 (British time). Somdet Chaofa Kromphra Naritsara hence was relieved of his duty as regent.

The government of prime minister Phraya Phahon Phonphayuhasena proceeded according to the constitution of the kingdom of Siam 1932 clause 9 which runs:

> The succession to the throne will proceed according to the intent of the Royal Household Act on the Succession, 1924 and with the approval of the Assembly.

It was the grace of King Vajiravudh (Rama VI) to have issued the Royal Household Act, 1924 which was re-enacted by the provisional constitution of 27 June 1932 and the constitution of the kingdom of Siam 1932.

Students who have studied the royal chronicles of Ayutthaya, Thonburi, and Rattanakosin will remember that previously after the death of a king very serious problems arose over the choice of a successor because there was no royal household law with a clear ruling. In the case that the *upparat* ("front palace" or heir apparent) was still alive, then the custom was followed for him to succeed. But there were many cases in the past when the heir apparent died before the king and no heir had been established.

When King Phutthaloetla (Rama II) ruled the country, he appointed Somdet Phra Anuchathirat formerly called "Chaofa Chui" as *upparat* with the name Somdet Phra Mahasenanurak. He had sons with various consorts. For instance, with Chaochom Samli, the daughter of King Taksin, he had many sons including Phraongchao Phong-itsaret, the founder of the Itsarasena family. With Chaochom Sap, he had Phraongchao Phumarin who was the founder of the Phumarin family (Momratchawong Chiak Phumarin entered the na Pombejra family as the mother of Phraya Chaiwichit Wisitthammathada, the father of Thanphuying Phoonsuk Banomyong). But this *upparat* died before his brother King Phutthaloetla (Rama II) who did not appoint another prince as *upparat*. Thus when King Rama II died, his son Krommun Chetsadabodin, who at the time held the rank of *phraongchao*, arising from the fact that his mother had been born as a commoner, ascended the throne before Somdet Chaofa Mongkut whose mother had the rank of *somdet chaofa*.

When King Phra Nangklao (Rama III) died without having appointed a son or any prince as *upparat* in place of Somdet Phra Mahasakdiphonlasep who had died earlier, members of the court and senior officials together invited Somdet Chaofa Mongkut to ascend the throne as King Mongkut (Rama IV).

When King Mongkut died without having appointed a son or any prince as *upparat* and successor in place of Somdet Phra Pinklao who died before the king, members of the court and senior officials together invited Somdet Chaofa Chulalongkorn to ascend the throne under the name King Chulalongkorn (Rama V), and later invited Phraongchao Yotyingyot (who had another name as Phraongchao "George Washington"), son of the late *upparat*, to have the title as *upparat*.

This *upparat* passed away. Then King Chulalongkorn issued a decree abolishing the position of *upparat*, and appointing his son Somdet Chaofa Vajirunhis, son of Queen Savarintra, as crown prince. When this prince died, King Chulalongkorn appointed his son Somdet Chaofa Vajiravudh, son of Queen Saowaphaphongsri. The king later elevated her to a higher rank than Queen Savarintra, the mother of Somdet Chaofa Vajirunhis who had passed away already.

When King Chulalongkorn passed away, members of the court and senior officials together invited Somdet Chaofa Vajiravudh to ascend the throne as King Vajiravudh (Rama VI).

King Vajiravudh appointed Somdet Chaofa Chakrabong, his younger brother from the same mother, as heir. But he passed away before the king.

Hence he appointed Somdet Chaofa Atsadang, another younger brother by the same mother, to be heir. But he also passed away before the king. So he appointed Somdet Chaofa Prajadhipok, younger brother by the same mother, as heir. Somdet Chaofa Chuthathut, another younger brother born to the same mother before Somdet Chaofa Prajadhipok, had passed away earlier.

## III

The cabinet deliberated for five days from 2 to 7 March [1935] over which member of the Chakri royal family was appropriate for the government to propose for the approval of the Assembly as the future king. The constitution stated the succession must proceed "according to the intent (*doi nai*) of the royal household law". At that time there were several princes with the rank of *phraongchao*, sons of several different *somdet chaofa*. Many ministers had not studied the royal household law to gain a clear understanding. I had studied it somewhat in order to teach the course on administrative law at the law school of the Justice Ministry in 1931. So I explained the major principles of the royal household law which prescribed the order of succession for various cases, that is: 1. where the king has sons or grandsons; 2. where the king has no son or grandson but has younger brothers by the same major queen (*phraratchachonnani*), or sons of such a brother; 3. where the king has no son, grandson, or younger brother by the same major queen, but has elder or younger brothers by another major queen, or sons by such brothers; 4. where the king has no son, grandson, younger brothers by the same major queen, or brothers by another major queen, but has other siblings (*prachao phiyathoe* or *phrachao nongyathoe*) or sons by such siblings; 5. where the king has no son, grandson, younger brother by the same major queen, or brother by another major queen, or other siblings, but has uncles (who are sons of kings) or sons of such uncles.

But the details of the succession order (which the royal family calls *pochiam*), were unknown to almost every minister except Phraya Woraphong (M.R. Yen Itsarasena), minister of the palace, who had knowledge about these things. The others did not know the details of the sons and fathers of each prince; whether they had ranks as *momchao*, *phraongchao*, or *somdet chaofa*; how some sons of the king were *phraongchao* and some were *somdet chaofa*; how sons of a *phraongchao* might be *phraongchao* or *momchao*. So it took some time to study before they could grasp royal custom. The rank on the mother's side also had to be taken into consideration. The son of a king whose mother has the rank of *phraakkarachayathoe* or above had the rank *somdet chaofa*. Then among *somdet chaofa* there were different levels of seniority, depending on whether the mother was *somdet phrabaromma ratchini, somdet phranangchao phrabarommaratchathewi, phranangchao phraratchathewi, phranangthoe,* or *phra akkarachayathoe.*

As for sons of a *somdet chaofa,* the mother had to be taken into account. If she was *phraongchao,* the son became *phrachao worawongthoe phraongchao.* If the mother was a commoner, the son of a *somdet chaofa* used to be ranked *momchao.* But on 8 November 1927 King Prajadhipok made an announcement raising the existing and future sons of many *somdet chaofa* to be "*phra worawongthoe*" *phraongchao,* which was the royal rank below "*phrachao worawongthoe*" *phraongchao.*

As for sons of a ruling king (*phrachao lukyathoe*) who were born as *phraongchao,* if the mother was *phraongchao,* they received the title of *phraworawongthoe phraongchao* from birth. An example was Phraongchao Prempurachat, son of Krom Kamphaengphet and Phraongchaoying Praphawasit. If the mother was a commoner, he would be only *momchao.*

Apart from that, there were still *momchao, phraongchao, somdet chaofa* in the household of the heir apparent and many other high-ranking royal family members.

The first point which the cabinet studied was whether King Prajadhipok had an elder brother by the same mother who had sons still living.

1. Phraongchao Chula Chakrabong was son of Somdet Chaofa Chakrabongphuwanat who had been heir to the throne during the Sixth Reign. The cabinet studied the phrase "according to the intent" in the royal household law of 1924 to see whether Phraongchao Chula Chakrabong should be excluded according to clause 11(4) of the royal household law on grounds that his mother was of foreign nationality. According to a strict reading, the law excluded only successors who had a foreign wife (at the time Phraongchao Chula Chakrabong had no foreign wife). Some cabinet members considered that the exclusion had been applied to other heirs but had not been applied in the case of Somdet Chaofa Chakrabongphuwanat who was appointed heir by King Vajiravudh when he already had a foreign wife who had been properly accepted as a royal daughter-in-law. However, the majority of the cabinet interpreted the words "according to the intent" to indicate that the exclusion should also apply in the case of a successor who had a foreign mother.

2. Phraongchao Waranon was son of Somdet Chaofa Chuthathut, who was brother of King Prajadhipok by the same mother. But ministers considered that his mother was a commoner and not the major wife of Somdet Chaofa Chuthathut, whose major wife had been a *momchao,* had been granted a royal wedding ceremony, but had had no son. The cabinet meeting left Phraongchao Waranon out of consideration.

Then it was discussed whether the case following King Prajadhipok's abdication was a case "where the king has no son, grandson, or younger brother by the same major queen, but has elder or younger brothers by another major queen, or sons by such brothers".

At that time, Chaofa Boriphat Kromphra Nakhonsawan Woraphinit was still alive. But he had gone to live abroad at the request of the People's Party. Hence the cabinet did not consider him and his many sons, by referring to the words "according to the intent". Thus the meeting discussed the sons of King Prajadhipok's brothers by different mothers. Information was obtained from Chaophraya Woraphong that there were sons of Somdet Chaofa Mahidol and Somdet Chaofa Yukhon.

Between these two *somdet chaofa*, the mother of Somdet Chaofa Mahidol had the title of *somdet phrabarommaratchathewi*, which was higher than the mother of Somdet Chaofa Yukhon. But among their sons, the mother of those of Somdet Chaofa Yukhon was *phraongchao*, while the mother of those of Somdet Chaofa Mahidol was Mom [denotes a commoner] Sangwan (her name at that time), but she had been granted a royal wedding ceremony, properly accepted as a royal in-law, and elevated by Somdet Chaofa Mahidol as his only wife (*phrachaya*). Taking into consideration that Somdet Chaofa Mahidol had done beneficial deeds for the people, had been a royal family member who conducted himself as a democrat, and had been accorded love and respect by most people, the cabinet unanimously agreed to propose to the Assembly to approve inviting Phraworawongthoe Phraongchao Ananda Mahidol. On 8 November 1927, King Prajadhipok had already elevated Momchao Ananda Mahidol and many *momchao* born of *somdet chaofa* to be *phraworawongthoe phraongchao*. Hence on 7 March 1935, the Assembly approved the government proposal to invite Phraworawongthoe Phraong-chao Ananda Mahidol to ascend the throne, with the resolution backdated so that he succeeded from the day and time that King Prajadhipok abdi-cated, that is 2 March 1935 at 13.45 (British time).

The backdating of the announcement of King Ananda Mahidol's ascension to the throne followed the international royal practice which considers that the throne is not shaken by any circumstance even the death and succession of a new king. Thus people in many countries bless the king with the cry "*the king is dead long, live the king*" which means that the king has passed away but at the same time may the king prosper.

# IV

At that time, King Ananda Mahidol was nine years old and still a minor. He could not administer royal affairs and he could not appoint a regent. Hence there had to be one or more persons to act as regents according to clause 10 of the constitution of the kingdom of Siam 1932. If the parliament has not yet appointed anyone as regent, the constitution allows the cabinet to undertake that duty temporarily.

The cabinet at that time had General Phraya Phahon Phonphayuhasena as prime minister and also commander of the army; General Luang Phibunsongkhram as minister of defence and deputy army commander; Commodore Luang Sinthusongkhramchai as minister without portfolio and chief of staff of the navy; myself as minister of the interior with command over the police department because at that time Police General Adundetcharat was deputy director of police; and other ministers who had no part in overseeing armed forces. This cabinet did not in any way grasp the opportunity offered by the constitution to fail to propose regents, and carry out the duty itself. This happened on a later occasion. When King Bhumibol Adulyadej was travelling by ship from Singapore through the Gulf of Siam before reaching Bangkok around the end of November and beginning of December 1951, the Radio Coup took place. This caused the regents appointed by the king to relinquish their posts. The cabinet which had Field Marshal Phibunsongkhram as prime minister carried out the duty of regent. Hence Phibun attended in audience at Ratchaworadit pier twice—once as regent and again as a member of the cabinet. (At that time I was in Beijing. I turned on the radio to listen to the Bangkok station and heard these events which I still remember. I expect some in Bangkok can still remember.)

Phraya Phahon's cabinet decided it should propose to the Assembly to appoint a regent immediately after the Assembly on 7 March had approved inviting Phraongchao Ananda Mahidol to ascend the throne. In this matter they had to sound out in advance those whom the cabinet considered suitable as regent. They entrusted the prime minister and myself as minister of the interior to attend in audience on Somdet Chaofa Naritsaranuwattiwong to ask him to become regent for the new king. But Somdet Chaofa Naritsara said he had been a regent for King Prajadhipok. If he agreed to become regent for the new king, people would gossip that he wanted to be regent all the time. He asked the cabinet to consider other princes and suitable senior officials.

The cabinet met and decided there should be three regents as a council, with a royal family member as chairman, another as council member, and another senior official with knowledge and expertise about government of the realm.

In the discussion over which royal family member would be suitable as chairman of the regents, it emerged that most of the royal family members at that time had gone to live overseas following the event known as the Boworadej Rebellion. Those still in Siam apart from Somdet Chaofa Naritsara included one with a *krom* rank, that is Phraongchao Otsakanutit

Krommun Anuwatchaturon, who was a son of Somdet Chaofa Chakra-phatdiphong. General Phraya Phahon knew him well because they had served together as royal guards of King Prajadhipok. As for me, the prince knew me since I was a student in Paris. He accompanied Somdet Chaofa-ying Walai-alongkorn Kromluang Phetchaburi Ratchasirinthon, elder sister of Somdet Chaofa Mahidol by the same parents, on the occasion she went for medical care in France. Krommun Anuwatchaturon asked me to take him sightseeing in Paris many times. I held him in very high regard as someone who behaved as an exemplary democrat and did not conduct himself like a prince of high rank. Sometimes he did the cooking in the embassy kitchen himself. I still remember that there were some delicious dishes which I learned from him by buying the fresh food he wanted and acting as his assistant.

When General Phraya Phahon and I went to his department to ask permission to propose his name to the Assembly for approval as chairman of the Regency Council, he gave his consent.

Then Phraongchao Athit Thippha-apha, the royal secretary in the time of King Prajadhipok, came to see Gen. Phraya Phahon and me at the Parut-sakawan Palace, bringing various documents for Gen. Phraya Phahon and me to study. Gen. Phraya Phahon and I saw that he had cooperated well with the government so we sounded him out about proposing his name as another regent. He was pleased. (As for my part, he knew me from the time he was studying in England. He came to Paris many times and sometimes asked me to be his guide. I saw that he did not conduct himself like someone of high rank but acted as a model democrat, different from some people at the tail end of the royal court who puffed themselves up as royal family even more than the *momchao*.)

As for senior officials, the cabinet considered principal grand councillor, Chaophraya Yommarat Chatsenangkhanarin. He had previously served King Chulalongkorn and earned the royal confidence in important positions such as acting chargé d'affaires of Siam in London at the time Siam had a dispute with France in 1893, later commissioner of Nakhon Si Thammarat mon-thon which also administered the area of the seven Thai-Islam provincial centres, and later minister of public works in the Ministry of the Capital. While he was studying in England, King Vajiravudh elevated Chaophraya Yommarat to the status of his preceptor (*phra achan*) as detailed in the golden tablet (*suphannabat)* granting him a high rank. In the reign of King Vajiravudh, the Ministry of the Capital was combined with the Ministry of the Interior, and Chaophraya Yommarat was appointed as minister of the interior. In the new system, he continued to serve through to the reign of King Prajadhipok and then asked to resign. Hence he was the most senior among the high officials. Gen. Phraya Phahon asked me to sound him out, but I asked to excuse myself fearing that people would criticize me for favouring my own relatives (see appendix [not included here, but the details are the same as those appearing in selection 3 above]). I asked Gen. Phraya Phahon to sound him out himself. After being sounded out, he was pleased to allow his name to be proposed to the Assembly for approval as a member of the Council of Regents.

After the Assembly on 7 March approved the government's proposal to invite Phraongchao Ananda Mahidol to become king, the Assembly approved the appointment of a Regency Council consisting of: Krommun Anuwatchaturon, chairman; Phraongchao Athit Thippha-apha, regent; principal grand councillor Chaophraya Yommarat (Pan Sukhum), regent.

# V

News that saddened me greatly arrived at the time the ocean liner "Caen Verde" [Pridi transliterates this in Thai as *kong werde*; Caen is a guess] in which I was travelling to Europe to negotiate the reduction of interest on government loans and sound out foreign countries on amending the unequal treaties, docked at Brindisi in Italy on 13 August 1935. A foreign fellow passenger bought an English newspaper to read and came upon the headline that Prince Anuwat, regent of Siam, had committed suicide. This foreigner brought the newspaper for me to read. I did not believe the news was true and told him this news was not credible because before I left Siam I had gone to say farewell to him and saw no sign that he would commit suicide. The foreigner replied that the news from the reliable press agencies must be true. I travelled in that ship to Trieste in order to visit a shipyard where a Thai naval officer was stationed. Then I postponed my meeting with Mussolini and quickly travelled by train direct to Lausanne to attend on King Ananda Mahidol, his younger brother, Somdet Phra Anucha (Rama IX), and their mother. I requested Luang Siriratchamaitri, royal secretary, to show me the telegram from the government. The contents were the same as I had read in the newspaper already mentioned. There were no details on how or why he had committed suicide. So I hastened to Paris and received a report from General Luang Adundetcharat. Luang Adun himself had performed the autopsy on Krommun Anuwat. It appeared he had shot himself in the mouth by putting the gun in his lips and pressing the trigger with his own finger. The bullet had passed through the roof of his mouth killing him. Interrogation of his wife and people in the household revealed that before his death he had once said "now if we do anything even bending a finger there are people who complain". Later I had further information that some royal family members had disparaged him for becoming chairman of the Regency Council with the support of the People's Party. Someone wrote an anonymous letter with various denunciations. (If the police department has kept its investigation records, they might be disclosed now. At that time almost every newspaper in Bangkok carried details of the suicide but people skilled at shouting in cinemas had not yet appeared in Siam.)

Later, on 20 August of that year, the cabinet proposed to the Assembly to approve appointment of Chaophraya Phichaiyentharayothin to the vacant post of regent, and the Assembly agreed. The Council of Regents from then on consisted of:

> Phraongchao Athit, chairman
> Chaophraya Yommarat, regent
> Chaophraya Phichaiyentharayothin (Um Intharayothin), regent

Chaophraya Phichaiyentharayothin was descended from Chaofa Thonginthon who was son of King Taksin of Thonburi. He did not join the People's Party. By chance on the morning of 24 June 1932, he went for his usual morning walk (he had already left government service) and arrived in front of the railings of the Ananta Samakhom throne hall. He saw Gen. Phraya Phahon, who had already announced the seizure of power in the name of the People's Party, using an iron bar to force the lock on a chain around the gate in the railings. Gen. Phraya Phahon had very strong muscular arms. Chaophraya Phichaiyen walked up to look and said "this lot *are* capable". Then he went away. Later when the People's Party held merit-making ceremonies, he often took the trouble to attend. He thus earned the respect of the People's Party.

# VI

Later Chaophraya Yommarat passed away. The Assembly had not appointed anyone to the vacant post. The Japanese who had seized the country since 8 December 1941 informed Phibun, the prime minister, that I was obstructing friendly relations between Japan and Thailand, and requested the Thai government to arrange for me to relinquish the ministership and take a post which had no executive power. Phibun had Police General Adundetcharat inform me that I was requested to relinquish the post of minister of finance, and that if I agreed, a resolution would be proposed to the Assembly to appoint me to the vacant post among the regents. I agreed for my name to be proposed to the Assembly for this position, because I saw that the post of regent was really a small burden. This would give me time secretly to organize the anti-Japan resistance movement later known as the

Seri Thai movement. Also I would be relieved from taking part in a government which cooperated with the Japanese.

The Assembly passed a unanimous resolution to appoint me as regent on 16 December 1941. I took the oath before the Assembly to assume the new office on the 23rd of the same month.

Later on 21 July 1942 Chaophraya Phichaiyentharayothin passed away and the Assembly did not appoint a replacement. So only two persons remained on the Regency Council, namely Phraongchao Athit Thipphaapha as chairman and myself.

Later on 31 July 1944 Phraongchao Athit resigned for reasons described below.

The Assembly hence passed a resolution on 1 August of the same year to appoint me as sole regent.

## VII

King Ananda Mahidol reached his majority on 20 September 1945. But because communications were not easy, he could not travel back to Bangkok and could not appoint a regent. The Assembly exercised its power under clause 10 of the constitution of the kingdom of Siam 1932 by passing a resolution on 6 September of that year appointing me to continue as regent until the king returned.

I quickly sent a telegram requesting the king to return, and got the Allies agreement to provide an aircraft. A westerner has written a book about this and has printed a copy of my telegram and the royal reply in detail. These show my innocence in not clinging to the post of regent. King Ananda Mahidol returned to Bangkok on 5 December 1945 and graciously issued a royal command on 8 December conferring on me the post of senior statesman.

## VIII

The duty of looking after royal affairs belongs to the office of the royal household department which comes under the prime minister's office. The Regency Council does not have executive power but must work through the office of the Royal Secretariat which contacts the prime minister's office to and on behalf of the office of the royal household. But the royal secretary may agree to act on requests from the Regency Council, with the office of the royal household being responsible to the prime minister. Even Phraongchao Athit who was a member of the royal family and wanted to help the royal family did not have direct power. For me it was even more difficult to get anything done through the official procedures.

The royal secretary at that time was Phraya Chatdet-udom, and the deputy secretary was Nai Chalieo Pathumrot, who was a fellow promoter of 24 June. Phraongchao Athit entrusted me with the duty of looking after the safety of Queen Savarintra, because he thought I could ask Nai Chalieo Pathumrot to take over the work as Chalieo was directly under the prime minister's office. If the queen had to travel to provincial towns there were places in the care of the crown property office, whose director was Nai Pramot Phungsunthon, a 24 June promoter. If she stayed in Ayutthaya, there was a place belonging to the division of royal property in the Finance Ministry, of which Nai Sanit Phiunuan, deputy under-secretary of finance, was the director. Apart from this, Phraya Thewathirat, division head in the office of the royal household, knew me well enough to help out further in affairs connected with the royal family.

Looking after the safety of the royal family during the war sometimes required prompt action because of danger from aircraft. I had to use shortcuts by asking those named above to help take responsibility to get things done at my request.

## IX

Phraongchao Athit and his wife Mom Kopkaew were sports players but I was not good at sport so I did not go to play with them much except a few occasions when they invited me to play badminton. But Phibun was a sportsman and had the opportunity to play with Phraongchao Athit. This helped them to become more friendly and sympathetic to each other.

I did not know that Phibun sent a letter of resignation from the prime ministership to Phraongchao Athit as president of the Regency Council. Athit thought that Phibun was hurt over some personal problems, not a government problem, so he sent the resignation letter back without letting me know.

Later around February 1943, Phibun sent another resignation letter direct to the chairman of the Regency Council, and left Samakkhichai House [his official residence] without anyone knowing where he had gone. Perhaps Phraongchao Athit knew that Phibun wanted to resign really in order to shuffle a new cabinet. So he sent the resignation letter on to me to consider. I thus wrote my opinion on the cover of the file as: "This resignation letter is correct according to the constitution. Agreed. He may resign." I signed at the bottom, leaving a space above for Phraongchao Athit to sign, which he did. I then invited over Nai Thawi Bunyaket, who was then a minister and secretary of the cabinet, and asked him how Phibun would change the cabinet. He replied that Phibun probably would change it, and that he was looking for Phibun but could not find him. When the Regency Council forwarded the approval of Phibun's letter of resignation, the cabinet secretariat which oversaw the publicity department had Phibun's resignation announced over the department's radio.

Wherever he was at the time, Phibun was furious when he heard the publicity department radio announce the resignation. A number of military officers attended on Phraongchao Athit at Amphon Palace where he was staying at the time, and asked for the resignation letter to be returned to Phibun. It was natural that when Phraongchao Athit saw the mood of these military officers, his heart sank, because he could not return the resignation letter to Phibun. Hence he and Mom Kopkaew came to the house where I was staying which was on the bank of the river near the Tha Chang Wang Na, and asked to stay the night at my residence. I asked my navy friends to help give the protection he wanted and this gave me protection also. Navy friends sent a patrol boat under the command of Lt. Cdr. Watcharachai Chaisitthiwet to moor in front of my residence. The unit of Maj. Luang Ratchadecha, my official bodyguard, and Lt. Gen. Praphan Kulaphichit, the official bodyguard of Phraongchao Athit, came to help give protection also. We observed events until the afternoon of the following day but saw no army or air force officers come and make any threat. So Phraongchao Athit and Mom Kopkaew went back to the Amphon Palace.

Later Phibun retrieved his letter of resignation. He ordered the publicity department radio to announce that the broadcast of the resignation had been inaccurate, and that he still held the post of prime minister because the evidence of resignation had disappeared.

Phibun blamed Nai Thawi Bunyaket for broadcasting his resignation over the radio. Nai Thawi thus resigned as minister and secretary of the cabinet.

Then Phibun in his role as supreme commander of the armed forces sent an order to Phraongchao Athit and myself to go to the Supreme Command Headquarters. This was equivalent to having the regents take an order from the supreme commander to report themselves within twenty-four hours.

Phraongchao Athit went to report himself to Phibun as ordered.

As for me, I refused to go on grounds that I held the position of representative of the king who was the commander in chief (*chom thap*) according to the constitution. If I reported myself in submission to the supreme commander, it would be equivalent to reducing the royal authority of the king below that of the supreme commander. Some ministers advised Phibun to withdraw the order, and he agreed. Phraongchao Athit and I were hence able to continue carrying out our duty on behalf of the king as commander in chief according to the constitution.

# X

Later around July 1943, Phraongchao Athit went to rest at Klai Kangwon Palace in Hua Hin, and invited me to visit him at the weekend. I went once on this invitation.

At that time I heard the overseas radio broadcast the news that King Victor Emmanuel of Italy could no longer ignore Mussolini's deeds which had made the country experience defeat in war and had led Italy to disaster. The king thus commanded Mussolini to appear in audience at the Quirinal Palace. Those like-minded with the king arrested Mussolini, put him in an ambulance, put on the siren, and left the palace so that people on both sides of the road where the vehicle passed would not know that this vehicle was taking Mussolini to prison. Then the king appointed Field Marshal Badoglio as prime minister to establish a new Italian national government.

Phraongchao Athit and I discussed this event, and he observed that there was nobody in Thailand who would dare do such a thing. For fun I replied it needed someone old like Badoglio. I said further that in the afternoon on the train to Hua Hin, I saw Lieutenant General Phraya Wichitwongwuthi-krai standing at Huai Sai station. He was as old as Field Marshal Badoglio and he could do it. Then we laughed over the joke.

One day after Phraongchao Athit had returned from Hua Hin, Nai Chalieo Pathumrot rushed to see me and said that Phibun had called an urgent meeting of the 24 June promoters, and announced that Phraongchao Athit had reported that I was thinking of arresting Phibun just like Mussolini had been arrested, by arranging for Lieutenant General Phraya Wichit to lead the arrest. Phibun asked the meeting to consider charging me. The meeting requested to delay taking a resolution on grounds it could not believe Phraongchao Athit. It set up a committee to investigate me. The committee was already leaving Suan Kulap Palace making for Tha Chang. Before long the committee arrived. As far as I can remember, three people came: vice-admiral Sin Kamonnawin, General Chuang Chawengsaksongkhram and one other I cannot remember. The committee interrogated me. I admitted I had said those things but Phraongchao Athit had started the conversation and it was meant as a joke. If I were really going to arrest Phibun, I would not tell Phraongchao Athit because I had friends which I trusted much more than Phraongchao Athit. Also, how could I use someone old like Lt. Gen. Phraya Wichit to do what was claimed. The committee went back and reported to Phibun that Phraongchao Athit had reported some nonsense to him. And so the matter ended. Phraongchao Athit was rather embarrassed with me, and after that I had to be more careful in speaking with him.

After the war when Phraongchao Athit was badly ill one or two days before passing away, he had Nai Chalieo Pathumrot invite me to visit him at

Rattanapha Palace on Setsiri road. Before passing away he wanted to ask forgiveness for wronging me. I went to see him. He asked me to forgive what he had done. I replied that I had already forgiven him. I asked him to put his faith in Buddha's grace, cleanse his mind, and not worry about anything at all. Later he died peacefully. I did not harbour any ill feelings at all which might disturb his mind. If he has a special power of perception, he should know that I did nothing to disturb his mind.

## XI

Thai public opinion became more dissatisfied with Phibun. He wanted to make Thailand a great power by forcing men and women to wear hats in public places, forbidding the chewing of betel, moving the rafts on which people lived along the rivers and canals onto land on grounds that advanced countries did not live on rafts since rafts had no toilets. Labour was conscripted to construct roads. The cost of living rose many times above the pre-war level. Consumer goods were in shortage. MPs of both type 1 and type 2 became more dissatisfied all the time.

The publicity department radio broadcast praise of Phibun along with slogans and songs such as "Believe the leader, the nation will escape danger", "Wherever the leader goes, I will follow", features from Samakkhichai House, and so on. Instead of being popular with the majority of people, these made them even more dissatisfied. Then the "four pillars", the four people whose names people strung together as a phrase which meant they were supporting Phibun to act wrongly (those who want to know the names should ask those who can remember), suggested the authorities order cinemas to show a picture of Phibun after screening a film, and have those watching stand up in respect, as in the cinemas in Italy during Mussolini's time. The dissatisfaction of the majority of the people reached such a height that there had to be a change of prime minister. The majority of MPs of both type 1 and type 2 were aware that the people wanted Phibun's government to quit and be replaced by a new democratic government.

The Japanese did not sit quiet and watch without concern. They listened carefully to know when the Thai people became dissatisfied with Phibun, because Phibun had cooperated with the Japanese and this would mean that the dissatisfaction which the people already had with the Japanese would also increase. Hence the Japanese thought about finding a prime minister to establish a new Thai government. Police General Adun came to inform me that he saw something was up when the Japanese brought an ambassador from the time of the absolute monarchy into Thailand and he had gone to pay his respects to various members of the royal family and old aristocrats.

Also some former ministers who were in Japan had been encouraged to speak on the radio once in a while. Perhaps the Japanese were thinking of changing Phibun.

Then Phibun arranged a ceremony for the Japanese to swear an oath with him before the Emerald Buddha that they would be faithful to one another to the end. Most Japanese believe in Bushido not Buddhism. But they agreed to attend the oath-swearing ceremony at the Temple of the Emerald Buddha. A friend who had contact with the Japanese told me they were getting suspicious why Phibun had to invite them to swear an oath, and felt perhaps he was thinking of stabbing the Japanese in the back.

The British radio from Delhi used a stratagem to make the Japanese even more suspicious of Phibun by broadcasting a rhyme repeatedly for several days, and speaking slowly to allow listeners including the Japanese to write it down. The rhyme caught my ear so I still remember it was as follows:

> Why does a field marshal act like a field mouse
> Has he made a mistake he can't hack
> Why does a great hero, the man of the house,
> Let his enemies dance on his back

I learnt from a Thai who had contact with the Japanese that they took down this rhyme and were more suspicious of Phibun. In addition, General Kat Katsongkhram travelled to China, and the Chinese had General Daili, head of the Chinese Gestapo in Chungking, welcome him. For their conversations they had an interpreter who had been born in Thailand. Even though General Kat told General Daili he had travelled to China of his own accord, this news made the Japanese suspect that Phibun had sent him.

The Thai who had contact with the Japanese rushed to tell me that the Japanese army was preparing to seize the Thai government.

# XII

In July 1944 Phibun proposed a draft law to approve the royal decree on the administration of Phetchabun and Phutthaburimonthon [a planned Buddhist city at Saraburi]. Phibun planned to build these cities in areas of forest infested with malaria. People would be conscripted to labour on public works. The majority of MPs of both type 1 and type 2, who were already aware of the people's dissatisfaction, voted not to approve this law.

The problem arose within the government whether or not this vote amounted to a vote of no confidence in the government. Most ministers took the stance that the government should resign in accordance with etiquette, but the parliament might advise the Regency Council to reappoint it. Hence Phibun submitted his letter of resignation to the Regency Council. On this occasion Phraongchao Athit did not sign accepting Phibun's resignation. He invited the speaker of the parliament to sound out MPs about who should be the next prime minister before he would consider the resignation letter. Leading MPs came to ask me who was suitable to become premier. I advised them to sound out Phraya Phahon. Later the speaker of parliament, acting on the majority opinion of MPs, proposed to the Regency Council that Phraya Phahon should be prime minister. The Regency Council asked Phraya Phahon whether he was willing, but he declined.

Then those MPs who had joined the Seri Thai movement came to consult me about who would be appropriate for the sake of the Seri Thai movement. Mostly they felt that Nai Thawi Bunyaket was the appropriate type to be prime minister. The MPs had once voted for Nai Thawi to be speaker but Phibun had opposed it. Nai Thawi was straightforward and capable, and was a veteran in the People's Party. He had joined since 1927 when he was still studying in Paris. (Nai Khuang joined the People's Party only in 1932 a few months before the 24 June. Nai Khuang admitted this fact in his speech at the Teachers Council.) But Nai Thawi was someone who spoke forthrightly. This made it difficult for Nai Thawi to put on a front with the Japanese. Hence they agreed to sound out whether or not Nai Khuang would agree to become prime minister and put on a front with the Japanese, while entrusting the work of the government to Nai Thawi as overseer of the prime minister's office. So I invited Nai Khuang to see if he was willing. He agreed to these conditions. Then a majority of MPs passed an internal secret resolution for the speaker to propose to the Regency Council to appoint Nai Khuang as prime minister. Phraongchao Athit quibbled, refused to make the appointment, and asked to see Nai Khuang's policies and the ministers he would invite to join the government. Nai Khuang replied that the Regency Council should appoint him as prime minister first and then he would propose the ministers in the new government. I agreed to appoint Nai Khuang as prime minister first. The matter dragged on for several days.

Do people with common sense think that from the time Phibun tendered his resignation until the appointment of a new prime minister, the Japanese sat around idly? In truth, the Japanese had a hand in things. As noted, the Japanese were already suspicious that Phibun was not playing straight with them. The military and naval attachés came to see me at the Tha Chang house, displaying the proper etiquette. Because the Japanese respect their emperor, they showed respect to me as representative of the king of Thailand. The Japanese asked me whether I had any opinion on the appointment of a new prime minister in place of Phibun. I replied that it

225

should proceed according to the Thai constitution. The Japanese should consider it as an internal matter, so that the Thai would understand that the Japanese did not interfere in Thai internal affairs. This would add to the good reputation of the Japanese. They replied that if that were the case, then I should proceed according to the Thai constitution. The Japanese would not get involved. Let the new prime minister cooperate with the Japanese in future. Then the Japanese asked me what Nai Khuang Aphaiwong was like. They did not know him. I replied he was cheerful and good-natured, and I expected he could cooperate with the Japanese.

So people of common sense should understand that the Japanese who were in control of Thailand would not easily have agreed to let the Thais change the government unless they had first been made to understand as described.

# XIII

Phraongchao Athit was still standing firm and refusing to sign the appointment of Nai Khuang as prime minister. But finally he asked to resign from the post of chairman of the Regency Council, as he felt that Nai Khuang would not go all the way, and before long Phibun would return as prime minister again, and I would have to leave so he (Athit) could return to the Regency Council.

The parliament passed a unanimous resolution on 1 August 1944 appointing me as the sole regent.

On that same day I signed the royal command on behalf of King Ananda Mahidol appointing Major Khuang Aphaiwong as prime minister, with the speaker of the parliament countersigning the royal command according to the practice.

Nai Khuang Aphaiwong appointed a cabinet with several ministers. In particular, in line with Nai Khuang's agreement with me, Nai Thawi Bunyaket became both minister of education and also minister overseeing the prime minister's office with the duty of processing the work of the cabinet in the background of Nai Khuang. Nai Khuang had also agreed that on any matter concerning the government and the Seri Thai movement, of which Nai Thawi was the commander of the forces inside the country, Nai Thawi would discuss and decide directly with me. Nai Khuang requested not to know anything about it unless it required legislation or an announcement to the parliament. Hence there were many matters which Nai Thawi discussed with me first and then informed Nai Khuang to carry out, such as the announcement that the declaration of war against Great Britain and the USA was null and void. Nai Thawi Bunyaket countersigned the royal command as appeared in the government gazette, not Nai Khuang. Nai Thawi was the mainstay of drafting the law for pardon and amnesty of political offenders. Although I informed the Allies that there should be a pardon and amnesty for the sake of unity of the Thais who had the ideology to oppose Japan, as M.C. Suphasawat suggested, when it came to real implementation it was not an easy matter. Nai Khuang spoke at the Teachers Council saying that as soon as he became prime minister he ordered the release of political prisoners. In truth, Nai Khuang countersigned the royal command but the drafting of the law needed an understanding with Police General Adun, head of the police department, who was the person ordering the arrest of political offenders. He had to be made to see it was appropriate to give pardon and amnesty for the sake of unity between all the parties involved, and for the benefit of work on behalf of the nation. Police General Adun had the nickname "General Fierce-Eyes" because he was someone not easily outsmarted by anyone. If Nai Khuang, who had just become prime minister in the way described above, had wanted for no apparent reason to show his authority (*bunbarami*) by ordering the release of political offenders without consulting and coming to an understanding with General Fierce-Eyes who had arrested them, that would make Adun seem like the bad guy and Nai Khuang the good guy. This would make things complicated and would result in the political offenders, who were in the situation described by Nai Puey Ungphakorn in his article [on "Royal family members in the Seri Thai movement", included in the original volume with this piece], facing even more delay in getting released. Hence to secure a quicker release for the political prisoners in jail, Nai Thawi Bunyaket and I had to come to an understanding with General Fierce-Eyes. We called on Nai Puey Ungphakorn to explain the contents of the secret telegram I sent to inform the Allies. General Fierce-Eyes agreed in principle and entrusted Nai Thawi Bunyaket to draft the law of pardon and amnesty for all political offenders, omitting only those charged after the Japanese army entered Thailand. This was for their own safety, because the Japanese would catch them if they were released. As for Kromkhun Chainat whose rank had been withdrawn to become Nai Rangsit, apart from being pardoned, his old rank was restored.

Some of the offenders had the insight to understand the truth without I or Nai Thawi boasting to them. When they came out of Bang Khwang prison they came directly to see me at my house. For instance Phraya Udomphongphensawat (M.R. Prayun Itsarasak), former monthon commissioner, former minister of the interior and a leading poet, brought a present to give me. This was a small sheet of paper which he said he had written in Bang Khwang prison when he heard the news of the amnesty and pardon. His composition as far as I can remember was as follows:

Hail, the just regent!
Amnesty for those accused
Release from physical and mental hardship
Escape from the jail of deepest hell

I informed him that he should thank Nai Thawi Bunyaket who was the mainstay of that pardon and amnesty. Please could he change the hail to Thawi Bunyaket and help inform all those released about the goodness of Nai Thawi.

Several days later, Phraya Thep-hatsadin came to tell me he had just learned the truth that Nai Thawi Bunyaket and I were the mainstays in this matter.

Nai Thawi Bunyaket made merit by "pasting gold on the back of the Buddha". He did not show off claiming what he had done in this matter. Nai Thawi has passed away now. Let me record his goodness in this affair.

## XIV

We were not rough on Phibun because we had no desire to have a war among Thais. Hence when Phibun tendered his resignation from the prime ministership, I as regent approved his resignation in line with the constitution. Phibun still held the post of supreme commander. It was not announced immediately that he was dismissed from this position.

But Phibun gathered together troops at Lopburi to intimidate the new government. Vice Admiral Sin Kamonnawin, minister of defence and commander in chief of the navy, came to tell that we should quickly announce the dismissal of Phibun from the post of supreme commander and appoint General Phraya Phahon as army commander and Lt. Gen. Chit Mansinsinatyotharak as deputy. After sounding out Gen. Phraya Phahon and Lt. Gen. Chit to accept these posts, the navy arranged for an ambulance secretly to take Gen. Phraya Phahon, who had been suddenly taken ill, to the navy headquarters at the old palace in Thonburi.

As for me, for safety I secretly went to sleep at Thammasat University. I signed the royal command dismissing Phibun from the post of supreme commander and appointed him as adviser to the government (*thi pruksa ratchakan phaendin*), a post with high status but no command over troops. I also signed a royal command appointing Gen. Phraya Phahon as army commander and Lt. Gen. Chit Mansinsinatyotharak as deputy. To keep tight secrecy, this matter was told only to Nai Khuang who countersigned the royal commands and to Nai Thawi Bunyaket who drafted the royal commands and took responsibility for making a radio announcement in the morning. He entrusted Nai Phairot Jayanama to have the publicity department radio broadcast ready early in the morning. The radio broadcast went according to this plan.

Gen. Phraya Phahon as army commander issued an order for the troops in Bangkok and Thonburi to assemble around Wat Phrasirattanasatsadaram. When these troops assembled as ordered, Lt. Gen. Chit Mansinsinatyotharak on behalf of the army commander, told the troops to listen for the orders of the army commander and to remain peaceful. The troops obeyed the orders of the army commander and deputy. The possibility of bloodshed among Thais hence did not arise. This was not a miracle performed by Nai Khuang as he said at the Teachers Council. Many soldiers still living at present may remember the incident.

As for Phibun, he obeyed the royal command and moved from Lopburi to Lamlukka amphoe for the remainder of the war. As regent I ordered the palace officials to provide Phibun, who held the post of adviser to the government, with all the facilities appropriate to his status.

After the war, Phibun sent a letter to me with the following contents.

Laksi

Date [unspecified]

Dear respected teacher,

I see that you have a lot of work and I don't want to bother you at all. But at present I'm out of luck. I don't know who I should turn to, so I must ask for your consideration. First, I want to alter your understanding. Some time you may think a bit kindly of me. If you feel vengeful towards me for some old matters, you may not have an understanding of the truth. Maybe you had understood that I helped to close the parliament and exile you in connection with the communism charge. I was not the person who did this. Phraya Mano called me to attend at the closing of the parliament [1 April 1933]. At that time I was very much a child in politics. He persuaded me to sign as the last person. I saw all the others had put their names. I feared that if I did not put my name with them it would be very dangerous. So I put my name following Phraya Phahon. As for exiling you, ask Luang Adun to see who fixed it up. You'll find it was really Phraya Songsuradet. Luang Adun and I were charged with being communists. One day I went to meet Phraya Song and he still asked whether Adun and I were becoming redder. When I opened the parliament, Phraya Ratchawangsan still phoned to ask what I was up to. I replied that I was opening the parliament. Then he said, so you are not red? Or you're red already? I put the phone down.

In the events of that time, four or five people held meetings with Phraya Mano as leader. Whatever they wanted to do, they just went ahead.

I always knew the truth later when nothing could be corrected, because I was very much a child in politics. Over the resignation of the four army tigers [Phahon, Song, Ritthi, Prasat: 10 June 1933], I did not know the cause at all. They just simply resigned. I did not know what they were up to. I only knew that people often came to tell me Phraya Song would quit. Apart from that, I didn't fix up anything. Then after resigning, I did not know anything. After the change to a new government, I was still weak in politics. Phraya Mano asked who was suitable to be supreme commander and chief of staff. I replied with the truth, that according to army principle it should be Phraya Phichaironnarong and Phraya Dintharap. He agreed and accomplished it with a royal command. The truth of these old matters is like this. When Phraya Song left, I was stationed at the Norasing Coffee at night. I remember I went with Luang Adun. I heard later that Phraya Ratchawangsan, Phraya Ritthi, and Phraya Mano wanted the navy to imprison me there. I understand that Maj. Gen. Khamhiran was persuaded. The truth of these old matters is like this. Please understand I was not someone to make trouble for old friends. Others did it themselves. I helped whenever there was an opportunity.

When the Japanese came in, it made trouble for you. Ask Luang Adun. I never contacted the Japanese or asked for the authority to make trouble for you. I proposed you as regent.

What I have said here, let the Buddha and holy articles be my witness that it is the truth in every respect. If you don't believe me, the future itself will be my witness.

I hope you will receive what I have said here somewhat kindly. In my politics, now or in future, I've learned a lesson. I feel stupid and not capable enough. Going on with it will bring danger to me again and again. I prefer to be a farmer. Please do not be worried about me in politics. I've learnt my lesson. Being an ordinary fellow is better for me.

I've said a lot already. If there is anything wrong which bothers you, let me apologize. I have written about dealings with the Japanese and sent it for the speaker of the parliament and friends to read. My sole intention is to help friends not be made war criminals, including myself, according to the human instinct for self-preservation. Please excuse me over this too. Because if I do nothing, people will not know the reasons why we acted and will always think of us as selling the country. Our reputations are gone. I'm glad that despite what we did, at least the Emerald Buddha is still here; the Japanese did not carry it off somewhere else.

With the utmost respect,
P. Phibunsongkhram

# 17. SPEECH OF NAI PRIDI BANOMYONG

in the Assembly on 7 May 1946

Mr Chairman,

On the occasion that the Assembly session comes to an end today in accordance with the 1932 constitution, may I take this occasion to invite all the members of the Assembly to recall the grace of King Prajadhipok who granted the constitution in 1932 after the change in government. Before the grant of the constitution, the king had a wish which became known to the People's Party only six days after the change in government, that is on 30 June. Phraya Phahon Phonpayuhasena, Phraya Prichachonlayut, Phraya Manopakon Nitithada, Phraya Siwisanwacha, and myself were summoned to attend in audience on the king. Chaophraya Mahithon, who was the royal secretary, took down the record. The king said that he had wished to grant a constitution, but when he consulted high-ranking officials of the time, they disagreed. Finally when he returned from a visit to America he asked someone who attended in audience on that day to consider the issue. That person offered his opinion that it was not yet time, and the advisors agreed. The People's Party had no foreknowledge of the royal wish and performed the change honestly, not to steal a march on someone as certain people have pretended, twisting the truth. The complete truth appears in the record of the meeting on that day. The fact is that King Prajadhipok had a prior wish but there were people who advised against it. Hence when the People's Party asked the king to grant a constitution, the king was pleased to make this gracious gift to the Thai people. I would like all present and the Thai people as a whole to remember the king's graciousness and to have high esteem for His Majesty at all times.

At this point, those who promoted the grant of a constitution, and those who joined to help as type-2 members, have come to the end of their term as members. I feel it is necessary to re-establish an understanding of the democratic principles in accordance with the constitution which the People's Party requested King Prajadhipok to grant. By the constitutional system, we mean democracy with the rule of law, morality, and honesty, not that sort of democracy which has no rules and no morality, and which uses the right to freedom to generate disorder, the breakdown of peace, and moral decline. That system is called anarchy, not democracy. Take care. Do not confuse democracy with anarchy. Anarchy is a major danger to society and nation. To be secure, the democratic system must comprise law, morality, and honesty—or what in the old days was called government through unity. Rights without the limitations of law and morality, or rights without honesty—these are not the principles of democracy, not the principles for which the People's Party requested the grant of a constitution and for which King Prajadhipok granted the constitution to the Thai people. The king did not wish for anarchy. Let me take the example of Italy. Before the time of Mussolini, Italy's democracy had no rules. It was chaotic. This created the cause—or allowed the fascists to claim as cause—for the establishment of dictatorship in Italy. I do not wish to see dictatorship in Siam. Thus it is necessary to prevent or oppose anarchy, which provides a way for dictators to assert themselves. I believe that if we help one another to uphold the democratic system according to law and order as I have stated already, dictatorship cannot arise. I am one of those who joined with friends in the People's Party to request the granting of a constitution. I have always supported the democratic system according to the constitution, even in opposing Japan. That opposition might have made it necessary to form a provisional government. But I chose the route of setting up a government in accordance with the current constitutional system. I have no reason to become an enemy of democracy. I notice that there are people who misunderstand the democratic system and introduce anarchy in its place, which is a serious danger to the nation. I have no wish to make anyone believe me without opposition. I want opposition, but opposition which is honest, which does not raise up lies as truth. Telling lies or falsehoods is wrong. In politics, rights under a democratic system must be used with a pure heart, in the pursuit of the true common benefit, not personal benefit, or the jealousy which has its origin in egoism. Then unity or true democracy is possible. Anyone who has idealism with honesty—I have respect for that person. We can work together. I believe that if each party honestly pursues the common benefit of the nation, not personal benefit, even if each takes a different route to their objective, we will meet one another in the end. Let me refer to many royal family members *(chao nai)*. In the past, they went in one direction and I went in another direction. But many of these old royal family members aim for the common benefit of the nation not for themselves. In the end we can team up to work together well in the service of the nation, and love one another more closely than someone who uses the nation as a cover but really pursues personal interest. Some people are jealous when they do not get what they hoped for. They destroy activities which are of benefit for the country, instead of being constructive for the benefit of the country as a whole. Some are hostile to the People's Party out of an ideal of being honest to the person of the king. I respect that honesty. There are many examples of such honest people who joined together with me in activities in the service of the nation. These people have no reason for concern. But there are those who give an external appearance of loyalty to the king, but internally have a personal objective or benefits to be obtained. Their dissatisfaction is personal, hence I fear that these people may turn whichever way gives them the greater personal gain.

I hope that all of you members of the Assembly will use your rights with a pure heart and hold to the principles of law, morality, and honesty. Do not support the advent of anarchy. Let me entrust all you members of the Assembly with my thoughts on the future of the nation. I desire to see the nation free of dictatorship and free of anarchy, with only democracy complete with unity. Democracy with unity is the objective of the People's Party which requested the grant of the constitution. It was also the wish of King Prajadhipok who granted the constitution.

May I thank the members of the Assembly for their cooperation and good assistance to the government. May I wish that you all meet with happiness and joy. Finally may I invite all of you to wish success for democracy with unity, in accordance with the constitution, to continue in Siam for ever.

# 18. UPHOLD THE AIM FOR FULL DEMOCRACY OF THE HEROES OF 14 OCTOBER

As the committee to organize the 1973 meeting of Thammasat people in the United Kingdom (England) wants an article or message *(kham khwan)* from me for the memorial volume which will be published, I am happy to respond to this request with the message: "Uphold the aim for full democracy of the heroes of 14 October". I have composed the following essay as a brief explanation of this message.

I

The fourteenth of October 1973 is an important day in the history of the Thai nation—the day of the first stage of victory of Thai youth. The leadership came from university and school students of many educational institutions. They received support and cooperation from many million Thai people of all ethnic groups and all classes who love the nation. Together they combined as a movement to demand a fully democratic constitution for the Thai people. The clique controlling the power of the state ordered that section of the military and police which agreed to be their tool, to use modern weapons to suppress this movement whose members had only empty hands, or sometimes only sticks, to protect themselves. But the movement was not frightened. They remained firm in their readiness to sacrifice their lives and give up their personal happiness for the nation and people which they love and respect in the highest degree. Large numbers of the heroes were killed or injured or disappeared. Those who remained alive and received no bodily injury were badly exhausted both physically and mentally. As a result of the sacrifice of all the heroes in the righteous struggle, the first stage of victory was achieved. That is, the government of Field Marshal Thanom Kittikhachon as prime minister and Field Marshal Praphat Charusathian as deputy prime minister had to resign, including their positions as supreme commander and deputy supreme commander of the armed forces. Then there was a royal command to appoint Nai Sanya Thammasak as prime minister. He publicly confirmed that he would arrange for a democratic constitution and elections within six months.

I would like to join with the Thai people who love the nation to offer homage and praise to all these heroes. The Buddha preached a sermon which in one part conveys the important meaning that virtuous people *(sathuchon)* should conduct themselves with gratitude towards those who have done good deeds to them. Thais who are Christian or Muslim also live by a code of righteousness which is the same as the Buddhist one. Hence it is fitting that all we many Thais who love the nation show in our bodies, our words, and our hearts grateful acknowledgement of the good deeds of the heroes; and we should do good works in homage to the dead *(bamphen kuson thaksinanuprathan)*, including joining together to build a monument as a memorial for all the heroes.

The Buddha also said that good deeds should be both acknowledged and repaid. Hence, upholding the aim for full democracy of the heroes of 14 October so that they are safeguarded and developed further is an even more important obligation which virtuous people who love the nation should undertake.

## II

Virtuous people who love the nation and elevate the nation above personal benefit should be able to judge the aim for full democracy of the heroes of 14 October from the vision and standpoint of the mass of the people. The heroes do not include people of only one particular birthplace or class status. Rather, they include those with birthplace, economic status, and political status of different types. They include the poor, factory workers, casual workers, farmers, minor government officials, people who earn enough to get by, small capitalists, and patriotic capitalists who raise the nation above personal benefit. They are from all Thai ethnic groups *(national minorities)* who have Thai nationality. Thus the aim of all these heroes is for a constitution of full democracy in politics and economy, and for a vision based on Buddhist doctrine to serve as the guiding principle for achieving prosperity for all classes and all ethnic groups who love the nation.

As I have stated in many essays and speeches, the history of humanity from the primeval age onwards demonstrates that the economy is the important foundation of human society. The political system is only the superstructure which must be consistent with the economic needs of the mass of people in society. If the constitution which is the origin *(mae bot)* of law is in accord with economic needs, then a social crisis will not arise, and the country will progress peacefully in an evolutionary way *(evolution)*. If the constitution does not accord with the economic needs of society, a crisis must arise according to the natural law of conflict between two things which are in opposition to one another. If virtuous people who love the nation study thoroughly, they can see that the reason why the heroes sacrificed their lives and gave up their personal happiness to demand a constitution of full democracy is because the mass of the Thai people has undergone extreme hardship. A political system with no constitution—or a constitution in name only—conflicts with the economic needs of the mass of the people. The heroes thus sacrificed their lives and personal happiness in the wish for the Thai nation to have a political system with a fully democratic constitution which accords with the economic needs of the people, so that every ethnic group will join together in the unity of the country.

Virtuous people who love the country should be heartbroken to see that even before the smell of the blood of the heroes had completely disappeared, already people from some parties were trying to grab the first stage of the heroes' victory for the benefit of their party alone. For instance, as a model for drafting a new constitution, they introduced a constitution which their group had made, instead of beginning from the aim for full democracy of the heroes from all classes and ethnic groups which have Thai nationality. This creates a situation where those who want to uphold this aim of the heroes must find a way to fight either gently or with violence, depending on the method of the lead organization of each class and each ethnic group. Those groups which have already used violent methods could mobilize the mass of the people by claiming that this situation clearly shows that the method of drafting the constitution will serve the benefit of the privileged class alone, and hence the mass cannot rely on a constitutional system which is not fully democratic to solve the difficulties of the people as a whole. Thus, for the peace and happiness of the country, I appeal to the government and those involved in drafting this new constitution, to refrain from a drafting method which is biassed towards a constitution for the benefit of the privileged class, and to establish a vision in accord with the aim for full democracy of the heroes of 14 October.

III

The majority of the Thai people, who are poor, needy, and grievously oppressed by reactionary dictatorial power, have learnt to question whether they can really rely on anyone to solve their problems. Hence they rely on themselves, under the leadership of the Student Centre, to fight for their democratic rights. This is in keeping with the Buddhist saying, *attahi attano nāthō*, which translates as "what you can rely on is yourself". This dhamma principle is the same as the Christian teaching "God helps those who help themselves". Islam has a similar thought among the sayings of Mohammed.

To uphold, safeguard, and develop further the first stage of victory of the heroes, the people should not put their hope and trust in any one single individual or any one single group. They should rely on the power of the people themselves which is the true power. The centre has strengths both in terms of quality and quantity to serve as the vanguard of the people. They must fight for much longer yet in order to prevent the reactionary dictatorship which has been defeated in name only and whose framework of power still remains. They must fight against the remnants of various anti-democratic forces even though they are not the direct enemy—the dictatorship, which has lost power in name only.

The people and the centre which is their vanguard must hold on tightly to their victory. Everyone must have the discipline which comes from consciousness about their aims. They must take special care to prevent the enemies of democracy luring them away to the other side. They must base their vision firmly on a vision of full democracy, which will be the guiding principle to progress towards full democracy for the mass of the people. Anyone who holds a vision of semi-democracy will work towards semi-democracy only. Anyone who has a vision left over from the slavery era will work towards a government which resembles slavery; they will support the revival of dictatorship which governs people like slaves, as has happened in history.

I have described in many articles and speeches how in the past before the democratic system of the West and other modern versions, man had many social systems—the primitive democratic community, the slave system, and feudalism.

History shows that although a social system collapses, whether by force through the establishment of a new system or whether by law, in practice the vision born in the old system does not completely die. Rather, it gets passed down to some groups of the new generation even though they are born after the legal demise of the old system. In modern democratic countries and socialist countries, the new generations are born under the new society. But the corpse of the old vision, especially the slavery vision, persists and penetrates into the mind of some groups of the new generation for a long time. They strive to revive the old system which governs the people as slaves. This accords with the law that things which are dead or dying still leave behind a corpse. They struggle to stay alive or to bring what is dead in name back to life again.

In Thailand, the system of slavery was ended legally by the royal decree of 1906. King Rama V also abolished several customs which followed from the slave system. Yet the corpse of the vision created under the slave system still remained. It was not entrenched in everyone of the old order. Many members of the royal family and Thai aristocrats of the old order truly progressed according to the king's wish. They shed the corpse of the old vision, either wholly or in part. But among some groups from the old order, the slavery vision was deeply entrenched. They passed on the old vision as a legacy to the minds of some groups in the new generation. See the example in France. Some one hundred years after the abolition of absolutism in law, some groups of the new generation conducted themselves as *"ultra royaliste"*, as "more royalist than the king". (I dealt with this in the book about the royal family members and inside the Regency Council, printed in 1972). In Thailand we can see that some groups of the new generation which have the slavery vision approve of certain dictators who rule the people like slaves. These people never consider that such dictators have reduced the power which the king had under the democratic system. They do not reflect that such dictators wield more power than the king under absolutism. They support dictators who rule the people like slaves. Sooner rather than later, they help to revive slave-ruling dictatorship, as happened in Thai history over the past twenty-six years.

To help students and patriots study how to preserve and develop the aim for full democracy of the heroes of 14 October, let me propose that you all study the mistakes of the People's Party and other groups in history which were unable to uphold their first stage of victory and develop to full democracy. You may take it as a lesson not to make the same mistakes again. At the same time, you should study the methods by which other groups and organizations were able to uphold and secure their first stage of victory, and were able to develop and progress to completion, so that the correct course can be applied according to the conditions of time and place in Thailand.

1. The People's Party made many mistakes which had one clear result—disunity inside the party. The problem to be studied is why the People's Party was disunited. This disunity arose because of differing attitudes to self-sacrifice; because of selfishness which arose after the first stage of victory; and because of differences in social vision among various individuals and groups which had either a small or large hangover from the old mentality. The members were all in agreement only on the vision of bringing down absolutism, and they all dedicated their lives to that. When they had the first stage of victory, they split up according to how backward or advanced was the vision of each person and group. One camp with a static vision was satisfied when absolutism had been felled. A progressive camp wanted to develop the country further towards full democracy. A backward faction

wanted to rule the country by dictatorship, which might appear superficially different to slavery, but if analysed clearly, was really a slavery system, even more backward than feudalism.

2. Disunity inside this party or other parties is a common occurrence. There is no party or group in this world, either in the past or present, whether conservative, moderate, socialist, or communist, which has no internal conflict between its members. We hear of parties where internal conflict caused sections to split off and form new parties; parties where some members were expelled; and parties which had state power, such as the Soviet Communist Party and the Chinese Communist Party, where certain members were purged for betraying the ideology of the party by reviving an old direction. So if we hear that inside the Student Centre there is conflict over vision, or over the way to uphold and develop the victory, we should not be discouraged that this has come about, because it is something common according to the natural law of conflict between an old vision and a new.

The problem is whether the party or the movement's centre can overcome the conflict completely, or reduce it somehow, and keep acting according to its ideals rather than making the mistakes which led the People's Party to dissolve. It would be worth studying the methods of various parties which experienced internal conflicts but were able to solve them, either by keeping the party intact, or if necessary by preserving that section which held tightly to the party's ideals to ensure the party or centre survived until its aims were fully achieved.

The means that will help the party or centre to survive, despite the natural law of internal conflict, are: holding firm to the vision of full democracy as the guiding principle to achieve this righteous aim; undertaking constant self-scrutiny to correct mistakes; not resorting to unwarranted self-justification; and helping friends to do the same.

3. It is a reality that one military group in the People's Party used military power to make themselves big in the government and to rule the people by dictatorship. But truly there were many other military members of the People's Party who were loyal to the party's democratic ideals. For instance Phraya Phahon Phonphayusena, whether during the time he was commander in chief of the army or when he was prime minister, never did anything against democracy. Nor did he cling onto position. When it was time for him to leave according to the constitution, he resigned calmly. Many other army officers and People's Party members were loyal to the democratic ideal. It was only a small group of soldiers who, when they had power, joined forces to pervert democracy into dictatorship. Many civilian members of the

People's Party who had a selfish outlook hoped to make a windfall from dictatorial power and so turned to support it.

Hence the problem was not that those who were soldiers were pro-dictatorship while those who were civilian were pro-democracy. The problem was that the residue of the slavery vision was embedded in certain people, whether military or civilian, and this residue tended to make them want and support the dictatorial system which rules people as slaves.

In truth, since 1913 the Conscription Act has laid down clearly that all Thai males must do military service. When someone reaches seventeen, he must register as a conscript and has a chance of being called up for regular military service. The wish of King Rama VI was that Thai males should be soldiers of the Thai people. In the later period under dictatorship, military training made regular soldiers a tool of dictatorship. The intention of senior officers in the People's Party was to make the Thai army like the Swiss army, where males become soldiers to look after their locality as a people's army. The party took first steps in this direction by setting the highest rank in normal times as colonel. There was only one general who was the commander of the royal bodyguard. The military was organized by monthon and province, not by divisions, brigades, armies as in the absolutist period. At the start of the People's Party time, some people referred to the Thai army as the provincial army. If the pro-dictatorship military officers had not objected, the plan to organize Thai males as a people's army would have succeeded, and would be a power on the side of the people for upholding and developing full democracy.

The French revolutionary movement of 1789 could not make use of the old royalist army, apart from some soldiers who sided with the people. Hence the movement armed the French people to fight against the enemies of the people inside the country, and against foreign countries which raised reactionary armies to invade France and destroy democracy.

Subsequent revolutionary movements in many countries were able to uphold and develop their victory by organizing the people into a people's army. They welcomed soldiers from the old order who put the benefit of the people above their private benefit by volunteering to join the people's army.

In many movements which fought dictatorial power in Thailand, commissioned officers, NCOs, and enlisted men who were pro-democracy joined up on the people's side.

Hence, the problem is not that the revolutionary movement denies the importance of soldiers, but that soldiers should be soldiers of the people, who come from the people, who are trained to work for the people, and who refuse to be a tool of the dictatorial power which rules soldiers as slaves.

The histories of some countries show examples where conscript soldiers understood that the revolutionary movement acted for the benefit of their own distressed fathers and mothers. For instance, soldier sons of peasants knew that the movement would bring benefit to their peasant parents; soldier sons of poor people and labourers, or of petty businessmen, or of petty bureaucrats, knew the movement would bring benefit to their parents. Such an army refuses to be a tool of the privileged group which oppresses their parents. This army turns to be a force of the true people's movement of the nation (not a movement to preserve power, to expand power, or to expand the power of other nations).

4. The People's Party invited old aristocrats *(khun nang)* to help form the government headed by Phraya Manopakon. On 1 April 1933, Phraya Manopakon received a royal decree, as printed in the government gazette, to prorogue the Assembly and revoke several clauses of the constitution of 10 December 1932. An Anti-Communist Act was introduced to punish anyone with socialist thinking of various types, even if not communist.

Many people of good will at that time criticized me for not having learned a lesson from Sun Yat Sen who, after the revolution of 1911 had won a first stage of victory, entrusted power to Yuan Shi Kai, an aristocrat of the old Chinese order, as head of state. This enabled Yuan Shi Kai to overturn the first stage of victory of the revolution. He proceeded in a very backward way and set himself up as the emperor of China (temporarily until his death). I admit I alone made the mistake of proposing to the People's Party to invite Phraya Manopakon to head the government. Other members of the People's Party were not as familiar with Phraya Manopakon as I was. I had worked together with him in the law-drafting department and several times on the examination board for law students. In conversation he showed he was pro-democracy. And his conduct as chief judge of the appeal court showed he dared to make judgements without fear of absolutist power. Hence many law students of that time appreciated him. I saw him as a different type from Yuan Shi Kai who betrayed the Kwangsu Chinese emperor who had a desire to grant a constitution for China. I made the mistake of not analysing deeply that Phraya Manopakon still retained some of the thinking of the old order. But I ask for fairness for Phraya Manopakon. He could not have opposed the democratic constitution on his own. He was supported by some elements inside the People's Party whose vision still had the residue of the old order, and by other old aristocrats who had been invited to join the government.

My mistake should be a lesson to the students and new generation of today not to repeat. You must study the true make-up of people who you ally with and put your trust in, so that the first stage won by the heroes can be developed further. Some people may appear democratic for a while. But when the time comes to develop the democratic victory to another stage, they may act according to their old vision and inherited way of thinking. This may wreck the foundations for preserving the victory won at the first stage.

5. Colonel Phraya Phahon, who was prime minister after Phraya Manopakon, conducted public affairs totally according to the democratic system. And when it came to the point that he had to quit according to the constitution, he resigned, and was succeeded by Colonel Luang Phibun-songkhram.

When Colonel Luang Phibun was first prime minister, he conducted public affairs according to the democratic system. There was just one thing over which he departed from the earlier ideals of the People's Party. In normal times the highest military rank was only colonel, but Phibun was appointed by the regents to the rank of major-general.

Not long after, some people whose vision was inherited from the age of slavery encouraged Luang Phibun to govern the country by a nazi or fascist dictatorship, and to rule the people as slaves. Rumours were passed around that some people who went to pay their respects to Luang Phibun saw miraculous rays of light emanating from his body. This rumour became widespread. The truth was like this. One evening there was a drama performance at Suan Kulap Palace on the occasion of Luang Phibun's birthday. I and many promoter friends were also invited. Some still alive today may remember that Luang Wichitwathakan was the presenter of the drama and acted himself in some scenes. One scene depicted the dance of the chickens (Luang Phibun was born in the year of the cock). This dance signified that people with merit are born in the year of the cock, which is the tutelary spirit of the Thai nation. In another scene, Luang Wichit acted as a crippled old man. When he saw Luang Phibun and recognized a man of merit, he made a deep obeisance and his deformity disappeared. Luang Phibun turned to me with a look of embarrassment, then turned back to acknowledge Luang Wichit's obeisance. I saw that at that time Luang Phibun did not think of being a dictator. But later he was supported several times by people of the old vision, including a group known as the "four pillars" *(chatusadom)* who were intent on praising him beyond reason. Although he had been a democrat, Luang Phibun was gradually led astray into a new direction.

6. After peace was concluded in the war with French Indochina, some people supported Luang Phibun for a higher rank. Luang Phibun spoke with me and many other people that he should probably have the rank of major-general only. But the Regency Council, which then consisted of Phraong-chao Athit and Chaophraya Phichaiyen, promoted Luang Phibun from

major-general to field marshal on the signature of King Ananda Mahidol. They requested Luang Adundetcharat to countersign the royal command. Luang Phibun did not know about this matter in advance. But when he learnt from the announcement in the government gazette, he was not willing to accept the rank of field marshal, and for several months refused to go to receive the field marshal's baton from the Regency Council. Later Phraongchao Athit brought the baton to present to Field Marshal Phibun at government house in Suan Kulap Palace.

Later the Regency Council appointed Field Marshal Phibun as supreme commander of the armed forces. This created an even bigger opportunity for Field Marshal Phibun to govern the country as a dictator, and to take the country into the Second World War.

We can observe that if the Regency Council had refused to appoint Luang Phibun as field marshal and supreme commander of the armed forces, how could he acquire that rank and position? In the case of legislation, the Regency Council can refuse to fix their signatures to a bill, even when a royal command has been received. The problem lay with the Regency Council. Did they place the benefit of the nation above their deference to Luang Phibun?

After Field Marshal Phibun's actions had created losses for the country both internally and externally, the MPs of both type 1 and type 2, including People's Party members whose ideal was to preserve democracy, made plans to remove Field Marshal Phibun from the prime ministership by correct legal procedure. As regent, I acted according to the requirements of the MPs. Later I announced the royal order removing Field Marshal Phibun from the post of supreme commander of the armed forces, abolishing this post, and creating a post of commander in chief (*mae thap yai*), a post authorized in military law. Phraya Phahon was appointed to this post to command the armed forces according to democratic principles (I have given details in the book referred to above).

# IV

The next events should be a lesson on how reactionary dictatorial power can be brought back to life.

On 9 May 1946, King Ananda Mahidol with the endorsement of the Assembly granted the constitution of full political democracy. The people elected members of the Senate by indirect election and members of the Assembly by direct election. In effect, the king granted sovereignty to his people, working through their elected representatives, in the place of the semi-democracy in which type-2 MPs and senators had been chosen by appointment. Opponents of democracy were not happy with this full political democracy. When they could not fight it by constitutional methods, they instigated a coup.

While King Bhumibol Adulyadej was still in his minority, the parliament passed a resolution to appoint two regents, Kromkhun Chainatnarenton and Phraya Manawaratsewi. Both took an oath before the parliament to preserve the constitution and act according to it. On 8 November 1947, a small handful of military men, acting against the democratic intention of the majority of soldiers who are sons of workers and peasants, made a coup and overthrew the system of full constitutional democracy which King Ananda Mahidol had granted with the endorsement of the Assembly. The coup group announced it would use the temporary constitution of 9 November 1947 known as the under-the-water-jar constitution. Kromkhun Chainat was the only person to sign on behalf of the king even though he himself did not agree. Phraya Manawaratsewi did not sign.

This under-the-water-jar constitution had one person to countersign the royal command, namely Field Marshal Phibun, in the post of "commander of the Thai armed forces". This post enabled Phibun, who had been removed from the post of supreme commander of the armed forces earlier during the Second World War, to return with increased power.

What lovers of a democratic nation could not anticipate was that the Supreme Council of State *(khana aphirathamontri)*, which according to the under-the-water-jar constitution carried out the duty of the regents, would appoint Nai Khuang Aphaiwong, head of the Democrat Party, as prime minister; that Khuang would form a cabinet composed of old aristocrats and several Democrat Party members; and that this government would propose many old aristocrats of high rank for appointment to the Senate by the regents acting on behalf of the king. (The name of the Senate was changed [from *phruthisapha*] to *wuthisapha*.) The names of these senators can be seen from the list appointed on 18 November 1947. This removed the rights of the mass of Thai people to elect senators under the 1946 constitution.

Removing rights from the mass of the people was not enough to satisfy the Democrat government. Under the under-the-water-jar constitution, the government used the Senate as a provisional parliament to amend the law for elections to the Assembly. The provisions of the 1947 provisional constitution of the kingdom of Thailand (under-the-water-jar) as amended were as follows.

> For elections in the first instance, the provisions of the electoral law of 1932, as amended (third edition) in 1936 shall be in force, with additional amendment of the age for electoral candidates under clause 16(1) of the

electoral law of 1932 as amended (third edition) in 1936, to be not less than thirty-five years, with the exclusions in clause 17(1) of the act.

After the first election, if any seat falls vacant for any reason besides the expiry of the parliament's term or a dissolution, and a new election is held, the provisions of the above paragraph shall be in force.

Signed on behalf of the royal command
Khuang Aphaiwong
Prime Minister

Students of constitutional law should explain to young people which countries in the world have a democratic constitution which limits the minimum age of MPs or members of the lower house to thirty-five years. They will find every country in the world sets the minimum age of electoral candidates for the lower house no less than twenty-five years; and for the Senate slightly higher at thirty to forty years. For instance in the United States, the Senate is thirty years, while the lower house is twenty-five years.

Once the Democrat government had its Assembly consisting of MPs of high age along with its Senate comprised mostly of aristocrats of the older generation, they drafted the constitution of 1949 claiming it was the most democratic. How could it be the most democratic when it was drafted by senators who were not elected by the people either directly or indirectly, and by MPs aged over thirty-five years? The 1949 constitution showed more kindness to the younger generation than the under-the-water-jar charter by amending the minimum age for MPs from thirty-five to thirty years. But this was not a lot of kindness, as this minimum age was equal to the minimum for the American Senate which was intended to be a body of more advanced age.

Let me inform young people that in the provisional constitution of Siam of 27 June 1932, the first-ever charter granted by King Prajadhipok, clause 11 fixed the minimum age for electoral candidates at twenty years, the same as the voting qualification. Later during the drafting of the electoral law for the constitution of 10 December 1932, the king commanded Phraya Phahon, head of the People's Party, and myself to attend in audience about the draft constitution and electoral law at Chitlada Palace. The king was of the opinion that Thai males had to serve in the army, and hence fixing the electoral qualification at twenty years would not be convenient. A large number of Thai males serving in the army would have to take leave to vote, and this would waste many days and months of service time. Hence it would be appropriate to raise the age to twenty-three years, so that army conscripts would have already been discharged into the reserves or into the monkhood for one year. Phraya Phahon and I endorsed the king's suggestion and drafted the electoral qualification as not less than twenty-three years. This electoral law was used until superceded by the electoral law of the Democrat Party.

I have another observation. Those who advertise themselves as admirers of King Prajadhipok and who rage against the People's Party over the king's abdication, why do they not respect the king's own wishes to grant such democratic rights?

We can see that Field Marshal Phibun and his group were able to return with increased power through the help of people whose vision was left over from the old order that opposed democracy.

Field Marshal Phibun allowed the Democrat government to remain in power for only a few months. Then a handful of military men requested Nai Khuang to resign from the prime ministership. The regents appointed Field Marshal Phibun as prime minister and installed a government in place of Khuang's. The senators who had been appointed, and the MPs who had been elected by the law which removed the rights of people aged below thirty-five, were still in place. They immediately expressed their confidence in Field Marshal Phibun as the executive.

Later, on 23 March 1949, this same Senate and Assembly passed a new constitution, in which were hidden several provisions which should be noted here. Clause 181 included:

> Senators appointed according to the constitution of the kingdom of Thailand (provisional) shall remain senators under this constitution, and their term shall be counted from the day of the royal command with their appointment.

Students of constitutional law can see with little difficulty that the 1949 constitution transferred senators appointed under the provisional under-the-water-jar constitution to be senators under the 1949 constitution. This was mutual back-scratching between the coup group and the old order.

On 29 November 1951, nine officers of the army, navy, and airforce announced over Thailand radio that they had set themselves up as the "Provisional National Executive Group". Later they asked the king to bring back the constitution of 10 December 1932. King Bhumibol Adulyadej granted the wish after having the Assembly make suitable amendments.

After Nai Chalieo Pathumrot, Nai Chit Singhaseni, and Nai But Patthamasarin were executed for the regicide of Rama VIII, Field Marshal Phibun had many new facts which showed the innocence of these accused. While I was living in China, he sent a representative to inform me that he would bring about justice by having the regicide case reviewed according to the practice in some advanced countries, and that he would conduct the government of the country according to the methods of full democracy. But whether Field Marshal Phibun truly acted this way or not is another problem.

Those with the vision of the slavery era at first maligned Field Marshal Phibun for not respecting the king. This made some of the new generation of the time have wrong ideas. They then supported Field Marshal Sarit to overthrow Phibun by coup, and helped broadcast that Sarit was the saviour of the throne.

At first, Field Marshal Sarit set up Nai Pote Sarasin and then General Thanom Kittikhachon as prime minister to rule the country under an amended constitution of 10 December 1932. But before long, Field Marshal Sarit's true substance was revealed. He was advised by Luang Wichit-wathakan to make another coup on 20 October 1958, to abrogate constitutional government completely, and to rule the country by what was called the "Revolutionary Party" which had more power than the king under the absolute monarchy. It could arrest and shoot people without court proceedings. Even though this group proclaimed martial law which provided for circuit courts (san sanam), they did not bother with them. Their group arrested some people and shot them against the wall of Wat Mahathat, the wat where Luang Wichitwathakan had entered the monkhood and studied for a theological qualification (parian). The incident made the monks and worshippers very dismayed. It did not accord with the propaganda by those of the slave mentality that Sarit and his people were great respecters of Buddhism of which the king is the defender of the faith.

The constitution granted by royal command on 28 January 1959 reduced royal power in many ways. For instance, clause 17 allowed government to execute any person without court proceedings. This abolished the royal power to grant a pardon, which had been a custom from the time of King Ramkhamhaeng, and was a tenet of modern constitutions including that of the military dictator, Mussolini. In truth, if the punishment under the old law was considered too little, the law should have been amended and the penalties increased. And if the process of criminal justice was too slow, the law should have been amended to speed things up. But Field Marshal Sarit and his group of the slavery vision, although they claimed to respect the king, reduced the power which the king once had under the democratic system and in accordance with the royal tradition of the ten ways of the king (thotsaphitratchatham).

In 1963, Field Marshal Sarit passed away, and Field Marshal Thanom Kittikhachon received royal appointment as prime minister. The Thanom government had to concede to the request from Thai patriots to look into the government accounts. It was revealed that Field Marshal Sarit had embezzled over two thousand million baht to nurture his harem. When dishonesty was revealed on this scale, some members of the royal family, who were not tightly locked into an anti-democratic point of view, came to understand that Field Marshal Sarit had not been loyal to the throne. But a number of young people who had the residue of the slavery system proclaimed an excuse for Sarit: "Although Field Marshal Sarit swindled many thousand million baht of the nation's money, the fact that he preserved the throne has the highest value". Wise people should see that this excuse for Field Marshal Sarit put out by the old reactionary group, both old and new, is lese-majesty. The Thai people are the protectors of the throne, and it is disrespectful to the king to say that the throne exists because of a field marshal who took the nation's money to pander to his own pleasure and to have almost a hundred Thai women as his courtesans.

Field Marshal Thanom Kittikhachon became prime minister in place of Field Marshal Sarit, with Field Marshal Praphat Charusathian as deputy prime minister. They governed according to the constitution which removed several powers from the king for several years until the promulgation of the constitution of June 1968 which took ten years to draft. This is a world record. No country has taken this much time to draft a constitution or required such a large expenditure of the nation's funds. Even the constitution of the dictator Mussolini took only a few months to draft. The constitution of 1968 was used for only around three years. In November 1971, Field Marshal Thanom and group made a coup, cancelled the constitution, and ruled the country by their own system of dictatorship. Around one year later, the constitution of 15 December 1972 was promulgated and remains in force up to the time of writing.

From this evidence, it can be seen that the slavery vision is a danger to the Thai nation and people. Sooner or later it provides the support for dictators to return with increased power and again govern the people as slaves. The dictator changes from person to person, but the dictatorship remains.

## V

Many students and representatives of journalists have written to ask whether I have any suggestion about the drafting of the new constitution. Let me reply with just the few following points for those interested to study.

As I have already said, let the new constitution be in line with the aim for full democracy of the heroes of 14 October, so that it may last a long time, and so that the mass of the people can concentrate on making a living, for the sake of economic prosperity and peace, instead of spending their time fighting to change a constitution which does not accord with this aim.

This aforesaid aim is in line with King Prajadhipok's wish, which was the important point-of-origin *(mae bot)* for the fundamental change from absolute royal power to constitutional democracy. Nobody should show disrespect for this important point-of-origin which changed the basis of the system.

In studying law, it is not enough just to study the provisions clause by clause. The interpretation of law must take into account the intention of the law as well. The intention appears in the preamble.

Some people have listened to misleading rumours from the enemies of the People's Party that King Prajadhipok simply put his signature on the constitution of 10 December 1932 which the government of that time proposed, as if he was only a royal signet stamped on the constitution and other legislation. In truth, the preamble of the constitution records that he "reviewed meticulously every process". That is, he sent a message to the government summoning Phraya Manopakon, Phraya Phahon, and myself to attend in audience to hear his opinions and proposals about the constitution, especially the preamble which states the major intention of the constitution. The People's Party asked the king himself to make a draft so that it would accord with the king's desire. The king accepted this responsibility. When the king's original draft was complete, he had Phra Sanprasoet (Nakha-prathip) bring it to see if I had any opinions. I asked Phra Sanprasoet to convey my reply that I agreed with the royal proposal on all points. The constitution drafting committee agreed that the preamble was in line with the intention of the people and the royal desire, and was also very elegantly expressed. The Assembly considered the preamble and approved it by unanimous resolution.

The royal wish for the Thai people to have full democratic freedom is apparent in the preamble as follows:

By royal command, the constitution of the kingdom of Siam bestows on the king's people full sovereignty from this day forward.

This constitution had a provisional section with MPs of type 2 as half of the total number. The king devised this as a necessity during the changeover from the absolute monarchy to constitutional democracy, because in any major change of the political system which alters the foundations of politics or of politics and economy, it is necessary to have a provisional section. But when the term of the provisional section was over, there would remain only MPs of one type, that is the type elected by the people, in accordance with the king's wish for the people to enjoy full sovereignty. The king had no wish to resume the power to appoint any members of parliament at all.

It should be explained also that when war arose in Europe, and the Thai government of the time was preparing to mobilize the army reserves and special reserves into the regular forces to deal with the situation that might arise in Indochina, this meant that those Thai males would not easily be able to exercise their electoral rights on an equal basis with those not mobilized. As there was no knowing how long the danger of war would continue, the government of the time proposed to the Assembly to extend the provisional section from ten to twenty years. The meeting of the Assembly proceeded according to the rules on constitutional amendment in every detail. Not only type-2 members alone took the resolution to extend the provisional section, but type-1 members who had been elected directly by the people also voted unanimously in favour of the resolution. Then when the provisional section had been in force for fourteen years, there was no longer any necessity to keep it up to the full twenty years. The preamble of the constitution of 9 May 1946 runs as follows:

> Then Nai Pridi Banomyong who at that time held the office of regent, remarked to Nai Khuang Aphaiwong, prime minister, that the constitution of the kingdom of Thailand granted by the king to the Thai people was now in its fourteenth year; government under the democratic system in accordance with constitutional democracy had brought progress to the country in many respects; the people had come to know the benefit of this system of government truly well; yet the political situation has changed considerably; the time had come when the provisional section of the constitution should be abolished, and the constitution of the kingdom of Thailand should be amended. The prime minister thus discussed the issue with type-2 MPs and with the promoters of the constitution. When agreement had been reached, the government of Nai Khuang Aphaiwong's party proposed a resolution to the Assembly on 19 July 1946 to appoint a special sub-committee to research and study how the constitution of the kingdom of Thailand should be amended to bring it into line with the political situation of the country and to make the government yet more fully democratic.

Nai Prakop Hutasing, chairman of the drafting committee of the new constitution [i.e. the 1974 constitution], has stated in interview to some newspapers that they would select good things from Thai constitutions in the past to consider for the new draft.

To help the constitution drafting committee, the government, and the legislative assembly which will consider the draft constitution at the final stage, to receive opinions broadly from university and school students inside Thailand and studying overseas, and from the mass of the people who will come under this new constitution; and to remove misunderstandings arising from propaganda which appeared in some newspapers which are the voice of certain parties, that the constitution which they are drafting will be the most democratic; I think university and school students and the mass of the people should set up groups to study every constitution which Thailand has had, to consider in great detail whether any version is or is not truly the most democratic, and then to report to the drafting committee, the government, and the legislative assembly.

To this end, these various study groups must have copies of every Thai constitution. That being so, the government must print a book collecting together all the constitutions to serve as a tool for the drafting committee, the ministers, and the legislative assembly in their process of deliberation. I thus propose the government should print this book for these study groups also, for sale at a moderate price, even printed on proof paper. Also it should be printed quickly in order to be timely. The printing cost should not be very much when compared with the meeting allowances and expenses of drafting so many constitutions already.

In the past, some people have misappropriated the royal command for personal benefit, sometimes without understanding and sometimes by feigning not to understand. This came about because some constitutions were written in a way that made people misunderstand, especially about countersigning the royal command. In the new constitution, please have it written clearly in what cases the king has power to initiate something himself, or on the advice and approval of whoever and whatever. This has already been done in legislation which clearly states "with the approval of parliament". In the drafting of royal decrees and royal commands to make various appointments, it should be written clearly in the constitution that this can be done by the king himself or with the approval of whoever or whatever organization. For example, suppose that the king is to appoint senators as in the 1949 constitution which some people claim was the most democratic. Let it be written that "the king shall appoint the senators as proposed by the chairman of the Privy Council or by the Privy Council". It should not be written "the king shall appoint" and then "the chairman of the Privy Council shall countersign the royal command" because this makes the mass of the people misunderstand that the king first chooses people according to the royal disposition and then has the chairman of the Privy Council countersign the royal signature. The mass of the people know that the privy councillors themselves choose the people they think should be senators and propose them to the king for signature. In the same way, if senators are appointed as in the 1968 constitution whereby the government countersigns the royal command, then write clearly in the constitution that the senators are proposed by the government for the king to appoint. For instance, during the time the under-the-water-jar and 1949 constitutions were in force, there were some senators who falsely claimed that they accepted the position of senator because they could not go against a royal command, even though they themselves knew well in their own hearts that the Privy Council or government had proposed their own people to the king for royal signature.

The constitution of 9 May 1946 respected the wish of King Prajadhipok to give his people "full sovereignty". This is the point-of-origin of constitutional democracy. Thus it laid down that the members of both the Senate and Assembly would be elected by the people, because if senators are people the government or Privy Council proposes to the king for appointment, it goes against the royal wish to infringe the full sovereignty of the Thai people. Such appointment is no different at all to the system of type-2 members which had already been revoked. It is even worse because type-2 members were only provisional and when the provisional term was over, there remained only the members elected by the people. As the system of appointive senators probably lasts for as long as a constitution is used, this system is "semi-democracy", not "full democracy".

In Japan and almost all European countries which have monarchs as head of state and parliaments consisting of Senate and Assembly, senators are elected by the people by direct election or by two-stage election in which the people elect an electoral college and then this organization elects the senators. The exception is the British *"House of Lords"* which can be incorrectly translated into Thai as "assembly of nobles *(khun nang)*", giving the wrong idea that the old Thai nobles should be appointed as senators. But *"Lord"* in Britain is a feudal lord *(chao sakdina)* who has inherited from his ancestors one of the large or small landed estates which were combined under the United Kingdom. They are not nobles who are government officials with high rank in the Thai fashion. The British House of Lords is comparable to the assembly of a federation of feudal lords whose territories were united under the British monarchy in old times. In the period from then until the present, there are some members of the British House of Lords who were granted by the monarch the title of lord in name only and who do not hold power over any territory.

The kingdom of Denmark has a single chamber called the *"Folketing"* whose members are elected by the people.

The kingdom of Sweden has a single chamber called the *"Riksdag"* whose members are elected by the people.

The kingdom of Norway has a parliament, the *"Storting"*, with two chambers, the *"Lagting"* and the *"Odelsting"* which are elected by the people directly and indirectly.

The kingdom of the Netherlands (Holland) has two chambers, with members of the upper chamber elected by the provincial councils, and the lower chamber directly elected by the people.

The kingdom of Belgium has two chambers. The Senate includes members elected by the people and also the king's sons, who are members by virtue of their position but who in practice do not exercise this right. The House of Representatives has members elected by the people.

Some newly independent black kingdoms in Africa have constitutions giving the monarch power of appointing the members of the upper chamber.

Concerning the appointment of senators under the 1949 constitution by the chairman of the Privy Council countersigning the royal command, we should consider what is the general principle of constitutional law, and what has been the result in practice, in order to make things clear in concrete terms for university and school students and the mass of the people also.

a. In what monarchical countries around the world does the constitution have provisions as in the 1949 constitution?

b. Thai students in Britain should know full well that the British Privy Council has over three hundred members, and the chairman does not have the power to countersign the royal command to appoint members of the upper house. Yet in Thailand by the 1949 constitution, the Privy Council had no more than nine members including the chairman.

c. Although it was written in the 1949 constitution that the king appointed the Privy Council yet the president of the parliament countersigned the royal command. Students interested in constitutional law should know what countersigning the royal command means.

d. In practice, the chairman cannot countersign for the appointment of senators on his own, but he must consult the Privy Council of no more than nine persons.

e. In practice, we must consider the real situation of who the privy councillors are. As far as I can recall, at present there is Krommun Phitthayalap as the chairman, Chaophraya Sithammathibet, Phraya Manawaratsewi, Phraya Srisena, General Luang Suranarong, and Nai Sanya Thammasak (if I have made any omission or mistake, please let the reader complete the list).

I am trying to recall those who used to be privy councillors who have passed away or resigned to take up other positions. I can think of General

Luang Senanarong (father of Lieutenant General Sawaeng Senanarong), Phraya Borirakwetchakan, and General Luang Kampanatsaenyakon (formerly minister in the cabinets of Field Marshal Phibun and Field Marshal Sarit). It seems Luang Chamrunnittisat was once a privy councillor but resigned to take up the post of minister of justice. If I'm wrong please excuse me.

·Students and the mass of the people should use their discrimination to see what was the real effect in practice of the method of appointing senators under the 1949 constitution.

During the drafting of the constitution of 10 December [1932] there was a problem over whether it should be written into the constitution that the king had the duty to uphold the constitution. The king had Phraya Phahon and myself attend in audience at Chitlada Palace. The king said that the constitutions of many countries with presidents as heads of state laid down that the head of state had the duty to uphold and protect the constitution, and must take an oath to that effect before assuming office. The king said that such a provision was not necessary for Siam as the king's grant [of the constitution] was already equivalent to a vow. Besides, by royal custom the king made vows during the coronation ceremony. I asked whether, now that the system of government had been changed to a constitutional monarchy, he would like to add something to the royal vows in the coronation cere-mony of future kings. He said there already was a passage in the preamble which enjoined members of the royal family to join together with the common people to protect and abide by the constitution. Those who would be kings in future would be drawn from the royal family and so would have the duty to uphold the constitution.

Then the king commanded a page to bring a special issue of the Royal Gazette for 1925 for me to read a passage of the royal [coronation] oath as follows:

Then the king speaks in Thai words from the Pali as follows:

"Oh Brahmans. Now that I have assumed the full responsibility of government, I shall reign in righteousness for the good weal of the populace. I extend my royal authority over you and your goods and your chattels, and as your sovereign do hereby provide for your righteous pro-tection, defence, and keeping. Trust me and live at ease."

The high priest *(phraratchakhru)* is the first to accept the royal command as follows:

"I do receive the first command of Your Majesty."

"It is done . . . "

"I make the vow to set the royal heart to maintain the ten ways of the king, the imperial observance of moral precepts, and other matters in accord with royal wish." [Part of this translation is adapted from *The Coronation of His Majesty Prajadhipok of Siam B.E. 2468*, pp. 15, 17.]

King Prajadhipok explained that the royal wish at the end [of the above passage] was already clear, that is, future kings must protect the constitution.

Later this coronation ceremony was conducted again in the reign of the present king.

The final passage of the royal preamble to the constitution of 10 December 1932 runs:

Let all the royal family members, all government officials both military and civilian, and all the people in the kingdom be united and harmonious in protecting and abiding by the constitution of the kingdom of Siam so it may last together with the territory of Siam in eternity, according to the royal wish in every way.

Phraya Phahon asked how the king would uphold the constitution. King Prajadhipok said that if the government proposed anything against the constitution, the king would return it without affixing the royal signature. Phraya Phahon continued that the People's Party was worried that military officers who had been dismissed from the reserves would think of overthrowing the government and presenting a new constitution of their own for the royal signature; what would the king do? The king said he would consider that group in rebellion *(khabot)*, and in his status as commander in chief he would hold that group were enemies of the crown in defiance of the royal command. If they forced him to affix his signature, he would abdicate and let them find another king to affix the royal signature.

Later in 1933, a number of officers of the military reserve under the leadership of Phraongchao Boworadej raised troops from some provincial centres and came to menace Bangkok in order to overthrow the government. King Prajadhipok gave royal permission for the government to call this group a "rebellion", and did not lend the royal name to this rebel group in any way. This was the royal graciousness to uphold the constitution which the king had granted. The king was ready to use his power as commander in chief if the government troops were unable to suppress the rebellion.

The case of regents differs from that of the king who takes the aforementioned vow in the coronation ceremony. Hence regents have to swear an oath to the parliament before assuming office as follows:

to protect and abide by the constitution of the kingdom of Siam (Thai).

In other essays, I have talked about the occasion, at the time I was regent, when I opposed the government for acting against the constitution, and refused to declare war against Britain and America. I would not put my name to the declaration and hence it was not valid.

The constitution of 9 May 1946 did not arise from a coup, but was written in accordance with the constitution of 10 December 1932, as already noted. At that time King Ananda Mahidol was a minor. The regents appointed by the parliament in accordance with the constitution of 1946 swore an oath to the parliament "to protect and abide by the constitution of the kingdom of Thailand". Hence if Kromkhun Chainat had acted according to his oath, he would not have agreed to sign on behalf of the king on the under-the-water-jar constitution, and would have carried out his duty as commander in chief in place of the king who was in his minority. Then there might have been no under-the-water-jar constitution, which was the point-of-origin for Thailand subsequently having so many constitutions that people cannot remember how many. The system could have been upheld under which the Thai people had full democracy in accordance with the wish of King Prajadhipok.

The temporary constitution of 27 June 1932, which was drafted by the People's Party itself, and presented to the king to grant to the Thai people for the first time, laid down only that the *"kasat"* was the supreme head of state, and had no clause giving the king power as commander in chief.

One day during the drafting of the constitution of 10 December 1932, Phraya Phahon and I were summoned by the king to attend in audience at Chitlada Palace. The king said that the word *kasat* was incorrect because it meant only a warrior. To be correct it had to be written as *"phramahakasat"*, that is the great warrior who holds the weapons to protect the country. This was the royal custom from old times. Phraya Phahon and I agreed with the king and suggested that not only should it be written that the head of state is the king *(phramahakasat)*, but also that he should be commander in chief with power over all the military. The king said this was correct since the presidents of various countries were commanders in chief over the whole military; this was a matter which went together with the royal power to protect the country and to uphold the constitution, because the king had the power to command the military forces in action, and to order the military to act in ways that they should act, and to refrain from actions that they should refrain from.

Subsequent constitutions laid down the power of the king as the supreme head of state and as the commander in chief.

Even though the reactionary dictators reduced the power of the king in the constitution on many points, that group still agreed to the provision that the king was the head of state and held the position of commander in chief, which are powers passed down from the constitution of 1932.

Some people interpret the word "supreme" *(sung sut)* as meaning the highest. But in Thai *"chom"* means the topmost *(yot ying)*, hence *chom thap* (commander in chief) means the topmost over the supreme commander *(phu banchakan thahan sung sut)*, a position which is not in the constitution, but was established by royal decree and is subordinate to the commander in chief *(chom thap)*.

During the Second World War when I was regent, there was conflict between the powers of the commander in chief and the supreme commander. As I have written in the book referred to above, acting on behalf of the king in his status as commander in chief, I gave orders to the supreme commander to take certain actions and to refrain from actions which should be refrained from. For instance the fact that he wanted to raise troops to suppress patriots brought about the dismissal of Field Marshal Phibun from the office of prime minister. I personally requested Nai Khuang, the prime minister, to go and negotiate with Field Marshal Phibun at Lopburi. But Phibun did not accept, and was preparing to raise troops from Lopburi. I saw that unless there was a royal command issued to make things clear, Field Marshal Phibun might bring forces to slaughter people. Thus for documentary evidence, I signed on behalf of the king on a royal command dismissing Field Marshal Phibun from the post of supreme commander, rescinding that post, establishing the post of commander in chief *(mae thap yai)* in accordance with the act on military affairs, and appointing General Phraya Phahon to hold this post. Phibun had considerable forces under his command, but when he saw the royal command he did not dare disobey.

There are comparable examples from countries with kings as heads of state where the king can order the whole military, as follows.

In 1936, the Japanese Young Military group mutinied, seized certain areas of Tokyo, and used weapons to kill politicians and innocent people. The military command could not restrain this Young Military Group. Emperor Hirohito used his power to order the Military Group which gave rise to this evil to lay down their arms and surrender to their superiors. He had them punished as an example. Peace returned for the Japanese people. Nobody complained that the emperor contravened the constitution.

In 1945 the Allies dropped atomic bombs on Hiroshima and Nagasaki. People were killed, injured, and devastated. Emperor Hirohito saw that fighting on against the Allies would bring no chance of victory but would only cause the death of more of the emperor's people. He agreed with some politicians that they should surrender to the Allies in order to find a way to revive the Japanese nation at a future opportunity. A violently minded military group used force to seize power over some parts of the military headquarters, and opposed the emperor issuing a royal command to his people over the radio. Emperor Hirohito used his royal power decisively to order the suppression of this violently minded military group. The Japanese radio was able to broadcast the royal command according to the emperor's wish. Although Japan was submitted to the Allies, before long Japan developed economically, bringing prosperity to workers, farmers, and all classes of Japan. If the emperor had not agreed to use the royal power decisively against the violently minded Japanese soldiers, the Japanese nation would have been devastated, and it would have been difficult to revive the country. The history of Japan hence praises the emperor rather than condemning him for contravening the constitution. This was because the emperor considered the Japanese nation over and above the emperor.

In Europe there is the example of King Victor Emmanuel III of Italy. Under the fascist constitution of the dictator Mussolini, the king was head of state in name only. But when in 1943 he saw that Mussolini was bringing ruin to the Italian nation, he used his power as head of state decisively to order people loyal to himself to arrest Mussolini, and he issued a royal command dismissing Mussolini from various positions including prime minister in order to rescue Italy from the fascist system. When the Second World War was over, he abdicated in favour of the crown prince, Umberto.

History and current events in several countries have examples of the head of state becoming like the statue of a guardian spirit adorning a shrine or spirit house, so that others can have dictatorial power.

In the eleventh century in Japan, some people displayed such great reverence for the emperor that they worshipped him as a guardian spirit descended from the god of the sun. The emperor ceased to exercise his power and duty in the kingdom, but devoted himself to religious ceremonies, and affixed the royal seal in accordance with whatever the dictator of the "shogun" system wanted. The shoguns took over the power of governing the realm, consolidated a dictatorial system, and passed this inheritance down to their descendants for eight hundred years. Japan fell behind the Western countries in this period. Around the mid nineteenth century, patriotic Japanese who desired progress and prosperity for their nation, overthrew the dictatorship of the shogun and revived the royal power which the emperor should have in accordance with a democratic constitutional system. Later when the Meiji emperor passed away, the residual slavery vision of the shogun system reduced the power of the emperor in practice to the point where Japan was defeated in the Second World War. At present, the emperor has the power and duties which he should have under a democratic constitution. This has made Japan have more economic progress and prosperity than many Western countries.

In Bhutan before 1907, the head of state was venerated as a "righteous king" *(thammaracha)* whose duties consisted only of religious ceremonies. The royal seal, the power to govern the realm, effectively fell into the hands of dictators who held the position of "god-king" *(thepracha)*. In drafting the 1959 constitution, which was the model for that of 1972, perhaps someone advised Field Marshal Sarit to include some residual traces from the Hindu kingdoms around the Himalayan region, so that he acted in the same style. Although the Thai dictators did not call themselves "god-kings", in their behaviour they were comparable with the "god-kings" of Bhutan before 1907.

In Nepal before 1951, the head of state was elevated as the "great royal king" *(maharacha-thi-racha)* but only had power to stamp the royal seal on certain national documents. The real administrative power rested with another "great king", the prime minister. The post was inherited in the "Rana" family. It should be noted that Thai dictators from Field Marshal Sarit onwards were not Sarit's descendants, but they belonged to the same family of dictators and passed on the dictatorial power by inheritance. We all know also that if Field Marshal Thanom had quit normally, the dictatorial power would have been inherited by Field Marshal Praphat and Colonel Narong, the son of Field Marshal Thanom.

The drafters, the government, and the legislative assembly which will take the resolution over the new draft constitution must jointly take responsibility to ensure that the new constitution does not open a route for people to assume dictatorial power following the examples from the histories of many countries and from the Thai past, by doing away with the power which the king should have in a constitutional democracy. The transfer by King Prajadhipok of power from the absolute monarchy to a monarchy under a democratic constitution is a point-of-origin which is sacred. No person has the right to show disrespect for this sacred point-of-origin.

The mass of the people surely want constitutional judges who maintain what is fair and just *(tham)*. The major problem in appointing constitutional judges is what method to use to have judges who are fair and just in interpreting the constitution. The 1946 constitution gave parliament the power to appoint constitutional judges because the senators and MPs were elected by the people. But under the 1949 constitution, senators were appointed. Wise people should use their discrimination to consider who the judges appointed under this constitution were, and whether the interpretations of those appointed by political office had any bias in favour of the government. May I propose that all the high court judges should form a convention of constitutional judges which is not under the influence of the government. The mass of the people would have a good assurance about interpreting the constitution, and preventing the government from any infringement of the constitution.

## APPENDIX

1. Many Thai students overseas have asked me whether the appointment of senators by the chairman of the Privy Council countersigning the royal signature in accordance with the 1949 constitution had any effect in practice. I explain that the provisional section of that constitution transferred the senators from the under-the-water-jar constitution to be senators under the 1949 constitution also. But there was a provision that half of the senators had to be changed every three years by drawing lots. Those who lost their seats could be reappointed. Hence, on 17 November 1950, fifty senators who drew lots lost their seats, and on 18 November 1950, another fifty received royal appointment in their place with the chairman of the Privy Council countersigning the royal signature in accordance with the 1949 constitution. Broken down by title and by rank they were as follows:

    a. By title: Momchao, 6; Momratchawong with the title of Mom (prior to Phraya), 1; Phraya, 14; Phra, 11; Luang, 5; no title, 8.

    b. Broken down by military rank and non-military: those with military rank from major up to general, 21; no military rank, 29.

2. The names of senators appointed by the chairman of the Privy Council countersigning the royal signature on 18 November 1950 were: 1. Lieutenant-General Phraya Aphaisongkhram; 2. Lieutenant-Colonel Luang Chai-asawarak; 3. Major-General Mom Sanitwongseni; 4. Phraya Borirakwetchakan; 5. Phraya Acharatsongsiri; 6. General Mangkon Phromyothi; 7. Phraya Sara-akkaphongthammaphilat; 8. Khunying Lekha Aphaiwong; 9. Phraya Suriyanuwongprawat; 10. Major-General Phraya Intharawichit; 11. Nai Banchong Sicharun; 12. Phra Nitinaiprasan; 13. Luang Prakopnitisan; 14. Phra Aphakantraphatphisan; 15. Luang Chalanutson; 16. Commodore Momchao Phonpricha Kamalat; 17. Colonel Phra Ramnarong; 18. Phraya Krittaratsongsawat; 19. Momchao Saritdet Chayangkun; 20. Momchao Chatchawit Kasemsan; 21. Phraya Anuman-rachathon; 22. Phra Phetcharakiri; 23. Momchao Disanuwat Ditsakun; 24. Phraya Methathibodi; 25. Major-General Phraya Phichaisongkhram; 26. Phra Chaipanya; 27. Momchao Upalisan Chumphon; 28. Major-General Momchao Pridithepphong Thewakun; 29. Major-General Phra Udom-

yothathiyut; 30. Commodore Luang Samruat Withisamut; 31. Lieutenant-Colonel Thanphuying La-iat Phibunsongkhram; 32. Nai Charin Krisanaphakdi; 33. Lieutenant-General Phraya Srisoraratphakdi; 34. Phra Manuphanwimonsat; 35. Major-General Ronnasanwisawakam; 36. Commodore Phraya Saraphaiphiphat; 37. Lieutenant-Colonel Phra Asasongkhram; 38. Major Luang Sorasitthayanukan; 39. Phraya Satchaphirom; 40. Nai Chulin Lamsam; 41. Captain Luang Chamnikolakan; 42. Rear-Admiral Lek Sumit; 43. Phra Chuangkasetsilpakan; 44. Phraya Prakitkonlasat; 45. Major-General Banyat Thephasadin na Ayutthaya; 46. Major-General Nom Ketnuti; 47. Phra Sukhumwinitchai; 48. Rear-Admiral Thawan Thamrongnawasawat; 49. Phraya Borihannititham; 50. Nai Chun Watchakhup.

3. I gave those students further opinions as follows.

At present the numbers of people related to the royal family with titles from Momchao upwards has fallen. Hence people lower down the rank order, that is Momratchawong, have a good opportunity.

At present, the number of people with titles has fallen considerably from before, because since 1932, nobody has received a title. As for the old holders, many people have surrendered them. Later there was an act to revoke titles except for those people who wished to preserve their own old title.

The 1949 constitution prepared to revive titles. Clause 12 ran: "the king has the power to establish titles and to grant royal decorations". On this matter it must be understood that the government could countersign the royal command and hence it was the government who would propose names to the king for appointment. However, this constitution was in force for only three years and then abrogated. The government did not ask the king to establish any new titles in time. However, there were some people and parties who appealed to Field Marshal Sarit to revive titles. This has continued to the present. Thus, if the constitution currently being newly drafted follows in the path of the 1949 constitution, we can expect to see a new generation of people with titles in numbers according to the government's needs, in the same way as the royal decorations which can be seen everywhere.

The 1949 constitution took over the senators from the under-the-water-jar constitution to become the first batch of senators under that charter. There is a problem that if the constitution being newly drafted follows in the footsteps of the 1949 constitution, will the members of the current legislative council become wholly or in part the first batch of senators under the new constitution?

# 19. EXCERPTS FROM: *MY CHEQUERED LIFE AND MY TWENTY-ONE YEARS OF EXILE IN PEOPLE'S CHINA*

[All proper names are spelled as they are in the original French.]

## CHAPTER IV
## THE UNDERGROUND KINGDOM OF SIAM

### XI

When King Ananda reached his majority *(sui juris)*, I invited him to return to Siam to fulfil the function of head of state. The king arrived in Bangkok on 5 December 1945. Hence my function as regent was automatically ended. The king conferred on me the title of "senior statesman" which is a purely honorific title with no executive power. That allowed me to take rest, which I had desired so much after my painful and difficult work throughout the war and the three months following.

On the recommendation of the government installed after the war, the National Assembly was dissolved. After the general election, a government was installed in which the prime minister and other ministers were reactionaries. Disputes between progressive and reactionary MPs multiplied in the parliament. The government resigned. The king asked me to form a government in which I would be prime minister. With the support of the progressive majority of the Assembly, a new constitution was passed, according to which parliament would be composed of a Senate and a chamber of representatives, with all the members elected by the people.

The disputes between progressives and reactionaries in no way diminished. On the contrary, they increased from the fact that the Supreme Court had acquitted Field Marshal Pibul by invoking the non-retroactivity of the law (promulgated after the war) on war crimes.

Hence Pibul at freedom resumed his vengeful political course in collaboration with the reactionary elements.

## XII

Some months later, that is on 9 June 1946, King Ananda died in his bedroom in the royal palace from a revolver shot in his head. After police investigation, and on the recommendation of the king's uncle, a communique was issued by my government announcing that the king had died accidentally from the bullet of a revolver which belonged to him.

Hence, I recommended to parliament to give its approval for the sole brother of the king to ascend the throne, under the name King Bhumibol. As the new king was still a minor, a Regency Council presided over by the king's uncle himself was nominated by the National Assembly. This Regency Council then requested me to form a new government.

After the partial parliamentary election at which I was elected MP without opposition in my constituency, I voluntarily resigned as prime minister. A new democratic government was installed composed of progressive and democratic ministers. But the reactionaries accused the new government of being my protégé. For this reason, the reactionaries directed their attacks against me personally by making campaigns of slander against me—among other things, that King Ananda had not died accidentally, but that the former secretary and valets, of whom I was an accomplice, had killed the monarch. These slanders were destined to deceive the people in order to prime the way for the reactionary coup d'état of which we will speak in chapter 7.

## CHAPTER VII
## THE REACTIONARY COUP D'ÉTAT AND MY FIRST ESCAPE FROM SIAM TO SINGAPORE AND CHINA

## I

In November 1947, a military coup d'état supported by the ultraconservatives and chauvinists, overthrew the legal government of Admiral Thamrong who was accused of being my protégé. They attacked my house in a merciless attempt to kill me along with my wife and my young children. They considered me an obstacle to their rise, and an accomplice in the killing of King Ananda. Field Marshal Pibul, who had been released some months earlier on grounds of the non-retroactivity of the law on war crimes, was nominated by the makers of the coup d'état as supreme commander of the armed forces, with total power of command over the authority of the state. The makers of the coup d'état proclaimed a new constitution according to which the senators were no longer elected by a two-stage indirect election, but were directly nominated by the head of state; and this nomination had to be countersigned by the leader of the coup d'état. The minimum age for electoral candidates for the chamber of representatives, formally fixed at twenty-three years, was pushed back to thirty-five years, thus corresponding to the minimum age for senators in the United States. Anyway, this measure was only temporary, as later Siam was governed over several changes by other constitutions which were fascist, semi-fascist, or neo-fascist. In addition, this constitution suppressed many political liberties. A new government was installed, with a majority composition of ultra-conservative elements. But some months later, the military asked this government to resign and Field Marshal Pibul again became the prime minister.

The night of the coup d'état, I made a miraculous escape from the soldiers who surrounded my house, and remained for some time with some naval friends in the base at Sattahip. Foreseeing a civil war, I decided to leave my homeland and take refuge initially in Singapore while awaiting a favourable moment for my peaceful return to Siam.

With my travelling companions, I went to see a friend who had fought under the command of Lord Mountbatten during the war, Captain Stratford Dennis RN, who had become naval attaché in the British embassy, to ask him to contact his ambassador to communicate my wish to go to Singapore as a political refugee. Thus Dennis, with the cooperation of his colleague, Captain Gardes USN, the American naval attaché, was charged with conducting us from the quay of the port of Bangkok to the high seas in a small motorboat belonging to Gardes, crewed by himself, his wife, and his sister-in-law. Then we embarked on a British oil tanker bound for Singapore. The captain and officers of the oil tanker received us cordially and provided us with every facility.

II

At that time Singapore was part of the British colonies. Although the British government had granted me political exile, I understood well that this would last until the day when it recognized the new regime in Siam. To that end, I had asked our ambassadors in London and Nankin (in disagreement with the new regime in Siam) each to provide me with a diplomatic passport with visas allowing me to enter various foreign countries. The two ambassadors agreed. Thus I had been able to obtain diplomatic visas from the embassies of China, USA, France, etc. I remained seven months in Singapore waiting for a favourable moment for my return to Siam. I then learnt that a certain number of my friends were secretly preparing a revolutionary uprising against the reactionary regime, which required a certain time before being executed. Thus I left Singapore to visit other countries while waiting for the event.


## III


At the end of May 1949, I left Singapore to go to Hong Kong where my Siamese friends, including the temporary consul general of Siam, received us cordially.

From Hong Kong we went to Shanghai where our Chinese friends, born in Siam, as well as some members of the Siamese embassy at Nankin, welcomed us.

Sanguan Tularaks, the former Siamese ambassador to Nankin, and myself went to the house of the Mexican ambassador to ask him for a visa which would allow us to visit his country—which he granted us without the least difficulty.

We thought of going to Mexico with a stop by San Francisco. While we were presenting our passports to the Chinese official in charge of immigration, a young American called Norman Hannah, vice-consul in Shanghai, arrived in a rush, wrenched my passport from the hands of the Chinese official, and cancelled the American visa given me by the American embassy in London. I then realized that a young American vice-consul had full authority over a Chinese official, and even over the American ambassador (later I learned that this vice-consul was a CIA agent). Besides that, I understood that the medal and citations bestowed on me by the American government were of no value, but in fact I was considered as a criminal on the accusation of their own enemies during the war (Pibul), in refusing me a transit stay of a few hours on American territory.

The Americans in Shanghai tried to contact me to clarify the incident, but I refused to meet them.

One day, one of my American friends, who had worked with me at the time of the resistance against the Japanese, invited me to dine with him in the name of friendship. I was surprised to meet there the American consul general who expressed his regrets for the incident of the visa and informed me that Marshal George Marshall, the American secretary of state, had commanded that the American visa should be replaced in my passport. A little later, the former American vice-consul, Norman Hannah, was transferred to Bangkok. It was the CIA which encouraged the reactionary Siamese police to arrest my wife and eldest son who were in Bangkok during my absence. My wife was then "interned" in the police headquarters for eighty-four days, while my eldest son Parl, aged twenty, was tried and condemned to twenty years imprisonment for a so-called plot against the security of the state. (He was released under a general amnesty law at the time of the 2500th anniversary of the Buddha).

Hannah was transferred to Afghanistan for a short period, and then again transferred to Bangkok as counsellor of the American embassy. One day the former Siamese ambassador in Paris gave me a copy of Hannah's report relating the incident of the visa. This report contained many lies. Among others, he wrote that after having cancelled the American visa in my passport, he came to see me at my hotel, that I received him amicably, and that we had dinner together.

Before Buddha, I swear that I have never seen Hannah's face again since the day of the incident.

I learnt that eventually at the end of 1970, Hannah left his post in Bangkok to return to the USA.

I have no rancour against Hannah. I would simply like the American tax payers to realize that the sums of money used for the petty expenses of the CIA correspond sometimes with the false reports on which basis decisions are taken which are prejudicial to the interests of the Americans themselves.

IV

Chiang Kai-chek, having been informed of the incident at the airport, expressed to me his desire to grant me hospitality in China, assuring me that he would not forget my contribution to the cause of the Allies during the war and that he would never extradite me, for he remembers that the Pibul government had acted with dishonesty and without scruple vis-à-vis China. As a result, he commanded some of his officials to grant me facilities for my stay in China.

V

On 1 October of the same year, I learnt that the Siamese government, thanks to the betrayal by one member of a revolutionary group, had arrested many officers and politicians who would make a revolutionary uprising on the following day. This rebel movement was led by General Netr Khema-yothin, former pupil of the Higher Staff College of France, who had been one of the members of the "Free Thai Movement" during the war. A certain number of my brothers were attached to this new rebel movement. This attempted uprising has been called the "Rebellion of 1 October 1949".

Those who were able to escape arrest sent their representative to discuss with me about establishing another plan for revolution against the reactionary regime. We agreed that I should personally lead another uprising in cooperation with our friends in the royal navy, my students from Thammasat University, some democratic elements, and some patriotic soldiers and police including some admirals and a general, the former head of the general staff of the royal army dismissed by the reactionary coup d'état.

When my friends in Siam advised me that the moment was favourable, we hired a boat of twenty tons to go secretly from the Chinese coast to the eastern coast of the Gulf of Siam.

## CHAPTER VIII
## THE DEFEAT OF THE GRAND PALACE REBELLION
## (26 FEBRUARY 1949)

### I

On 26 February 1949 around 9 P.M., accompanied by my friends I left the house where I was hiding in Bangkok to go to Thammasat University where the revolutionary advance party, consisting of a certain number of my students and other patriots, was waiting for me. I gave the order for our advance party to go and disarm the company of soldiers guarding the Grand Palace so that we could occupy it. The king had not lived in this palace for over a hundred years. It served only for grand ceremonies, official and religious. This palace consisted of the throne hall, former royal residences, the Buddhist temple housing the emerald statue of the Buddha, the Finance Ministry, the strong-room of the State Treasury, the Royal Secretariat, and a division of the Government Secretariat.

The commander of the palace guard was not able to resist the surprise attack of our advance party. Thus after fifteen minutes we controlled the whole palace. Simultaneously, our light mortar launched its projectiles on the headquarters of the reactionary forces. The first infantry regiment of the enemy tried to leave their barracks and were stopped by the shells of our grenade-launchers. The government radio station was occupied by our unit commanded by a colonel (a former fighter in our resistance movement during the war). Through the night from 26 to 27 February, there was sporadic fighting between the revolutionaries and reactionaries.

### II

Unfortunately our reinforcements promised by the naval division were stopped by forces loyal to the new regime.

Around six o'clock in the morning of 27 February, the troops of Field Marshal Pibul, commanded by General Sarit Thanarat, received the order to bombard the Grand Palace which we were occupying.

Seeing that our reinforcements had not arrived in time, and to avoid destruction of historic buildings and objects of great value to the nation found in the Grand Palace, I commanded our forces to withdraw into the headquarters of a naval command situated on the bank of the great river beside the Grand Palace. From there, I explained to my companions in arms that they must cross the river on boats placed at our disposal by an admiral, commander of a naval unit, while I remained in the headquarters of the naval detachment to await our reinforcements.

During this time, the government troops regained control of the whole capital. This was hence the defeat of my uprising of 26 February, named later the "Grand Palace Rebellion".

The government officers who took part in the struggle against our rebellion were promoted to higher ranks, notably General Sarit became field marshal in 1954. In 1957, the latter succeeded in making a coup d'état against Field Marshal Pibul, his own master, who took refuge in the USA and then Japan. At first, Sarit did not himself openly take the power of government. He entrusted the post of prime minister to his subordinate, General Thanom Kitikhachorn. A year later, Sarit made a new coup d'état and overthrew the Thanom government. He himself became prime minister and governed Siam until his death in 1962 [actually 8 December 1963]. Then when General Thanom Kitikhachorn, the subordinate of Sarit and Pibul, became prime minister again, he was promoted to the rank of field marshal and continued to govern Siam until our time, at first under another dictatorial constitution created by Field Marshal Sarit, later under another constitution according to which the Senate was nominated by the king on the recommendation of the prime minister. In November 1972, the constitution promulgated by Thanom himself was suppressed and replaced by a dictatorial regime.

III

On 27 February towards midnight, the frigate captain Manas Charubha conducted me to a secret place. From there my wife and my son Parl helped me go to the house of a patriot who kindly granted me hospitality for five months, even though the government had promised a large reward to whoever revealed our hiding place. This patriot had no inclination for this reward.

Two years later in 1951 the frigate captain Manas and another captain Anond Puntharikapa organized another uprising known as the "Manhattan Rebellion" because a detachment of sailors led by Manas boarded the American ship Manhattan during the ceremony in which the American ship would be presented to Siam in the presence of Field Marshal Pibul, the American ambassador, and leading figures of both countries.

Manas and his detachment arrested the field marshal under the eyes of the Americans and went on board a Siamese gunboat, the Sri Ayudhaya. Then a battle broke out between the marines and navy loyal to the revolutionary cause on one side, and the army and air force loyal to the reactionaries on the other. At first, it seemed that the revolutionary forces controlled the capital, but the air force sent aircraft to bombard the gunboat, the headquarters of the rebellion, without pity for Field Marshal Pibul who was there and who appealed to his loyalists not to use arms and to negotiate peacefully with the rebels. The aircraft bombarded the gunboat anchored in the middle of the great river, which soon sank. Field Marshal Pibul miraculously escaped by jumping into the river, and made it to the bank where he was welcomed by elements who were loyal to him. He was thus able to return to the headquarters of the government forces.

Other army units from neighbouring provinces joined up with those of the government and succeeded in fighting back against the naval units. Finally the government forces were able to retake control of the capital.

The government police arrested several naval officers including the navy commander in chief, along with some civilians suspected of having participated in the rebellion.

Captain Manas and Captain Anond, along with another army officer who was involved in the rebellion, were able to escape secretly and take refuge in Burma. Similarly a certain number of patriots were able to take refuge in Laos, Cambodia, and Singapore.

Some months later, Captain Manas returned secretly to Bangkok to take part in another rebel organization known as the "Peace Rebellion".

On this occasion Manas was arrested at the same time as my son Parl and my wife. Anond stayed in Burma and did not return to Bangkok until recently, thinking that he could benefit from the amnesty law which freed Manas, my son, and some other rebels. But unfortunately, the government authorities arrested him and tried him in the criminal court which condemned him to twenty years imprisonment, the same as Manas, etc. Then his penalty was reduced, and finally he was pardoned by the king in August 1972.


IV


After the defeat of our Grand Palace Rebellion on 26 February 1949, the police arrested every person suspected of having participated. Among them were some who were completely unknown to this rebellion. The criminal court condemned around fifty of our comrades to nine years imprisonment, and acquitted many others for lack of proof. Many comrades succeeded in escaping arrest and took refuge either in the countryside of Siam, or in neighbouring countries, or even better remained in Bangkok in full daylight with a certain nerve, thinking that no witness could testify having seen them taking part in the rebellion which took place during the night of 26 up to the morning of 27 February.

However, four former ministers were arrested—Tong-In, Thavil, Chamlong, Tong-Pleow—who did not take part in the actual rebellion, that is, at the time we occupied the Grand Palace.

On the eve of the rebellion, Tong-In, Thavil, and Chamlong were warned that they should remain in their houses and not enter onto the scene until after the success of the rebellion. For this reason they remained peacefully at home. As Pibul and the reactionaries wanted them for always being opposed to their government, they arrested them. Another former minister, Tong-Pleow, was in Penang (in Malaya) several months before the rebellion, and I never asked him to take part in our rebellion. However, Pibul's police reported having seen this man and sent him a false telegram under the name of one of his wives telling him to return to Bangkok. Far from imagining the subterfuge, he returned to Bangkok and on arrival was arrested by the police.

These four former ministers underwent torture by the reactionary police to the point they were going to die from wounds inflicted by lashes of the whip and blows from fist and foot. To disguise the wounds, on a particularly dark night the police placed these half-dead men in a truck guarded by soldiers with machine guns, followed by another police car commanded by a police colonel. When the truck arrived at a certain point around twenty kilometres from Bangkok, the two vehicles stopped, the police got out and machine-gunned the four innocents. On the following day, the police announced that during the transfer of the accused from one police post to another, Chinese bandits from Malaya had fired on the police to seize the prisoners. The police were thus obliged to respond using their machine guns, and bullets had mortally struck the four accused. Nobody in Siam gave any credence to this account for the simple reasons that the Malay rebels (at that time) were around a thousand kilometres away from Bangkok.

## V

Everything I have just related also accords with the official report of the police and the registered depositions of witnesses in the case of the rebels charged before the criminal court of Bangkok.

However, eighteen years after the defeat of the Manhattan Rebellion, or exactly twenty years after that of the Grand Palace, that is in 1969, an American named William Warren, employed as a teacher by one of the universities in Bangkok, wrote a book on the story of Jim Thompson known as the king of Thai silk, and in a passage about the death of the former ministers, he accused me of having jumped into the river to save my skin, abandoning my companions, at the time Pibul's troops attacked my headquarters.

This teacher spoke of me because his friend Jim Thompson knew me. He thought that his friend knew Siamese history well. However, Jim Thompson arrived in Siam several months after the capitulation of the Japanese and not during the war as W. Warren claimed. In addition, he confused me with Field Marshal Pibul who jumped into the water to save himself when the gunboat where he was interned during the Manhattan Rebellion was hit by the aerial bombs of his own troops. It was equally regrettable for Siamese students that this teacher was so unsuitable in carrying out his duty. In effect, he directed students in preparing their theses, which required a certain amount of research on facts and authentic documents such as the judicial files open to the public, but this teacher was content with simply the hearsay of the reactionaries of the same type. This might cast doubts on his own education.

## CHAPTER IX
## THE ADVENTURES OF MY SECOND ESCAPE FROM SIAM TO PEOPLE'S CHINA

### I

I hid at a patriot's house, as I have already mentioned in section 3 of the previous chapter, for five months with no possibility of organizing another rebellion. I decided then to leave Siam for Pei-ping which had just been liberated by the Chinese liberation army under the Chinese Communist Party.

I entrusted my wife with the difficult task of arranging my escape and those of my other companions, by asking the assistance of our loyal Siamese and Chinese friends.

The government had the land borders under strict surveillance. Thus we chose the maritime route for our escape, although this route presented many risks, for we would have to cross various surveillance posts established at several places at the mouth of the great river "Menam" which we would have to pass through to reach the sea. Besides, in Siamese territorial waters there were the government's naval patrols. Similarly there were control posts on the coasts of British Malaya and the Indonesian islands which at that time were Dutch colonies. We would have to take further new risks before our secret embarkation on an ocean-going steamer to Hong Kong, and from there, take another steamer to go to Tsing-Tao, occupied by the people's forces of China.

A friend placed at our disposal a little motor trawler of five tons displacement. A patriot loyal to the cause of the people, a retired naval ensign, voluntarily requested a leave from the shipping company where he worked in order to help us by himself taking command of the little trawler.

My wife asked a non-communist Chinese friend, who after the war had been under our protection against the threat of death by extremist nationalist Chinese, to kindly help us organize secretly our embarkation on a steamer at Singapore to go to Hong Kong. From there a representative of the Chinese Communist Party had to help us change steamers bound for Tsing-Tao. The steamer had to manoeuvre as well as possible to avoid the naval patrols of the nationalist Chinese who still controlled the south of China at that time, and made its wake across the China sea.

My wife had thus agreed with our overseas Chinese friend that if ten days after my departure from Bangkok, he had received no news of our arrest, that meant we had already passed the limit of Siamese territorial waters. Then our Chinese friend would tell his faithful secretary to take the plane to Singapore where he would meet us at an assigned rendezvous, so that the British authorities would know nothing of our presence in Singapore.

II

On 6 August 1949 around 6 P.M., we embarked on our little trawler. We had chosen this time in order to arrive at the first customs post at nightfall and a few minutes before it closed, so we would not run the risk of being inspected minutely. In fact we passed through without any difficulty. Our little trawler continued its course right in the centre of the estuary of the river where a government torpedo-boat was anchored to check on boats. With cool nerves our captain brought our little trawler alongside the torpedo boat, and two sub-officers came down to examine our boat. They found nothing abnormal in respect of contraband goods, and their captain ordered that our boat should be allowed to pass. Our trawler thus continued on its voyage by following the coast towards the south.

As the Siamese law does not allow fishing boats of less than five tons displacement registered in Bangkok to go beyond 250 kilometres along the maritime coast of the south, we would have to break the law to go even beyond 1,500 kilometres. This obliged us to take all sorts of precautions to avoid being intercepted by a naval patrol. One fine morning when we had reached around 800 kilometres from Bangkok, I saw that there was a government gunboat ahead of us, anchored at the mouth of a small river on the coast. In such a situation, we were in great difficulty. If we continued on our route, we would doubtless be arrested by the gunboat. If we went back towards the north, the gunboat could be suspicious of us and fire on us. In both cases, we risked being arrested by the gunboat. Fortunately, by a miracle, a fishing boat came out from the coast in the direction of stakes where traps were fixed for catching fish. These stakes were situated between the gunboat and our trawler. Our captain steered our boat in the direction of the buoys where we made fast while waiting for the arrival of the fishermen.

When they arrived, we bought some fish so that the gunboat would be convinced that we had come solely to do business with the local fishermen. After this camouflage, we turned our boat northwards to give the appearance of returning to Bangkok.

In fact, after we had travelled ten kilometres, we stopped at a curve in the coast which hid us from the gunboat until 11 P.M. Then we decided to take the risk of going eastwards onto the high seas, outside Siamese territorial waters. Fortunately that night the sea was very calm, and when we had gone sufficiently far, we turned towards the south, and on the following day, reaching the limit of the Siamese maritime frontier, we turned east [he must mean west] and entered the territorial waters of British Malaya.

There we followed the eastern coast of Malaya and stopped at an islet for rest, and then left towards the south. At nightfall there was a storm. We were obliged to land our trawler near a village on the coast of British Malaya. Some Malay policemen came to examine our boat and threatened to arrest us. After we talked with them and gave them a bribe, they allowed us to remain during the storm. We thought that they would inform against us despite this, but that there was no risk of being taken during the storm. Thus even before the storm had completely abated, we left the coast to sail on the high seas, outside the territorial waters of British Malaya. From there we continued our route towards the south and at the end of two days reached the territorial waters of Singapore. As our trip had lasted less than ten days and our Chinese friends would not yet be at the rendezvous, we went to the island of Balaik in Indonesia which was under Dutch administration. This island was a smuggling centre where the Dutch administration provided facilities for boats of any nationality. We remained there for two or three days until the delay of ten days was up. From this island we returned to the port of Singapore to meet our friend. While approaching the port we were examined by two patrols commanded by the Malays, but they found nothing abnormal concerning our merchandise. With cool nerves throughout, our captain anchored our little trawler in the roads of Singapore, and our Chinese friend from Bangkok met us there to discuss the plan for our journey to Hong Kong. While waiting, we disembarked on the island and were put up at a friend's house situated near the police headquarters, without them knowing anything.

Some days later, with the aid of our Chinese friends (non-communist) we secretly took the steamer for Hong Kong.


# III


At Hong Kong, the representative of the Chinese Communist Party sent Sun, an overseas Chinese, to wish us welcome and to accompany us on our future voyage up to Pei-ping. Sun is the brother of the former nationalist officer Liang, to whom the Chinese nationalist government had entrusted the care of entertaining our missions sent to Chungking during the war, and who is in fact a communist sympathizer about whom we have spoken in chapter 4, paragraph 6.

We were put up in an apartment rented by the former Siamese ambassador Tularaks, where Admiral Thamrong, the former prime minister of Siam, had taken refuge after the defeat of the rebellion of October 1948.

On the morning of 12 September of the same year [1949], my four companions and myself embarked on a steamer of three thousand tons displacement belonging to Chinese merchants but registered under the formality of an English vessel. So that the steamer would not be seized by the navy of the Chinese nationalists, the British authorities gave a "port clearance" indicating that the port of destination for this voyage was Inchon in South Korea.

Other travellers—Chinese democrats from Hong Kong invited by the CCP to participate in the consultative political conference of the Chinese people—gradually embarked on the same steamer.

Some travellers knew how to come to an arrangement with the customs officers. As for us, believing in the honesty of the British customs and immigration officers, we had let them search our baggage in our cabin, thinking that the Hong Kong customs men would not dare to abuse the situation in front of their British superiors. They scattered our things around a bit and when they had left the cabin, we ascertained that some rare medicines which were very expensive at that time and which we had bought for our stay in China, had disappeared.

The customs men not only stole our precious medicines, they also threatened to inform the immigration authorities that we were suspected of being communists and would have to pay them at least five hundred dollars per person. Sun thus had to contact the representative of the CCP to take care of them. A Chinese democrat from Hong Kong who travelled on the same steamer with me told me that there were many cases of corruption by the British officials in this colony, especially in the immigration service and the customs. The money that we would have to pay to these officials was known as "tea money". Later when the British government of Hong Kong established the lottery in the colony, friends who lived there told me it was well-known in Hong Kong that, if someone won the grand prize in the lottery, he could sell his winning ticket to the agents of these corrupt officials for a price higher than the prize itself. For example, if one won the grand prize of a million dollars, one could sell the ticket for 1,200,000 dollars. These officials bought the winning tickets to justify the amount of money which they transferred to England so that the British authorities would not pursue them for corruption.

Returning to the account of our voyage, before leaving the port of Hong Kong, some minutes after the payment of the "tea money", two other Chinese came on board the steamer. They threatened Sun that they would denounce him at immigration so that he could not travel further unless he gave them a sum of money. Sun gave them all the remaining money in his pockets, but the two gangsters were not satisfied. Sun was obliged to let them search his clothing, while asking them to leave him a few dollars to "buy some tea" in the course of the voyage.

## IV

Another representative from the Chinese Communist Party who was responsible for our voyage and that of all the Chinese democrats on the steamer, seeing that the plan for the voyage would run aground if they continued to load cargo, thus asked the captain of the steamer to leave the Hong Kong roads as quickly as possible, leaving the remainder of the cargo for another steamer which would come the following day. It was thus that, paying no attention to the bad timing, our steamer left the Hong Kong roads in the afternoon of the same day.

The captain of the steamer specified to us that in the event we were inspected by a Chinese nationalist ship, we should tell them we were going to South Korea and not to the part of Chinese territory under the control of the communists.

When our steamer was outside the territorial waters of Hong Kong, the captain received a radio communication reporting a big storm. To avoid this danger, the captain had immediately to steer the steamer between an islet and the Chinese coast still held by the nationalists. We had to remain there around twenty-four hours before continuing our voyage.

One fine morning when we had reached the China sea, I observed on the horizon a black speck having the shape of a naval vessel coming in the direction of our steamer. The captain informed all the passengers that they must hold themselves ready to be inspected by a nationalist naval vessel. As a result, those who possessed documents or papers which the nationalists could make use of to suspect that one or other of them was a communist or simply a sympathizer, had to destroy them immediately, otherwise the owner of such documents could be arrested and taken to Taiwan. Many passengers thus burnt their documents in the boiler of the steamer's engine, but we did not do the same for we thought that in case of inspection we would show our Siamese passports while explaining that we were going to Inchon in South Korea and not to the Chinese territory under communist control.

The warship approached closer and closer to our steamer. When it was around four hundred metres from us, we observed the British colours painted on its side. The officer of the warship announced by loudspeaker that he surveyed this area to protect British commercial shipping and that if our steamer were intercepted by the nationalist patrols, we should inform them immediately by long wave so they could come to our aid. Everyone was relieved. However a Chinese professor from Hong Kong expressed to me his regrets for having hastily burnt his precious documents including several volumes of his private journal which he had kept since his youth.

One fine morning, that is to say on 18 September 1949, our steamer entered into the roads of Tsing-Tao, where communist officials of the port came on board to welcome all the passengers. After some formalities, our steamer was moored at the quay. The other Chinese, invited to participate in the consultative political conference of the Chinese people, rushed to continue their journey by railway to arrive at Pei-ping in time for the opening of the conference on 21 September.

We others, on the invitation of comrade Ma (the communist mayor of Tsing-Tao) prepared ourselves to visit the recently liberated town. He put us up in a grand hotel of the town.

# GLOSSARY

| | |
|---|---|
| amphoe | an official territorial unit, subdivision of a province |
| *ariya* | civilization |
| *kalapaphruk* | a mythical tree whose fruits are everything that man can desire |
| *kamnan* | the official headman of a tambon |
| *khlong* | canal |
| *krom* | department; also a royal rank (see appendix 3) |
| *kuti* | monks' residential quarters in a *wat* |
| monthon | an official territorial division, larger than a province, often translated as "circle", used in the nineteenth and early twen-tieth centuries |
| *muang* | traditional term for a political unit which can range from a town to a country; an official territorial division later replaced by province |
| *parian* | the exam certificate given to a graduate of Buddhist theology |
| *phra si-ariya* | the once and future Buddha, Maitreya, the focus of utopian and millenarian beliefs |
| *phrai* | a peasant and bondsman under the *sakdina* system |
| *phuyaiban* | village headman |
| *rai* | area of measurement equal to 0.16 hectare (0.4 acres) |
| *ratchathinnanam* | conferred titles often used as names |
| *sakdina* | literally "power over fields"; the old official ranking system; the Siamese version of feudalism |
| *sala* | a hall, especially in a *wat* |
| *salung* | monetary unit equal to one quarter of a baht |
| Sangha | the Buddhist monkhood |
| *sen* | old unit of length equal to forty metres |

| | |
|---|---|
| *seri* | free |
| tambon | an official territorial division for a group of villages, sometimes called a "sub-district" |
| *tamlung* | old monetary unit equal to four baht |
| dhamma | religion, religious teaching, religious texts |
| *that* | slave |
| *ubosot* | the ordination hall in a *wat* |
| *upparat* | the King of the Front Palace, the "Second King"; the designated successor from the late Ayutthaya period until the Fifth Reign |
| *wat* | Buddhist monastery or temple |

# APPENDIX 2

# SOURCES

## PART I: BEFORE THE REVOLUTION

1. *Sakun Phanomyong* [The Banomyong family], pp. 163–75 in *Chiwaprawat yo khong nai Pridi Phanomyong* [Concise autobiography of Nai Pridi Banomyong], Bangkok: Project on Pridi Banomyong and Thai Society, second edition, 1992 (not in the first 1983 priting).

2. *Kan phraratchathan nam sakun "na Pomphet"* [The royal grant of the surname na Pombejra], pp. 185–9 in *Chiwaprawat yo khong nai Pridi Phanomyong* (1992 edition, not the 1983).

3. *Prasopkan lae khwam hen bang prakan khong ratthaburut awuso Pridi Phanomyong: achan Chatthip Nartsupha samphat ratthaburut awuso Pridi Phanomyong mua wan thi 10 mesayon pho. so. 2525* [Some experiences and opinions of senior statesman Pridi Banomyong: Chatthip Nartsupha's interview with senior statesman Pridi Banomyong on 10 April 1982], Bangkok: Project on Pridi Banomyong and Thai Society, 1983; excerpts from pp. 18–25, 34–40, 51–2.

4. *Chiwaprawat yo khong nai Pridi Phanomyong*, excerpts from pp. 3–5, 17–8.

5. *Kham athibai kotmai pokkhrong: suan thi 4, samai ratchakan patchuban* [Commentary on administrative law: part 4, during the current reign], *Nitisan* [law journal], year 4, volume 6, October 1931.

6. *Kham athibai kotmai pokkhrong*, lectures delivered at the law school, 24 February to 31 March 1932, printed in *Prachum kotmai mahachon lae ekkachon khong Pridi Phanomyong* [Collected public and private law of Pridi Banomyong], Thammasat University, 1983, pp. 275–99. Note that items 5 and 6 have the same title in Thai, but we have translated one as "commentary" and the other as "lectures".

## PART II: THE REVOLUTION

7. *Prakat khong khana ratsadon chabap thi 1* [Announcement of the People's Party No. 1], sometimes called the manifesto, distributed as a handbill on 24 June 1932, reproduced in Chai-anan Samudavanija and Khattiya Karnasuta (eds.), *Ekkasan kan muang kan pokkhrong thai (pho. so. 2417–2477)* [Documents of Thai politics and government, 1874–1934], Bangkok: Social Science Association of Thailand, 1989, pp. 209–11.

8. *Phraratchabanyat thammanun kan pokkhrong phaendin sayam chuakhrao phuttha-sakkarat 2475* [Provisional constitution of the kingdom of Siam 1932], signed and promulgated by King Rama VII on 27 June 1945, reprinted in *Naew khwam khit pracha-thipatai khong Pridi Phanomyong* [The democratic thought of Pridi Banomyong], Bangkok: Pridi Banomyong Foundation, 1992, pp. 265–70.

9. Letter from Pridi to Phoonsuk, 3 July 1932, private letter, courtesy of Thanphu-ying Phoonsuk Banomyong.

10. *Khao khrongkan sethakit* [Outline economic plan] was presented by Pridi in February 1933, debated in parliament on 30 March 1933, and then suppressed. We have used what is probably the first published edition by Sakdi Silpanon's press in April 1948. The plan and related documents have most recently been reprinted in 1999 by the project to celebrate Pridi's birth centennial.

11. *Bang ruang kieo kap kan ko tang khana ratsadon lae rabop prachathipatai* [Some aspects of the establishment of the People's Party and democracy], dated 24 June 1972, first printed by Pramot Phungsunthon, Bangkok, Nitivet press, 1972; reprinted in *Naew khwam khit prachathipatai khong Pridi Phanomyong*, pp. 1–24.

12. *Khana ratsadon kap kan aphiwat prachathipatai 24 mithunayon* [The People's Party and the revolution of 24 June], speech written in Paris and sent to be delivered in Bangkok on 24 June 1982 at the seminar on Half a Century of Democracy, first printed in the proceedings of the seminar, Bangkok, 1982, reprinted in *Pridi Phanomyong kap sangkhom thai*, pp. 333–62; and in *Naew khwam khit prachathippatai khong Pridi Phanomyong*, pp. 25–46.

# PART III: AFTER THE REVOLUTION

13. *Chiwaprawat yo khong nai Pridi Phanomyong;* excerpts from pp. 23–7

14. Speeches broadcast on Thai radio on 27 June of 1934, 1935, and 1936; printed in *Naew khwam khit prachathipatai khong Pridi Phanomyong*, pp. 249–59.

15. *Kan ko tang khabuankan to tan yipun lae seri thai* [Establishment of the anti-Japan resistance movement and Seri Thai], printed in the memorial volume of Pramot Phung-sunthon, 1981, reprinted in *Pridi Phanomyong kap sangkhom thai*, pp. 97–116.

16. *Khwam pen pai phai nai khana phu samret ratchakan thaen phraong* [What happened inside the Regency Council], printed in *Bang ruang kieo kap phraboromwongsa-nuwong nai rawang songkhram lok khrang thi song* [Some matters concerning the royal family during the Second World War], distributed on Pridi's 72nd birthday, published by Pramot Phungsunthon and Proeng Siriphat at Nittivet press, 1972, pp. 38–78.

17. Speech in parliament on 7 May 1946, printed in *Naew khwam khit prachathipatai khong Pridi Phanomyong*, pp. 260–2.

18. *Chong phithak chetanarom prachathihatai sombun khong wirachon 14 tulakhom* [Uphold the aim for full democracy of the heroes of 14 October], first printed by Nitiwet Press, and in *Anuson mahawithayalai Thammasat*, both in December 1973, reprinted in *Pridi Phanomyong kap sangkhom thai*, pp. 413–48.

19. *Ma vie mouvementée et mes 21 ans d'exil en Chine populaire* [My chequered life and my twenty-one years of exile in People's China], published privately in Paris in 1972, translated into Thai by Chamnon Phakworawut and Phornthip Toyai as *Chiwit phan phuan khong khaphachao lae 21 pi thi liphai nai satharanarat Chin*, Bangkok, Thianwan, 1986; extract from pp. 47–69, 85–107 of the French original.

# BRIEF GUIDE TO ROYAL AND OTHER TITLES APPEARING IN THE TEXT

I. Royal family titles by birth, in descending order

*Chaofa*
   Offspring of king with queen of *chaofa* or *phraongchao* rank
   Offspring of heir apparent or other *chaofa* with consort of *chaofa* or *phraongchao* rank
   *Phraongchao* elevated by the king

*Phraongchao*
   Offspring of king, heir apparent, or other *chaofa* with other consorts
   *Momchao* elevated by the king

*Momchao*
   Offspring of *chaofa* with non-royal wife
   Offspring of *phraongchao* (by birth) with any wife

*Momratchawong*
   Offspring of *phraongchao* (by elevation) with any wife
   Offspring of *momchao* with any wife

*Momluang*
   Offspring of *momratchawong* with any wife

*Mom*
   Former *chaofa* or *phraongchao* stripped of higher rank.
   Commoner elevated to princely status.

Note: *Somdet* is a superlative, rather like "majestic", often incorporated into the first two ranks above as *Somdet Chaofa* and *Somdet Phra.*

II. Non-hereditary titles conferred on certain members of royal family (queens, chaofa, phraongchao) in recognition of individual merit, in descending order

*Krommun*
*Kromkhun*
*Kromluang*
*Kromphra*
*Kromphraya*

III. Non-hereditary titles conferred on male commoners, momratchawong, and momluang in government service, in descending order

*Somdet Chaophraya*
*Chaophraya*
*Phraya*
*Phra*
*Luang*
*Khun*
*Mun, Chamun, Chaomun*
*Phan*
*Thanai*

IV. Other titles mentioned in the text

*Chaokhun*: honorific for officials of *chaophraya* and *phraya* rank
*Chaochom*: consorts (of king or heir apparent) who were commoners
*Mom* (for female): commoner wives of *chaofa, phraongchao,* or *momchao* princes
*Thanphuying*: principal wife of somdetchaophraya or chaophraya
*Khunying*: principal wife of phraya
*Nai*: adult commoner male over fifteen years
*Nang*: married or once-married adult commoner female over fifteen years
*Nangsao*: never-married adult commoner female over fifteen years

[Note: This appendix is condensed and adapted from the appendix by Thadeus and Chadin Flood in their translations of *The Dynastic Chronicles Bangkok Era: The First Reign* by Chaophraya Thiphakorawong, Tokyo, Centre for East Asian Cultural Studies, 1978–80; and *The Dynastic Chronicles Bangkok Era: The Fourth Reign* by Chaophraya Thiphakorawong, Tokyo, Centre for East Asian Cultural Studies, 1965–74.]

# APPENDIX 4

# CHRONOLOGY OF EVENTS MENTIONED
# IN TEXTS

| NATIONAL EVENTS | PRIDI |
|---|---|
| **1885** | |
| 8 Jan Petition to King Chulalongkorn on constitution | |
| **1900** | 11 May Born in Ayutthaya |
| **1910** | |
| 23 Oct Death of King Chulalongkorn. King Vajiravudh succeeds. | |
| 26 Oct Supreme Council of State formed | |
| **1912** | |
| 26 Feb Ro. So. 130 plot discovered | |
| **1917** | Enters Law School |
| **1920** | |
| | May Becomes barrister |
| | Aug Leaves to study in France |
| **1925** | |
| 26 Nov Death of King Vajiravudh. King Prajadhipok succeeds. | Oct–Nov Clash with ambassador. Almost sent home |
| **1926** | |
| 27 Oct King asks Privy Council to advise on national flag | |
| **1927** | |
| | Feb First meeting of People's Party in Paris |
| | Mar Returns to Siam |
| 30 Nov First meeting of Committee of Privy Council | |

| NATIONAL EVENTS | PRIDI |
|---|---|
| **1928** | |
| | 16 Nov  Marries Phoonsuk na Pombejra |
| **1931** | |
| Oct  King returns from visit to USA | |
| **1932** | |
| Mar  Royal advisers scuttle reform proposals | |
| | 12 Apr  Leaves for France |
| 24 Jun  Revolution by People's Party | |
| 27 Jun  Provisional constitution | |
| 30 Jun  People's Party audience with king. Discussion on constitution | |
| | 29 Sep  Returns to Siam |
| 7 Dec  People's Party formal apology to king | |
| 10 Dec  "Permanent" constitution | |
| **1933** | |
| 30 Mar  Assembly debate on Economic Plan | |
| 1 Apr  Assembly prorogued | |
| 2 Apr  Anti-communist law promulgated | |
| 20 Jun  "Second coup" (Phahon) | |
| 13–27 Oct  Boworadej rebellion | |
| Nov–Dec  First elections | |
| **1934** | |
| 12 Jan  King Prajadhipok leaves Thailand | |
| | 14 Mar  Act founding Thammasat University |
| | 21 Mar  Becomes minister of the interior |
| **1935** | |
| 2 Mar  King Prajadhipok abdicates | |
| | August  Trip to Europe for loan negotiation |
| **1937** | |
| | 9 Aug  Becomes minister of foreign affairs |
| 7 Nov  Elections | 13 Nov  New treaty signed with US (12 others follow) |
| **1938** | |
| 12 Dec  Elections | |
| 16 Dec  Phibun becomes prime minister | 20 Dec  Becomes minister of finance |
| **1939** | |
| | 29 Mar  Tax reform and revenue code passed |
| 24 Jun  Name changed from Siam to Thailand | |
| | 29 Sep  National banking bureau bill passed |
| **1940** | |
| 19 Sep  Provisional clauses extended | |
| **1941** | |
| 8 Dec  Japanese troops invade Thailand | 6 Dec  Removed from cabinet, made a regent |
| 11 Dec  Thailand and Japan sign military cooperation agreement | |

| NATIONAL EVENTS | | PRIDI | |
|---|---|---|---|
| **1942** | | | |
| 25 Jan | Thailand declares war on Britain and US | | |
| **1944** | | | |
| 26 Jul | Phibun resigns as prime minister | | |
| 1 Aug | Khuang becomes prime minister | 1 Aug | Becomes sole regent |
| **1945** | | | |
| 15 Aug | Formal Japanese surrender in Thailand | | |
| 17 Sep | Seni Pramoj becomes prime minister | | |
| Sep | Kukrit Pramoj forms Progressive Party | | |
| 5 Dec | King Ananda Mahidol returns to Thailand | 8 Dec | Awarded title of "senior statesman" by king |
| **1946** | | | |
| 1 Jan | Peace agreement signed with Allies | | |
| 6 Jan | Elections. Khuang becomes prime minister. | | |
| | | 24 Mar | Becomes prime minister until 3 June |
| 5 April | Democrat party formed. Kukrit merges Prog. Party. | | |
| 9 May | Constitution (Pridi's) | | |
| 9 Jun | Death of King Rama VIII | 8 Jun | Becomes prime minister until 10 June |
| | | 11 Jun | Becomes prime minister until 21 August |
| 9 Nov | People's Party dissolves itself | 3 Nov | Leaves Thailand for world tour |
| **1947** | | | |
| | | 20 Feb | Returns to Thailand |
| 8 Nov | Coup | 8 Nov | House attacked. Hides at Sattahip naval base. |
| 9 Nov | Under-the-water-jar constitution | 20 Nov | Escapes to Singapore |
| **1948** | | | |
| 29 Jan | Elections. Khuang becomes prime minister | | |
| 6 Apr | Coup against Khuang | | |
| 8 Apr | Phibun becomes prime minister | | |
| 1 Oct | 1 October Rebellion | | |
| **1949** | | | |
| | | Jan | Returns secretly to Thailand |
| 26 Feb | Palace Rebellion | | |
| 3 Mar | Murder of Thawin, Tongin, Chamlong, Thongplao | | |
| 23 Mar | Constitution (Khuang's) | | |
| | | 6 Aug | Escapes to Singapore |
| | | 21 Sep | Arrives in China |

| NATIONAL EVENTS | PRIDI |
|---|---|
| **1951**<br>29 Jun  Manhattan Rebellion<br>29 Nov  Silent/Radio coup | |
| **1952**<br>26 Feb  Constitution (1932 revised)<br>Nov    The "Peace Revolt" | |
| **1957**<br>16 Sep  Sarit's first coup. Constitution. | |
| **1958**<br>20 Oct  Sarit's second coup | |
| **1959**<br>29 Jan  Constitution (Sarit's) | |
| **1963**<br>8 Dec  Death of Sarit. Thanom succeeds. | |
| **1968**<br>June   Constitution (Thanom's) | |
| **1969**<br>10 Feb  Elections | |
| **1970** | 8 May  Arrives in Paris |
| **1971**<br>17 Nov  Thanom coup against own<br>government<br>15 Dec  Constitution | |
| **1973**<br>14 Oct  Student uprising | |
| **1974**<br>January  Formation of Legislative Assembly<br>5 Oct    1974 constitution approved | |
| **1976**<br>6 Oct  Massacre and coup | |
| **1983** | 2 May  Dies in Paris |

# INDEX